Brotherhood of Barristers

How did ideas of masculinity shape the British legal profession and the wider expectations of the white-collar professional? *Brotherhood of Barristers* examines the cultural history of the Inns of Court – four legal societies whose rituals of symbolic brotherhood took place in their supposedly ancient halls. These societies invented traditions to create a sense of belonging among members – or, conversely, to marginalize those who did not fit the profession's ideals. Ren Pepitone examines the legal profession's efforts to maintain an exclusive, masculine culture in the face of sweeping social changes across the nineteenth and twentieth centuries. Utilizing established sources such as institutional records alongside diaries, guidebooks, and newspapers, this book looks afresh at the gendered operations of Victorian professional life. *Brotherhood of Barristers* incorporates a diverse array of historical actors, from the bar's most high-flying to struggling law students, disbarred barristers, political radicals, and women's rights campaigners.

Ren Pepitone is Assistant Professor of History at New York University, with particular research interests in the history of gender and sexuality and modern Britain and its empire.

Modern British Histories

Series Editors:

Deborah Cohen, *Northwestern University*
Margot Finn, *University College London*
Peter Mandler, *University of Cambridge*

'Modern British Histories' publishes original research monographs drawn from
the full spectrum of a large and lively community of modern historians of
Britain. Its goal is to keep metropolitan and national histories of Britain fresh
and vital in an intellectual atmosphere increasingly attuned to, and enriched by,
the transnational, the international and the comparative. It will include books that
focus on British histories within the UK and that tackle the subject of Britain and
the world inside and outside the boundaries of formal empire from 1750 to the
present. An indicative – not exclusive – list of approaches and topics that the
series welcomes includes material culture studies, modern intellectual history,
gender, race and class histories, histories of modern science and histories of
British capitalism within a global framework. Open and wide-ranging, the series
will publish books by authoritative scholars, at all stages of their career, with
something genuinely new to say.

A complete list of titles in the series can be found at:
www.cambridge.org/modernbritishhistories

Brotherhood of Barristers

A Cultural History of the British Legal Profession, 1840–1940

Ren Pepitone

New York University

CAMBRIDGE
UNIVERSITY PRESS

CAMBRIDGE
UNIVERSITY PRESS

Shaftesbury Road, Cambridge CB2 8EA, United Kingdom

One Liberty Plaza, 20th Floor, New York, NY 10006, USA

477 Williamstown Road, Port Melbourne, VIC 3207, Australia

314–321, 3rd Floor, Plot 3, Splendor Forum, Jasola District Centre, New Delhi – 110025, India

103 Penang Road, #05-06/07, Visioncrest Commercial, Singapore 238467

Cambridge University Press is part of Cambridge University Press & Assessment, a department of the University of Cambridge.

We share the University's mission to contribute to society through the pursuit of education, learning and research at the highest international levels of excellence.

www.cambridge.org
Information on this title: www.cambridge.org/9781009456746

DOI: 10.1017/9781009456722

First published 2024

A catalogue record for this publication is available from the British Library

Library of Congress Cataloging-in-Publication Data
Names: Pepitone, Ren, author.
Title: Brotherhood of barristers : a cultural history of the British legal profession, 1840-1940 / Ren Pepitone, New York University.
Description: Cambridge, United Kingdom ; New York, NY : Cambridge University Press, 2024. | Series: Modern British histories | Includes bibliographical references and index.
Identifiers: LCCN 2023051139 (print) | LCCN 2023051140 (ebook) | ISBN 9781009456746 (hardback) | ISBN 9781009456753 (paperback) | ISBN 9781009456722 (epub)
Subjects: LCSH: Inns of Court–History. | Courts–Great Britain–History. | Lawyers–Great Britain–Societies, etc.–History. | Practice of law–Great Britain–History. | Culture and law–Great Britain–History. | Legal ethics–Great Britain–History.
Classification: LCC KD502 .P47 2024 (print) | LCC KD502 (ebook) | DDC 340.06/042–dc23/eng/20231108
LC record available at https://lccn.loc.gov/2023051139
LC ebook record available at https://lccn.loc.gov/2023051140

ISBN 978-1-009-45674-6 Hardback

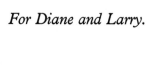

For Diane and Larry.

Contents

Figures

Preface: A Primer on the Bar

The following is intended as an orientation for readers who are unfamiliar with the peculiarities of the British legal profession. Readers who are already acquainted with the structure of the profession may wish to skip ahead.

This is a book about the bar, the upper portion of the British legal profession. In the body of this book I sometimes use the term lawyers as a synonym for barristers, and the legal profession as a synonym for the bar, but these terms are rectangles to the bar's square. The British legal profession is a broad entity that encompasses barristers and solicitors – both of whom are understood to be lawyers – to say nothing of the body of clerks, conveyancers, and other legal professionals who are not lawyers but who work for and with them in the field of law.

The historical legal profession was a split one, in which solicitors interacted with clients and then passed along briefs to barristers, who would then prepare these briefs and plead cases in court. The difference between the two was sometimes captured linguistically in the designation of barristers, and only barristers, as advocates. Barristers had an exclusive right of audience in the superior courts and fiercely (though not always successfully) combatted encroachment on their right to plead in the lower courts. Given their monopoly over advocacy, it was only barristers who were eligible for the most important judicial appointments because they were the only ones who had (and could have had) the requisite experience and training. Along with the increased prestige and opportunities to rise high, barristers tended to be better remunerated than solicitors.

In nineteenth- and twentieth-century Britain and its empire, there were multiple avenues of legal training available for someone who wished to work in the legal profession. Those who could not afford entrance fees required to become a barrister or solicitor – or, until 1919, women – were not entirely precluded from working in the legal field. Clerking for barristers was an occupation in and of itself and, while less prestigious, potentially quite lucrative. Barrister and clerk had a mutual interdependence, the clerk securing briefs for his barrister and in return receiving a portion of the barrister's fee. In the nineteenth century, a small number of women found legal work that did not require being qualified as a barrister or solicitor, including conveyancing, patent work, and estates.

Those who wished to be solicitors began an apprenticeship of sorts as articled clerks. The requirements for becoming a solicitor changed across the century, particularly with the formation of the Law Society, a formal regulatory association. Founded in the 1820s, the goal of the association was to raise the reputation of the profession by ensuring standards of practice and to discipline dishonest practitioners. Royal charters and subsequent legislation gave the society authority over the lower half of the bar. Between the second half of the nineteenth century and the first half of the twentieth, the society instated required examinations alongside apprenticeship and eventually formed its own law school. These efforts successfully enhanced the prestige of the lower half of the legal profession, though it remained subordinate to the bar.

This book deals exclusively with those who wished to be called to the bar, that is, who wished to qualify to practice as barristers. In order to do so, they would have had to join one of the four Inns of Court – ancient legal societies that regulated admission to the upper half of the legal profession. The Honorable Societies of the Inner Temple, Middle Temple, Lincoln's Inn, and Gray's Inn each occupied their own grounds in central London – the two Temples nestled in the crook of the Thames and the City of London's western border; Lincoln's Inn, north of them off Chancery Lane; and Gray's Inn, north still along Holborn.

In order to understand what the Inns of Court were, it is important to clarify what they were not. Readers unfamiliar with the British legal profession might find their names confusing. The Inns were not inns in the sense of hotels or places a traveler might lodge, and they had no formal connection to either the law courts or the members of a monarch's court. Likewise, the Inner and Middle Temples were not places of worship or devotion – they were called Temples because their grounds had once belonged to the Order of the Knights of the Temple of Solomon of Jerusalem, or Templars. Though sometimes fodder for dark legends, the connection between the land and the Knights Templar had been severed by the early fourteenth century, at which point the grounds were leased to lawyers. These lawyers organized themselves into two formal associations, adopting the names of their location, hence the Inner and Middle Temples.

The Inns of Court were also not law schools in any recognizable sense, though they could be sites of legal learning. A law school is an accredited institution that: offers a program of systematic learning, usually via courses taught by experts; tracks progress via examination; and requires measurable proficiency in the subject matter to award a degree. At the start of the Victorian period, the Inns of Court did not offer any program of systematic learning, let alone courses of any kind. They did appoint senior barristers, known as readers, to deliver a lecture or series of lectures across a term on a particular legal topic. Attending these lectures was optional, however, and there was no examination given on their content. Indeed, in the 1840s, at the start of this study, there were no examinations at all, either during term or before a call to the bar. The Inns did not (and still do not) award law degrees. Those who read law at university and then went on to practice as barristers surely found the training helpful. But a law degree was not necessary to become a barrister, and a person with a university law degree could not practice law without first going through the Inns of Court.

So what, then, *were* the Inns and what were the requirements to become a barrister? The Inns were professional associations whose primary function was to preserve the prestige of the bar by regulating the admission and behavior of law students and barristers. That is to say, the societies were more invested in members' social standing and conduct than their knowledge of the law. These priorities might sound warped, but they make sense given the history of the societies. The early modern Inns served as finishing schools for the sons of the aristocracy, most of whom would never practice as barristers but might find a smattering of legal learning useful for managing their estates. The intellectual liveliness of the Inns was disrupted by the civil war, however, never to be fully revived. With the decline of formal education at the Inns, wealthy young men began replacing time in Georgian London with time touring abroad. Meanwhile, as the wealth of Britain's commercial classes grew, they saw sending their progeny to the Inns of Court as a way to boost their sons' social status from tradesmen to professionals.

These demographic changes meant that in order to maintain the status of gentlemanly professionals, the Inns needed to monitor the makeup of the bar. They did so via several policies, the first of which were admission fees, term and dinner fees, and a £100 deposit. This latter sum would be returned once a student had been called to the bar, but the outlay of so much money could deter even middle-class prospective candidates, to say nothing of the working classes. The fees did not, however, preclude the sons of the commercial classes from joining, and so in the early nineteenth century, the Inns took steps to distance themselves from the ungentlemanly taint of trade. The societies created new rules that prohibited any person engaged in a trade from joining the Inns and disbarred any barristers who pursued a trade themselves. Former solicitors were required to be out of practice three years before joining the societies – solicitors received fees directly from clients, which stank of providing a service. Barristers, by contrast, received honorariums (from the fees paid to the solicitor via the client, but exchanging money one step removed from its source was enough to erase the specter of trade).

Assuming a candidate was not engaged in trade and could pay the fees, once they joined an Inn, the only other requirement was to keep term by eating a certain number of dinners in the society's hall over a period of several years. To repeat: a law student did not need a university law degree, did not have to attend classes, and was never tested on their legal knowledge before being called to the bar. They paid their fees, ate their dinners, and after an appropriate amount of time (usually three years) received their call to the bar. What, you may ask, would prohibit a person who had learned absolutely nothing of law along the way from practicing as a barrister? Formally the answer was, nothing would. But when Victorian MP reformers asked the same skeptical question, the leaders of the Inns readily explained that a barrister who knew nothing would not receive briefs from any solicitors, whereas the accomplished barrister would. There was no need for the Inns to institute examinations, as practice sorted the wheat from the chaff.

The aforementioned leaders of the Inns were known as masters of the bench, or benchers, a body of the bar's elite that functioned as trustees of the societies. The benchers regulated admission to the Inns, calls to the bar, and served as a disciplinary body with the right to disbar offending members. Each Inn had its own bench, with new benchers elected by existing benchers. This antidemocratic structure meant that benchers were overwhelmingly drawn from the ranks of senior members of the bar, known as king's or queen's counsel, depending on the reigning monarch. When a barrister "took silk," that is, was appointed queen's counsel (and thus entitled to wear a QC's silk gown), it was de rigueur for the benchers of the Inns to ballot for them to be added to the bench. Junior members of the bar (marked by their woolen "stuff" gowns) were not prohibited from joining the governing bodies of the Inns, but they constituted only a sliver of each Inn's bench.

What types of law did barristers practice and where? Both barristers and solicitors had the right to plead in the lower courts, such as the petty sessions (now known as magistrates courts), which dealt with summary offences. The attraction of being a barrister rather than a solicitor, however, lay in barristers' sole right to plead in the superior courts, which are the High Court of Justice, the Crown Court, and the Court of Appeal. In terms of noncriminal law, that is, civil law (a term that can be confusing as it also refers to codified law, but is not used in that sense here), barristers pleaded cases at the High Court of Justice, currently broken into three divisions: the King's Bench Division, the Chancery Division, and what is now known as the Family Division. Pleaders at the King's Bench specialized in common law, a branch derived from precedents set by previous judicial decisions rather than statutes. Common law cases often involved principles of contract or civil wrongs. The Chancery Bar encompassed equity cases involving trusts, probate, real estate, and the like. Equity barristers pleaded in the Court of Chancery, but much of their work would have been conducted outside of court. The Family Division, created in 1971, is the amalgamation of the courts of probate, matrimony and divorce, and admiralty. Notably, the former two were institutions of Victorian creation, formed by acts of Parliament in 1857 to transfer jurisdiction over probate, marriage, and divorce from the ecclesiastical courts to specialized civil courts.

Barristers practiced criminal law at the Crown Court, which in London was the Central Criminal Court, or Old Bailey. Criminal cases were also heard at the assizes – traveling courts that met periodically to hear cases in regions outside the capital. These courts were divided into six circuits, each circuit covering a different geographic region. Barristers' practice on circuit was organized around the circuit messes – institutions that were part club and part professional association. While on circuit for four to six weeks twice a year, the members of the mess would travel, lodge, and dine together. Customarily, barristers could only join one circuit. Membership of the mess was open to any barrister who practiced on that circuit, though admission was via ballot and not guaranteed. The circuit messes developed their own rules and etiquette and could exert social pressure, fines (usually in bottles of wine), or even expulsion from the mess to enforce them. Unlike the Inns of Court, however, the circuit messes did not have the power to disbar barristers, and they regulated members' behavior only while they were on circuit a few months out of the year.

In the nineteenth century, the law, law courts, and lower branch of the legal profession all underwent significant reforms and restructuring, but the bar made it through the century with relatively few structural changes and the authority of the Inns over the profession remained largely intact. In the 1860s and 1870s, a few individual MPs tried to make a cause out of reforming legal education and the governance of the bar, but their efforts failed less because of resistance from the Inns than because of apathy from their fellow parliamentarians. The societies did make a few voluntary concessions to rationalization and reform, a way of reassuring the public they took their duties seriously. In 1875 they instituted an examination before call to the bar and, in 1894, formed the General Council of the Bar to coordinate policies across the four Inns. Rather than agents of meaningful change, however, these were nominal measures designed to appease those interested in reform while preserving the structure and authority of the Inns.

This is not to suggest that the bar was somehow static or changeless, however. Indeed, the nineteenth century saw significant demographic changes in the profession. Between 1835 and 1885, membership of the bar tripled, taking the bar from a relatively small profession with several hundred members to one with upwards of 7,000. Within these expanded numbers, fewer and fewer men came from the landed gentry, and those who did came from lesser estates; more and more were the sons of civil servants, businessmen, and professionals. Changes to the bar's demographics were also fueled by the expansion of the British empire, which both put and relieved pressure on the bar. In the latter regard, imperial outposts created new avenues for the swelling numbers of barristers to practice. If work at home was scarce, a man could try and make a career at the colonial bar. At the same time, the Inns of Court found trying to regulate the bar both at home and across the empire at best unwieldy.

White settler colonies like Canada, Australia, and Ireland developed their own bars, which released their citizens from needing to train at the Inns, and the Inns from having to regulate barristers practicing there. The first of these to be created was the Irish bar: King's Inn in Dublin was established in 1541. The Statute of Jeofailles 1542, however, required anyone wishing to be called to the Irish bar to first keep term at the English Inns of Court. It was not until three hundred years later, in response to pressure from both Irish law students and Home Rule MPs, that this requirement was repealed by the Barristers Admission (Ireland) Act 1885, and thenceforth Irish barristers could be members of King's Inn alone. In Canada and Australia, the qualifications for becoming a barrister varied by province, colony, or territory. As early as 1797, the Act for the Better Regulation of the Practice of Law created the Law Society of Upper Canada, which provided a pathway to professional practice that did not require a call from the Inns. Similarly, in 1848 the government of New South Wales created a Barristers Admission Board with the power to admit barristers to practice sans time in the UK if they otherwise met educational standards set by that body.

In India, by contrast, to practice as a barrister required a call to the bar from one of the four Inns. This requirement ensured that a steady stream of would-be legal practitioners flowed from India to train in London. For much of the nineteenth century, these law students were white Britons, many of whom began their careers as civil servants and hoped the bar would open new avenues within imperial hierarchies. By the century's end, however, spurred by the Raj's attempts to integrate more native Indians into its bureaucratic structures, a growing number of Indian men – usually from elite backgrounds – joined the Inns of Court. In addition to white and Indian barristers, practice at the bar in India was somewhat complicated by the existence of Indian legal professionals known as vakils. Vakils underwent rigorous training and examination, which allowed them some but not all of the privileges of barristers. They could plead in some superior courts, for example, but not those of the presidency cities Calcutta, Madras, or Bombay. For Indians pursuing a career in law, therefore, a call to the bar from Inns was understood to be an easier path to greater prestige and higher earnings – if they could find the time and money required to study in London, to say nothing of the cultural divides they might face upon arrival.

Acknowledgments

I would like to begin by thanking the Modern British History series editors at Cambridge University Press – Deborah Cohen, Margot Finn, and Peter Mandler – as well as Liz Friend-Smith and Rosanna Barraclough, for their help (and great patience). This book was much improved by the thoughtful comments of three anonymous readers. The generous support of several granting agencies made the initial research for the book possible. I am grateful to the Paul Mellon Centre for Studies in British Art, the North American Conference on British Studies, and the Doris G. Quinn Foundation. I could not have finished writing without the time provided by a Fulbright Visiting Fellowship at Lucy Cavendish College, University of Cambridge.

I am also indebted to a number of libraries and archives. I would particularly like to thank Lesley Whitelaw, Hannah Baker, and Siobhan Woodgate at the Middle Temple Archives for hosting me for so many hours. Sharing cups of tea with Celia Pilkington of the Inner Temple Archives made workdays a true pleasure. Additional thanks to the staff of the Lincoln's Inn Archive, the British Library and British Newspaper Library, the London Metropolitan Archives, the Women's Library, the Liddell Hart Centre for Military Archives, and the National Archives.

My work has benefited enormously from a number of seminars and workshops. Tremendous thanks to Eve Worth and Aaron Reeves for including me in the University of Oxford workshop on gender and elites in Britain since 1850, which helped me rethink how to frame some of my research. Thanks too to the Folger Shakespeare Library for hosting The Legal and Cultural Worlds of the Inns of Court, chaired by the late Christopher Brooks. Participants in the European Seminar at the Johns Hopkins University, and the History Department Brown Bag Luncheon at the University of Arkansas, provided insightful feedback. I am deeply grateful to all the members of the JHU Gender History Workshop, including Toby Ditz, Mary Ryan, and Mary Fissell, who offered thoughtful critiques and suggestions for some of the earliest drafts of this work.

Many scholars have discussed methodological questions, read drafts, pointed me in new directions, and generally shared their expertise with me. At Hopkins, John Marshall patiently and stalwartly directed me to and through long centuries of legal thought. Will Brown exceeded the call of duty as a friend and colleague in the generosity of his intellectual support. Jess Clark, Katie Hindmarch-Watson, Laurel Flinn, and Amanda Herbert supplied me with academic inspiration, considered feedback, and unwavering encouragement. Special thanks to Todd Shepard, and to Sara Damiano, Katie Hemphill, Norah Andrews, Jessica Walker, Adam Bisno, Jessica Valdez, David Schley, Elizabeth Imber, and Rachel Hsu.

At New York University, Guy Ortolano has offered unflagging support, and I could not imagine a better faculty mentor than Rebecca Goetz. I am so grateful for the support and friendship of the Junior Faculty Club. I am also fortunate to have generous colleagues nearby in Columbia. Thank you to James Stafford and especially Susan Pedersen, as well as the members of Columbia's British History Seminar, for their excellent feedback. I am grateful for the insights there of Seth Koven, who helped me see the forest and not just the trees. While at Cambridge, Peter Mandler, with characteristic kindness, invited me to speak at the Modern Cultural History Seminar, where I received helpful feedback from members, including Ben Griffin. Thanks to both Zoë Thomas and Heidi Egginton for thoughtful comments and infinite patience. I am ever grateful for the friendship and keen insights of Lucy Delap and Laura Carter.

I owe an unspeakable amount to two women whom I respect deeply as mentors, feminists, and friends. Lydia Murdoch inspired my love for Victorian Britain, helped me think critically, and modeled for me the kind of educator I wanted to be. She is why I am doing the work that I do. Judy Walkowitz encouraged me to explore, challenged me to push further, directed me to new ideas, and helped me refine my own. She has been an inimitable exemplar in her scholarship and a pillar of support for my own. I am so glad I get to be part of our reading group.

Finally, I want to thank the tremendous number of friends and family members who spurred me on throughout this undertaking: Jenna Krall, Rebecca Powers, Charlotte O'Donnell, and Ean Fonseca, who were there from its inception. A piece of me will always belong to Baltimore and the vibrant, weird, and wonderful friends there. I received unwavering encouragement from many members of the arts community, especially Sarah Lamar, Evan Moritz, and Susan MacCorckle. Bad Girls Lindsey Griffith and Stephen Karnes have made research trips that much more fun. I've been very lucky to have the two best dog wives, Tanja Heffner and Caroline Starr, cheering me on. Special thanks to long-time supporters Tammy Sforza, Dolores Kusman, Anthony and Joan Policastro. And lastly, thanks to Diane and Larry Pepitone, who have buoyed me in just about every way imaginable.

1 Introduction

In February 2019, Joanna Hardy, a junior barrister at the criminal bar, tweeted, "We talk a lot about retention of women at the criminal bar. We wring our hands and shake our heads … But what can we actually do?" She followed with a list of suggestions that received 280 retweets and was featured in news outlets including the *Daily Mail, Telegraph,* and *Standard.* Of Hardy's nine ideas, six related not to professional policies or procedures but to the culture of the bar. Hardy insisted that male barristers should not expect female colleagues to fetch coffee or organize case dinners. Men should not "make repetitive jokes about breasts or skirts," communicate in innuendo, or make comments like "You're worse than my wife." Her pithy sixth suggestion read, "Do not behave like you are on a stag-do."[1]

That male barristers might comport themselves like a group of ribald bachelors is deeply in keeping with the history of the legal profession. For the five centuries leading up to women's admission to the bar in 1919, law was an exclusively male occupation with a culture that emphasized eating, drinking, and fraternization in the truest meaning of the word. Nothing about the bar's masculine culture was accidental or incidental – all elements were carefully cultivated by the Inns of Court – the institutions that regulated, and still regulate, the upper half of the English legal profession. The Honorable Societies of the Inner and the Middle Temples, along with Lincoln's Inn and Gray's Inn, controlled the qualification for and discipline of practice as a barrister. The societies provided only limited aspects of legal training because they were guild-like professional associations dating back to the Middle Ages, not law schools. All barristers had to belong to one of the four societies, however, and many barristers practiced out of sets of chambers at the Inns.

---

[1] Joanna Hardy (@Joanna_Hardy), "We talk a lot about retention of women at the criminal bar. We wring our hands and shake our heads as females leave and leave and leave. But what can we actually do? A wee thread," Twitter, February 12, 2019.

As Hardy's list of recommendations indicates, to understand and overcome workplace discrepancies, we need to examine workplace culture. Yet most studies of professional inequality by sociologists and historians focus on the legal or institutional structures that created inequity and the formal processes by which women and minorities worked against these hurdles. They center around parliamentary acts or educational opportunities and in so doing consider women's and minorities' access to particular professional pathways. These studies cannot explain, however, why elite white male regimes persist after formal obstacles have been cleared away. Likewise, studies that acknowledge the importance of gender and race as operational categories often suffer from myopia, focusing solely on women and minorities.[2] Yet the fabric of legal culture, its very warp and weft, was made of ideas about and performances of Englishness and masculinity. To unravel it, scholarly enquiry needs to begin when the bar was composed entirely of men of almost exclusively British origin.

Taking the mid-nineteenth century as its starting point, *Brotherhood of Barristers* argues that the Inns of Court fused historicist ritual and Victorian strictures of gentlemanliness to cultivate everyday performances of professional masculinity. The societies then preserved institutional culture by adapting these principles to everything from demographic shifts to ethico-political questions of personal conscience in the face of metropolitan and imperial transformations across the early twentieth century. By anchoring its analysis in the Inns of Court, this book aligns itself with a wave of cultural historians who have reapproached institutional history to ask questions about gender, space, and materiality. These works move beyond one-dimensional renderings of institutions as totalizing, utilitarian, or stagnant to show the dynamic, uneven, and sometimes antipragmatic ways that institutions shaped individuals and society.[3]

---

[2] Richard L. Abel, *The Legal Profession in England and Wales* (New York: Blackwell, 1988); Jenny Daggers, "The Victorian Female Civilising Mission and Women's Aspirations towards Priesthood in the Church of England," *Women's History Review* 10: 4 (2001): 651–670; Carol Dyhouse, *Students: A Gendered History* (London: Routledge, 2006); Anne Logan, "Professionalism and the Impact of England's First Women Justices, 1920–1950," *Historical Journal* 49: 3 (2006): 833–850; Mary Jane Mossman, *The First Women Lawyers: A Comparative Study of Gender, Law and the Legal Professions* (Portland, OR: Hart, 2006); Patrick Polden, "Portia's Progress: Women at the Bar in England, 1919–1939," *International Journal of the Legal Profession* 12: 3 (2005): 293–338.

[3] Jane Hamlett, *At Home in the Institution: Material Life in Asylums, Lodging Houses and Schools in Victorian and Edwardian England* (Basingstoke: Palgrave Macmillan, 2014); Deborah Cohen, *Family Secrets: Shame and Privacy in Modern Britain* (Oxford: Oxford University Press, 2013); William Whyte, *Unlocking the Church: The Lost Secrets of Victorian Sacred Space* (Oxford: Oxford University Press, 2017); Amy Milne-Smith, *London*

This book insists that the study of the Inns and the legal profession is not a parochial pursuit but rather a means of unpacking the gendered logics that undergirded much of Victorian society. It holds masculinity as an essential category of analysis not just for understanding the bar but, more broadly, for making meaning of the operations of other venerable power centers such as parliament or the church.[4] Indeed, this work serves as a methodological model for explaining enduring conservatism and the ways that ancient, elite institutions have survived and thrived in modern Britain.

That a history of the bar would reapproach legal institutions by looking to the Inns of Court, rather than the law courts, may seem counter-intuitive. Time at the Inns, however, was *the* universal experience among all members of the bar, regardless of the kinds of law they practiced – if they practiced – or where. Examining the institutional power of the Inns, societies whose extra-legality made them uniquely invested in maintaining the status quo, reveals the epicenter of the deep-seated conservativism and resistance to change within legal culture. A focus on the Inns also grounds the study in two interrelated lines of inquiry: analysis of the built environment and of the gendered performances that took place within it. Indeed, one of the major preoccupations of this work is to advocate for the central importance not of men but of masculinity in shaping professional culture, as well as urban, imperial, and political history.

Unlike highly compartmentalized studies of the bar, therefore, *Brotherhood of Barristers* considers the Inns of Court from a variety of perspectives: as legal societies regulating access to an elite profession; as territories in London that maintained uneasy and contested relationships with the neighborhoods that bordered them; as artifacts of cultural heritage that took on national importance; and as producers of the gentlemanly liberal subject in the midst of Britain's great empire. The breadth of my chronological scope, from roughly 1840 to 1940, allows

Clubland (New York: Palgrave Macmillan, 2011); Vicky Long, *The Rise and Fall of the Healthy Factory: The Politics of Industrial Health in Britain, 1914–1960* (Basingstoke: Palgrave Macmillan, 2011); Louise Hide, *Gender and Class in English Asylums, 1890–1914* (Basingstoke: Palgrave Macmillan, 2014); Douglas Melvin Haynes, *Fit to Practice: Empire, Race, Gender, and the Making of British Medicine, 1850–1980* (Rochester, NY: University of Rochester Press, 2017).

[4] Ben Griffin, *The Politics of Gender in Victorian Britain Masculinity, Political Culture and the Struggle for Women's Rights* (Cambridge: Cambridge University Press, 2012); Lucy Delap, "Conservative Values: Anglicans and the Gender Order in Inter-war Britain," in *Brave New World: Imperial and Democratic National Building in Britain between the Wars*, ed. Laura Beers and Geraint Thomas (London: University of London, 2011), 149–168; Timothy Jones, "'Unduly Conscious of Her Sex:' Priesthood, Female Bodies, and Sacred Space in the Church of England," *Women's History Review* 21: 4 (2012): 639–655.

me to trace transformations with mid-Victorian roots that bore fruit in the early twentieth century and beyond. This chronology also allows me to consider women and colonial subjects in the same study, which other works on the bar have not done. The book employs sources utilized by other legal historians, such as institutional records and the legal press, but combines them with letters, diaries, memoirs, guidebooks, fiction, and the popular press to consider a broader context than most existing legal histories.[5] The book incorporates a diverse array of voices and historical actors, from the most successful and high-flying members to struggling law students, disbarred barristers, political radicals and dissidents, and women's rights campaigners.

This work examines institutions that, despite lying outside the realm of parliament or government bureaucracy, were deeply connected to powerful positions within the British state. In the nineteenth and early twentieth centuries, these four legal societies controlled access to the upper reaches of the legal profession in Britain and its colonies. As gateways to law, the judiciary, parliamentary, and cabinet positions, the Inns of Court were uniquely entrenched in the power structures of Great Britain and its empire. Other European nations, for example, did not divorce legal education and the regulation of the bar from the universities and the state.[6] In a split legal profession, barristers, who pleaded cases in court, held more prestige and higher salaries than solicitors, who interacted with clients. With specialized knowledge in law and the processes of using the courts, as well as professional connections to the governing elite, many leading politicians began their careers as barristers.

Members of the bar practiced all branches of law and were experts in a variety of forms of legal thought, but Victorian reflections on the power of the Inns of Court returned again and again to the unique status of precedent within British common law. Authors emphasized that the Inns governed the bar not because they were chartered to do so by the crown or any legislative body but because their uninterrupted governance of the bar from time immemorial gave them the right to continue. Similarly, they contended that the societies' centuries-old occupation and maintenance of their grounds justified the Inns' status as

---

[5] Daniel Duman, *The English and Colonial Bars* (London: Croom Helm, 1983); Raymond Cocks, *Foundations of the Modern Bar* (London: Sweet & Maxwell, 1983); Richard O. Havery (ed.), *History of the Middle Temple* (Oxford and Portland, OR: Hart, 2011).

[6] Michael Burrage, *Revolution and the Making of the Contemporary Legal Professions* (Oxford: Oxford University Press, 2006); Hannes Siegrist, "Professionalization with the Brakes On: The Legal Profession in Switzerland, France and Germany in the Nineteenth and Early Twentieth Centuries," *Comparative Social Research* 9 (1986): 267–298.

independent local authorities. For these interlocutors, often benchers of the Inns, precedent acted as a bulwark against other local or parliamentary authorities that infringed upon the Inns' rights over practice at the bar or their material environs. Precedent also dictated the standards by which the Inns governed their members. Rather than codified rules, the societies pointed to examples set by their forbearers. The absence of clear statutes afforded the Inns wide latitude in interpreting standards of professional practice, allowing them to adapt legal etiquette to shifting sociopolitical contexts. The societies' constant retrospective gaze created a culture centered on a deep valuation of history and its remains and connected the ancient material lineage of the Inns with their ties to ancient law. Importantly, the societies' respect for the inheritances of the past imbued the Inns with a conservative outlook, which presumed the infallibility of preceding decisions and resisted all but the smallest, most incremental changes.

It may sound surprising, then, to declare that the Inns of Court were actively engaged in processes of liberalism throughout the nineteenth century. Let me clarify. Firstly, I am using conservatism and liberalism in the sense of two broad ideologies, ones that historians such as Lawrence Goldman argue have been set more at odds by academics influenced by a partisan present than by the thinking of the Victorian past.[7] I take conservatism to mean an investment in tradition and its resultant hierarchies and structures of power, an investment held by the Inns of Court. This investment did not mean, however, that the Inns could ignore the increasing importance of standards of reason, economy, utility, and efficiency – that is, the standards of liberalism – to which more and more of Victorian society was held. The societies were reluctant to undertake changes that would dilute their authority over the bar, but they embraced policies that benefited public health and the well-being of their London neighbors, even at the Inns' expense. They did so in part because of the growing importance of public opinion: the best way to forestall parliamentary intervention and retain the rights they had gained as private associations was to take active steps to make it seem as if the Inns fulfilled public obligation and served the public good. In describing the Inns as at once imbued with conservative ideology but engaging in processes of liberal reform, this book stands with work like Goldman's that challenges the irreconcilability of the two concepts and pushes historians to reevaluate the approaches of public and private institutions in terms of ideological syncretism rather than polarization.

---

[7] Lawrence Goldman, *Science, Reform, and Politics in Victorian Britain* (Cambridge: Cambridge University Press, 2002), 264–266.

Indeed, despite their engagement in liberal reforms, this study illuminates how institutions independent of the central government fiercely
maintained their autonomy. William Joseph Reader and Harold Perkin
have charted the nineteenth-century ascendancy of reforms emphasizing
merit, training, and examination over systems such as the army's sale of
commissions, the civil service's use of patronage, and the exclusivity of
the Royal College of Physicians. According to this narrative, centralized
control and forced adherence to rules and guidelines rationalized these
professions and made them more meritocratic.[8] The Inns of Court,
however, firmly resisted the tide of centralization. Their ancient lineage
and the exalted status of the law in Victorian culture extended unique
cachet to the Inns and exempted the societies from sweeping parliamentary or press critiques. Furthermore, the societies neither needed to
legitimate their existence, as did the medical establishment, nor did they
experience dramatic failures in carrying out their function, as did the
army. Instead, throughout the nineteenth century, the Inns forestalled
parliamentary intervention through self-directed reforms. Theirs is a
story of longevity and continuity of institutional power. Similarly, the
societies maintained their authority on a local level. As liberties of
London, legally the Inns were independent from the City of London
and the greater metropolis. Centralized approaches to urban improvement in the mid-nineteenth century, such as the Metropolitan Board of
Works, presented a new threat to the autonomy of the Inns. The societies
warded off the City's and the board's endeavors to assert jurisdiction over
the Inns through a combination of law and ritual.

This book departs from earlier studies of the professions not only in
that it focuses on an occupation that bucked Victorian trends but also in
its insistence on the centrality of gender as an analytic category.
Historians of the legal profession rarely consider gender in their analyses,
taking it as incidental that the bar remained an exclusively male preserve
for five hundred years.[9] In contrast to these assumptions, I argue that in
legal culture, masculinity was not incidental but instrumental. The
Victorian Inns relied on a culture of fraternity to inculcate their members
with the values and attitudes appropriate to British barristers, encouraging members to take part in dining rituals, socialization in common
spaces, and volunteer drill corps. Fraternal rhetoric and praxis assumed a

---

[8] William Joseph Reader, *Professional Men* (New York: Basic Books, 1966); Harold Perkin,
The Rise of Professional Society (London: Routledge, 1989).

[9] Duman, *The English and Colonial Bars*; Cocks, *Foundations of the Modern Bar*. The bar was
opened to women only via parliamentary statute, by the terms of the Sex Disqualification
(Removal) Act 1919.

fundamental similarity between barristers not on the basis of their geographic origin, wealth, class, or religion but on the basis of their standing
as men. The Inns incorporated standards of gentlemanliness into both
informal expectations and codified rules for members' behavior. They
expected members to uphold masculine notions of honor, particularly as
related to trustworthiness and honesty. The societies presupposed legal
practitioners to be rational-minded and self-disciplined – qualities the
Victorians understood to be inherently male.

The societies used customs and traditions to promote both a particular
professional ethos and a culture of belonging based on fraternal bonds.
Eric Hobsbawm and others have argued that many Victorian rituals of
symbolic nature that were used to inculcate certain values and norms
implied continuity with the past, but really were of nineteenth-century
invention.[10] At the Inns of Court, the societies both reemphasized or
revived preexisting customs and established new ones with an ancient
semblance to instill a sense of brotherhood based on shared values in
their members. The societies also drew on the architectural remains of
their grounds, particularly emphasizing surviving medieval and
Elizabethan spaces and constructing new buildings or renovating old
ones to conform to these architectural styles. They used the logic of
precedent to maintain the bar as an all-male preserve: women never
had been admitted to the societies; therefore, they could not be admitted
to the societies. The Inns were further able to take advantage of new
developments in the Victorian era, such as the shift to a more robust
masculinity defined by participation in sporting culture, to tout fraternity
in the form of organizations like the Inns of Court Volunteer Rifle Corps.

In outlining the masculine logics of the bar, this book builds upon the
work of Paul Deslandes and others to investigate the role homosocial
institutions played in forging the values of the educated elite from the
tenets of British masculinities.[11] The Inns epitomized a "homosocial"
culture of affective same-sex bonds. In the usage proposed by Eve
Sedgwick, homosocial leaves room for erotic desire in relationships
between men, but does not necessarily assert claims of homosexuality.[12]
Historians have deployed Sedgwick's concept of homosocial to analyze a
variety of same-sex social interactions and institutions such as public

[10] Eric Hobsbawm, "Introduction: Inventing Traditions," in *The Invention of Tradition*, ed.
Eric Hobsbawm and Terrence Ranger (Cambridge: Cambridge University Press,
1983), 1.
[11] Paul Deslandes, *Oxbridge Men* (Bloomington: Indiana University Press, 2005); Milne-
Smith, *London Clubland*; John Potvin, *Material and Visual Cultures beyond Male Bonding,
1870–1914* (Burlington: Ashgate, 2008).
[12] E. Sedgwick, *Between Men* (New York: Columbia University Press, 1985).

schools and universities, sports teams, and gentlemen's clubs.[13] These fraternal worlds and activities would have been familiar to many members of the Inns; in fact, the societies would have been one of many homosocial spaces inhabited by law students and barristers.[14] Significantly, most studies that analyze homosociality focus on relationships cultivated outside the professional realm, arguing that spaces like clubs or secret societies provided respite from both the feminized domestic interior and the hyperrational world of the market.[15] Yet the bar was one of many professions – university professorship was another – in which friendship and sociability were as essential as, and often inextricably bound up with, learning and technical expertise.[16] The importance of affect at the Inns suggests that many Victorians did not hold clear distinctions between personal and professional relationships, and that the emotional separation between home and work may not have been as dramatic as some historians have claimed.[17]

Brotherhood of Barristers reveals the geographically and chronologically far-ranging impact of the bar's resolutely English, masculine culture. Located in the metropolitan center, the history of the Inns of Court simultaneously tells a story about London and a story that stretches beyond the metropole to the farthest corners of the British empire. With few exceptions, to practice as a barrister anywhere in the empire required joining an Inn and spending three years in London to qualify. No other profession demanded such centralized training. This consolidation socialized law students from across the empire into a resolutely masculine culture, and uniformly prohibited women from practicing as lawyers in all but a handful of white settler colonies.[18] At its height, the

---

[13] Deslandes, *Oxbridge Men*; Ben Griffin, *The Politics of Gender in Victorian Britain*; E. Showalter, *Sexual Anarchy* (New York: Viking, 1990); Milne-Smith, *London Clubland*.

[14] Duman, *The English and Colonial Bars*, 24; Alexander, *After Court Hours*, 65; A. Munby, *Munby, Man of Two Worlds*, ed. D. Hudson (Boston: Gambit, 1972), 10.

[15] John Tosh, *A Man's Place: Masculinity and the Middle-Class Home in Victorian England* (New Haven, CT: Yale University Press, 2007); Mark C. Carnes, *Secret Ritual and Manhood in Victorian America* (New Haven, CT: Yale University Press, 1989); Stefan-Ludwig Hoffmann, "Civility, Male Friendship, and Masonic Sociability in Nineteenth-Century Germany," *Gender & History* 13 (2001): 224–248.

[16] Christopher Hilliard, *English as a Vocation: The Scrutiny Movement* (Oxford: Oxford University Press, 2012); Emily Rutherford, "Arthur Sidgwick's *Greek Prose Composition*: Gender, Affect, and Sociability in the Late-Victorian University," *Journal of British Studies* 56 (January 2017): 91–116.

[17] Leonore Davidoff and Catherine Hall, *Family Fortunes: Men and Women of the English Middle Class, 1780–1950*. London: Hutchinson, 1987; Tosh, *A Man's Place*.

[18] Women practiced as barristers in parts of Canada, New Zealand, and Australia as early as 1900. Mary Jane Mossman, *The First Women Lawyers: A Comparative Study of Gender, Law and the Legal Professions* (Portland, OR: Hart, 2006), 14.

British empire encompassed approximately one-fifth of the world's population, making this book a comprehensive examination of exclusionary legal culture and revealing antecedents to disparities within the legal profession across the globe today.[19]

This study also reveals the societies' uneasy involvement in the processes of disciplining and ordering Great Britain and its empire. On the one hand, as ancient institutions that helped to mutually define and reinforce the values of the British elite, the Inns viewed themselves as responsible for shouldering certain burdens of imperial formation. As the societies understood it, admitting members from the empire would imbue colonial students with traditions and values of the Inns, eventually transporting these conservative priorities back to the empire. By instilling values central to the legal profession, such as fraternity and self-discipline, the Inns molded colonial subjects into what scholars have labeled the liberal individual. At the same time, however, the societies were also increasingly overwhelmed by the demands of an ever-expanding empire. Particularly in the early twentieth century, when faced with a growing number of politically radical or anti-imperial members, the Inns began to question the sustainability of their role as the central node of the legal profession.

Methodologically, this book weaves together several separate theoretical frameworks. It insists that an analysis of institutional power dynamics must be grounded in spatiality. Scholars and critical theorists have conceptualized space in a variety of ways. Inspired by the work of urban historians, art historians, and geographers, I begin this book with a focus on the built environment.[20] I argue that the buildings and grounds of the Inns created the conditions of possibility for producing the gentlemanly liberal subject, or in some cases failed to do so. I analyze the symbolic meanings of the societies' historicist architecture and the ways the Inns

---

[19] "A Current Glance at Women in the Law," *American Bar Association*, February 2013; "Trends in the Solicitors' Profession: Annual Statistics Report 2012," *The Law Society*, 2013; "Statistics," *The Bar Council*, 2006–10.

[20] Patrick Joyce, *Rule of Freedom* (New York: Verso, 2003); Chris Otter, *The Victorian Eye* (Chicago: University of Chicago Press, 2008); Lynda Nead, *Victorian Babylon* (New Haven, CT: Yale University Press, 2000); Judith R. Walkowitz, *City of Dreadful Delight* (Chicago, IL: University of Chicago Press, 1992); Seth Koven, *Slumming* (Princeton, NJ: Princeton University Press, 2004); Erika Rappaport, *Shopping for Pleasure* (Princeton, NJ: Princeton University Press, 2000); Nancy Rose Marshall, *City of Gold and Mud* (New Haven, CT: Yale University Press, 2012); Donald J. Olsen, *Growth of Victorian London* (New York: Holmes & Meier, 1976); John M. Picker, *Victorian Soundscapes* (New York: Oxford University Press, 2003); James H. Winter, *London's Teeming Streets: 1830–1914* (London: Routledge, 1993).

manipulated their built environment to retain cultural prestige and power. I am also indebted to Henri Lefebvre and Edward Soja, who insist that space cannot be reduced to mental construct or physical form, but must be considered as "the habitus of social practices."[21] Feminist anthropologists and geographers have critiqued Lefebvre and Soja for ignoring the operations of race and gender in favor of class, but nevertheless acknowledge the utility of retaining the maxim that "(social) space is a (social) product."[22] Indeed, this conception compliments many queer theoretical frameworks: if cultural categories like gender are a repetition of norms – a "doing" rather than a "having" – and space is created by practice, then the same everyday embodied performances that constitute gender likewise construct space.[23] Uniting the insights of Marxist geographers with queer theorists, I consider the use of space at the Inns, asking who was permitted access to which parts of the societies, and how ritual and the activities of social and professional life created classed, gendered, or racialized norms and marginalization. I do not contend that the halls, libraries, and chambers of the Inns merely hosted performances of a particular kind of professional masculinity, but rather that the spaces we think of as the Inns of Court were in fact *produced by* the dining rituals and other masculinist practices of the bar.

While Lefebvre and Soja are useful for connecting the built environment to the practices within it, their Marxism results in a dialectical conception of power particularly inappropriate for analyzing institutions that disdained both industrial and finance capital. Instead, this book understands the Inns of Court as participating in the processes that Michel Foucault dubs governmentality. In Foucault's conception, social control is not achieved by top-down interventions of the state, but instead emanates from a variety of nodes, especially institutions such as hospitals and schools. These institutions encourage members to internalize their values, at which point the individuals become self-regulating,

---

[21] H. Lefebvre, *The Production of Space* (Cambridge: Blackwell, 1991); Soja, *Postmodern Geographies*, 18.

[22] Rosalyn Deutsche, "Men in Space," *Strategies* 3 (1990): 130–137, and "Boys Town," *Environment and Planning D: Space and Society* 9 (1991): 5–30; Doreen Massey, "Flexible Sexism," *Environment and Planning D: Space and Society* 9 (1991): 31–57; Gillian Rose, "Review of Edward Soja, *Postmodern Geographies* and David Harvey, "The Condition of Postmodernity," *Journal of Historical Geography* 17: 1 (January 1991): 118–121.

[23] Judith Butler, *Bodies That Matter on the Discursive Limits of "Sex"* (London and New York: Routledge, 1993), 9. For examples of analyses pairing Butler and Lefebvre, see Deirdre Conlon, "Productive Bodies, Performative Spaces: Everyday Life in Christopher Park," *Sexualities* 7 (2004): 462–479; Melissa Tyler and Laurie Cohen, "Spaces That Matter: Gender Performativity and Organizational Space," *Organization Studies* 31 (2010): 175–198.

conducting themselves in accordance with the priorities of the established order. The Inns, inculcating members with the values of the bar and spreading them to the empire, were engaged in just such a process. Foucault conceives of power as "a multiplicity of force relations" and largely dismisses juridical discourse. His analyses therefore ignore legal institutions.[24] By giving serious attention to the built environment and embodied practice, however, my work considers legal institutions not as they shaped law but as they formed the privileged individuals that informed and upheld hegemonic discourses.

Foucault's insights on institutional power are valuable for describing the relationship between institutions and the individual and the role of institutions in society, but – like Lefebvre and Soja – his work is largely blind to the operations of race and gender within institutions. Sara Ahmed has argued that in both culture and scholarship, institutional whiteness and masculinity are often taken as a given and thus, in many accounts of institutional life, go "invisible and unmarked, as the absent center against which others appear as points of deviation."[25] To work against taking these categories as a given, this book relies on the work of black feminist and/or queer theorists like Ahmed, Sianne Ngai, and Lauren Berlant. These theorists remind us that narratives or tropes that are most familiar – for example, the white male professional – are ones that merit closest examination.

This book is also indebted to black feminist and queer theory for its work in highlighting the affective dimensions of institutional life. In *The Cultural Politics of Emotion*, Ahmed examines the use of metaphors (for example, the nation has a "soft touch") in contemporary British culture to show "how emotions become attributes of collectives."[26] Significantly, Ahmed understands emotions as originating neither within the self nor outside it, but as social and cultural practices that produce the very categories of interior and exterior. Ahmed thus analyzes the sociality rather than the psychology of emotion, tracing how "emotions circulate between bodies, examining how they 'stick' as well as move."[27] Following these trajectories, she insists, "allows us to

---

[24] Michel Foucault, "Governmentality," in *The Foucault Effect*, ed. Graham Burchell, Colin Gordon, and Peter Miller (Chicago: University of Chicago Press, 1991); Michel Foucault, *History of Sexuality, Volume 1* (New York: Vintage, 1978), 92; Joyce, *The Rule of Freedom*.

[25] Sara Ahmed, *On Being Included: Racism and Diversity in Institutional Life* (Durham, NC, and London: Duke University Press, 2012), 35.

[26] Sara Ahmed, *The Cultural Politics of Emotion* (Edinburgh: Edinburgh University Press, 2014), 2.

[27] Ibid., 4.

address the question of how subjects become *invested* in particular structures," a process which Foucauldian frameworks are unable to fully account for.[28]

Affect theory may seem a surprising framework for a book about Victorian legal institutions, but it is critical for explaining enduring power relations and resistance to change. Following Ahmed's insights, *Brotherhood of Barristers* holds that "brotherhood" was both a metaphor – lawyers were *like* kin – and an affective designation – lawyers should feel for one another the warmth, loyalty, and fundamental similarities of siblings. As Ahmed argues, within the metaphors that produce collective emotions, there is usually an implied us/them construction: citizen/immigrant, community member/terrorist, heterosexual/queer. In the case of fraternal rhetoric in the legal profession, if the "us" were male members of the bar, the most obvious "them" was women. Women were, by definition, not brothers. Whether or not people of color could be brothers remained a murkier question throughout the period of this study. In debates among both the bar's leaders and its rank and file, detractors almost always pointed to signifiers of masculinity – self-control, honesty, work ethic, or lack thereof – rather than racial determinism to argue against the inclusion of overseas members. By this logic, colonial members could not be brothers, not because they were people of color but because they were not fully men.

Importantly, just as Ahmed is not trying to access the subjective interior, this book makes no claims that every individual barrister felt strongly about the Inns. Instead, connecting Ahmed to Lauren Berlant, it considers how the metaphor of brotherhood created a set of expectations for members of the bar, both in the sense of who could conceivably be a member and in the sense of what men (and later women) could expect from their experience of membership. It understands members' responses to violations of these expectations – their distress, nostalgia, disgust, or condescension, expressed in word and action – to be affective reactions, or what Berlant calls "dramas of adjustment."[29] Examining these reactions and acknowledging that not all of them were grounded in rational logic – precedential thinking was important to the culture of the bar, but it can only account for so much – are essential for explaining the legal profession's resistance to change.

[28] Ibid., 12.
[29] Lauren Berlant, *Cruel Optimism* (Durham, NC: Duke University Press, 2011), 16, 3; Sianne Ngai, *Our Aesthetic Categories: Zany, Cute, Interesting* (Cambridge: Harvard University Press, 2012).

Background: An Exclusive Profession

The Inns of Court had long been elite and homosocial institutions, but the demographics of their membership varied by period. The Inner and Middle Temples' history, for example, began in the twelfth century, when members of the Order of the Knights of the Temple of Solomon of Jerusalem, or Templars, built a series of monastic buildings on the site. Their close ties to the English monarchy did not save the Templars from papal charges of heresy and depravity, and by 1314, the last member of the order was burnt at the stake. The property was then leased to lawyers who organized themselves into two formal societies, the Inner and Middle Temples. Though originally guild-like in nature, by the sixteenth century, the Inns served an important role as finishing schools for the sons of the aristocracy. John H. Baker and Wilfrid Prest have argued that as centers of learning and public ritual, the Elizabethan Inns were deeply engaged in civic life and the production of legal thought. Disrupted by the civil war, when many avoided London life if possible, legal moots, debates, and public rituals fell out of practice and went unrevived during the Restoration. In the late seventeenth and eighteenth centuries, with the decline of formal education at the Inns, wealthy young men began to replace time in London with a more fashionable "Grand Tour." At the same time, an increasing number of middle-class Britons could afford to send their sons to train as barristers. By the late eighteenth century, the middle classes accounted for two-thirds of the bar, whereas the gentry made up less than a quarter.[30]

Though there were no formal requirements for joining an Inn, several policies ensured the functional exclusion of those too far down Britain's social or economic hierarchies. Admission to the societies was primarily regulated by an applicant's ability to pay his fees. Each Inn required a £100 deposit returned at call, plus "admission and call fees, annual duties and term fees, term dinners, [later] examination fees, and certificate of call."[31] Such sums would have been prohibitive for almost all

---

[30] John H. Baker, *The Common Law Tradition* (London: Hambledon Press, 2000); Timothy Daniell and J. M. B. Crawford, *The Lawyers: The Inns of Court – The Home of the Common Law* (London: Wildy and Sons, 1976); Daniel Duman, *The English and Colonial Bars* (London: Croom Helm, 1983); Wilfrid Prest, *The Rise of the Barristers* (Oxford: Clarenden, 1986); David Lemmings, *Gentlemen and Barristers* (Oxford: Clarenden, 1990).

[31] In 1855 Middle Temple fees amounted to £60.12.0 for three years, and by 1920 the cost had risen to approximately £170; *Report of the Commissioners Appointed to Inquire into the Arrangements in the Inns of Court and Inns of Chancery* (London: George Edward Eyre and William Spottiswoode, 1855); MT 1 LBO 24, Letter to Richard Talemaye, July 19, 1920.

members of the working classes. In his demographic study of the bar, Daniel Duman notes that a rare few artisans' sons succeeded in entering the profession, but they were generally the children of highly skilled craftsmen such as jewelers. The bar could offer the possibility of social mobility to the sons of small businessmen, solicitors, doctors, teachers, and lower civil servants. Beginning in the 1820s, however, the societies instated rules to prohibit any person engaged in a trade from joining the Inns and disbarred any barristers who pursued a trade themselves. Former solicitors were required to be out of practice three years before joining the societies, and all prospective members had to provide character references signed by two barristers. As Duman argues, such regulations were intended to favor individuals who could weather several years without income during their studentship and early days at the bar. They also disadvantaged anybody without several barristers in their social milieu.[32]

While the Inns never made higher education a requirement for admission, they did privilege those with university degrees to encourage their membership. Noticing the decline of elite members but wishing to preserve the gentlemanly character of the bar, in 1762 the Georgian benchers passed regulations allowing Oxford or Cambridge graduates to be called to the bar after three years rather than five. The Inns also waved the £100 deposit for these individuals.[33] The Victorian societies responded to the growth in prestige of the regional universities by gradually broadening the list of exemptions to comprise a wider range of institutions.[34] In doing so they captured a wider swathe of graduates, but still excluded students who had taken degrees outside the UK, along with those who had not attended university. The required deposit and greater number of terms before call could be a financial burden for these students, and for overseas students, they were compounded with the cost of a voyage to London.

For those who possessed the means to join, the application process was fairly simple. A prospective student first chose which of the four Inns to which he wished to be admitted. Few memoirs or diaries explain why members selected their particular society. Some applied to the same Inn to which their fathers or families belonged, but some did not. Others may have applied to an Inn favored by graduates of their college. The Middle Temple, eager to drive up its lagging numbers at mid-century, readily

[32] Duman, *The English and Colonial Bars*, 19–21.
[33] By 1885, 58 percent of men at the Bar had studied at Oxbridge; Duman, *The English and Colonial Bars*, 20.
[34] MT MPA April 22, 1920.

admitted international students, making it a favorite with subsequent generations of overseas applicants. Men with no connection to an affinity group may have chosen at random. Having selected an Inn, the prospective student, or perhaps his parent, sent a letter of interest to the Under Treasurer of his chosen society, along with the two certificates of character signed by barristers and any requisite certificates related to examinations. Once all of this paperwork was in order, the student could pay his fees and begin keeping term.

Chapter Breakdown

Brotherhood of Barristers is a story of entrenched practices and resistance to change, of adaptation and, at times, accommodation. Of medieval origin, the Inns of Court derived their authority from common law precedent and privileged tradition and continuity with the past. In the 1850s, Victorian fiction established tropes of the Inns as decaying relics of Old London and sites of cultural heritage. Increases in membership spurred the Inns to undergo massive renovation projects; by the end of the century, most buildings were of Victorian creation. New social actors, urban developments, and increasingly complex global politics further challenged the seemingly unchanging nature of these institutions. Historically buildings, walls, and the Thames itself separated the Inns from the rest of London. Victorian infrastructural projects, such as the Victoria Embankment along the Temple riverfront, jeopardized the societies' freedom from urban encroachments. An increasing number of men from across the empire came to study at the Inns of Court, bringing with them unfamiliar religious, sumptuary, dietary, and cultural needs and practices. In 1919, parliamentary legislation forced the Inns to admit women. In the face of these changes, the trope of the Inns, their occupants, and their rituals as ruins of Old London endured and gained force in the twentieth century as writers figured the societies as bastions of continuity with the past.

Chapter 2 considers the Inns of Court in their relationship to the broader city, taking "London" to be both the people who lived, worked, visited, or otherwise circulated through the capital, and the variety of governing bodies responsible for regulating the city. The chapter highlights the societies' struggle to maintain their local autonomy while fulfilling obligations to the public good and, increasingly, to public opinion. The Inns were geographically and legally separate from the rest of the capital, but they connected with the central London populace via efforts to promote citizens' physical, moral, and cultural well-being. At the same time, the Inns clashed with newly created, centralized metropolitan bodies designed to unify and order the metropolis in the name of public health. Disputes between the Inns and entities like the Metropolitan Board of Works represented a conflict between an ancient system of local authority and processes of urban rationalization, a tension that defined metropolitan modernity in Britain. Historically the Inns of Court had warded off infringements upon their rights by citing common law precedent for their independence. But as competing strains within liberalism pushed institutions to engage in philanthropy in ways that could undermine institutional authority, the Inns found themselves unable to fully salvage their autonomy. As the priorities of the Inns seemed to diverge from the public good, divisions emerged between the benchers and the bar's rank and file.

These divisions were just one of many fractures within the increasingly heterogeneous population of the bar. Chapter 3 of the book examines how, particularly in response to their growing middle-class population, the Inns relied on their architectural spaces and social practices to ensure that all members of the bar embodied the ideal of the gentlemanly professional. In the absence of required classes, the societies stressed fraternization with older generations to inculcate new members with legal knowledge and the values appropriate to British barristers. The societies emphasized affective bonds and tried to cultivate fraternal relationships between their members. Yet in the mid-nineteenth century, the category of gentlemanliness was itself in flux, subject to divergent ideas of who could be a gentleman and how a gentleman should behave. Competing ideas of who belonged to the societies or what counted as gentlemanly behavior could result in unanticipated affective registers, including anger, indignation, and shame.

Questions of gentlemanliness became even more important as the Victorian rationalizing impulse that reformed the city similarly spurred Liberal MPs to inquire into the professions, debating whether or not the Inns of Court adequately governed the bar and effectively trained their members. The societies defended themselves from parliamentary assaults by insisting that legal etiquette ensured the gentlemanly character of the bar. Chapter 4 particularly examines disciplinary hearings for violations of etiquette at the Inns to consider the societies' direct assertions of their authority over the operations of the legal profession. It argues that, in the nineteenth century, breaches of legal etiquette largely pertained to illegal activity, especially fraud, or ungentlemanly behavior, such as engaging in trade. In the geopolitical context of the early twentieth century, faced with members holding new radical political commitments, the societies overlaid concerns about gentlemanliness with worries over personal political expression and national loyalty.

In the face of conscientious objection, colonial independence move-ments, and Bolshevik Revolution, the societies manipulated legal etiquette and rules to deliberately excuse or disbar members for similar offenses along lines that accorded more with members' seeming Britishness or foreignness than with the legality or illegality of their actions.

The Inns worried over political dissidents of all persuasions, but Chapter 5 examines their largest and most ongoing source of concern: Indian nationalists, whom the Inns sometimes conflated with Indian students more generally. Beginning in the mid-nineteenth century, men from throughout the empire, but in greatest number from India, came to London to study law. By the early twentieth century, burgeoning colonial nationalist movements gained visibility for their causes, some-times through violent actions in the colonies or in London. Members of the Inns came to distrust the potentially radical politics of their overseas members, equating all imperial subjects with anti-British actions. The societies collaborated with the British government to consider quotas limiting the number of Indian students in London. They debated whether or not colonial students were capable of being trained to be self-regulating subjects who would willingly submit to and replicate existing structures of power.

Chapter 6 considers how and why the societies resisted women even after their admission to the Inns in 1919 and the strategies women law students and barristers deployed to navigate the resolutely masculine culture of the Inns. It argues that beyond their gender, women's political commitments and social networks mitigated the degree of acceptance or resistance they faced from members of the societies. The chapter also examines the Inns' fraught reconciliation of the societies' concerns about overseas students with the new presence of women in their common rooms, gardens, and halls. It considers the complicated mapping of intersectional identities onto the existing culture of the Inns and traces how the societies manipulated space to privilege, protect, include, or exclude female members, colonial members, or female colonial members.

Each chapter in this book documents the Inns' unyielding though hardly static relationship with outside authorities in the face of demo-graphic, governmental, and geopolitical challenges. In Chapter 2, the societies repeatedly butted heads with municipal authorities, but were willing to cooperate with and accommodate both tourists and residents of local neighborhoods in the form of institutional noblesse oblige. Chapter 4 broadens the context to think about outside authority in the form of parliamentary pressures for bar reform in the nineteenth century, and geopolitical forces in the early twentieth. In both cases, the societies held their own, warding off parliamentary intervention with self-directed reforms and evaluating members' changing politics on a case-by-case basis. In the context of overseas students, however, the Inns' autonomy began to buckle. As Chapter 5 details, an expanding empire made demands on the societies that became increasingly difficult to accommodate, particularly in the face of nationalist violence. The Inns proved willing to not only cooperate with but also cede some authority to various arms of the state. Around the same time, as explored in Chapter 6, the Inns faced a crushing blow to their autonomy in the form of parliamentary intervention via the Sex Disqualification (Removal) Act 1919. Overall, however, these various challenges to the societies' independence changed the culture of the Inns in only minute ways. This book is a story not of decline but of the adaptability of powerful and conservative institutions whose longevity depended on the gendered, classed, and racialized underpinnings of institutional power.

2   The Metropolitan Inns

This chapter begins the study of the culture of the bar by focusing on the topography of the Inns of Court and their location in central London. Foregrounding the work of subsequent chapters that will examine the setting and crossing of social and cultural boundaries *within* the profession, this chapter interrogates the setting and crossing of the physical boundaries of the Inns and their environs. It explores strategies behind the shaping of the material spaces of the Inns, conflicts over which individuals outside the profession could be privy to those spaces and for what purposes. The Inns' contested relationship to the city at large was itself a result of the changing dynamics within and between the Victorian metropolis, Victorian public, and Victorian legal profession. To wit, all three were increasingly beholden to the values of the middle classes: middle-class tastes dictated public opinion and directed urban reforms; middle-class men largely filled the ranks of the bar. By examining the role class dynamics played in the development of the capital and expectations of the professions, this chapter identifies three key tensions at the heart of professional metropolitan modernity: veneration of the past versus the need for rationalization; the increasing importance of public opinion for dictating the operations of private entities; and the competing veins of centralization and localism within liberalism, an ideology whose political dominance at mid-century demanded that elite institutions engage in philanthropy and reform in ways that could both solidify and destabilize institutional authority.

The Inns' changing relationship to the public and the capital came about in part because of threats to the prestige of the upper branch of the Victorian bar. Historians have detailed the efforts of nineteenth-century professions to seek legitimation, particularly medicine.[1] Unlike medicine, however, which reinvented its plebian butchers as respectable

---

[1] Joan Lane, *A Social History of Medicine Health, Healing and Disease in England, 1750–1950* (London: Routledge, 2001), 11; Mary Wilson Carpenter, *Health, Medicine and Society in Victorian England* (Santa Barbara, CA: Praeger, 2010), 4–5.

experts, or even the lower branch of the legal profession, which created the Law Society to elevate the status of solicitors, Victorian barristers' social standing was downwardly mobile. The formerly aristocratic Inns of Court, finishing schools for the early-modern wealthy and titled, were by the early nineteenth century dominated by the middle classes. To describe the Inns as increasingly middle class is not to overstate the degree to which these were accessible spaces: membership of the mid-Victorian Inns was dominated by the sons of the professional and commercial classes, many of whom had the benefit of an Oxbridge education.[2] These men were a fraction of the overall population. Nevertheless, the Victorian bar saw a growing gap in both status and income between its highest-flying members and the hangers-on struggling to find work in an overcrowded profession.[3] Once the default realm of aristocrats, it became newly necessary for the Victorian Inns of Court to prove the bar a gentlemanly profession.

Emphasis on the Inns' ancient and aristocratic past proved effective ballast against the profession's increasingly middle-class membership. A wide variety of scholars have examined Victorian historicism as it manifested in everything from literary and artistic movements to capitalist enterprise.[4] The Inns of Court derived prestige from their ancient lineage and, therefore, devoted significant energy to keeping their connection to the past alive in the minds of members and in the cultural imaginary. The societies cast their environs as remains of Old London, their medieval church and Elizabethan hall material evidence of their ancient origins. At the same time, the needs of the modern gentlemanly professional demanded orderly, rational spaces fitted with modern conveniences. The Inns spent much of the nineteenth century restoring, repairing, and rebuilding their deteriorating environs. Architectural renovations and new constructions deliberately evoked the medieval and the Elizabethan, high points in the Inns' history and extremely popular periods within Victorian culture more broadly. Yet these buildings were also fitted with amenities such as heating, lighting, and running water – features emphasized in press reports across the century.

[2] Daniel Duman, *The English and Colonial Bars* (London: Croom Helm, 1983), 16, 24.
[3] Penelope J. Corfield, *Power and the Professions in Britain 1750–1850* (London: Routledge, 1995), 90.
[4] Peter Mandler, *The Fall and Rise of the Stately Home* (New Haven, CT: Yale University Press, 1997); Billie Melman, *The Culture of History* (New York: Oxford University Press, 2006); David Boswell and Jessica Evans (eds.), *Representing the Nation: A Reader* (New York: Routledge, 1999); Martin Wiener, *English Culture and the Decline of the Industrial Spirit: 1850–1980* (New York: Cambridge University Press, 1981); Rosemary Mitchell, *Picturing the Past* (New York: Oxford University Press, 2000); Paul Readman, "The Place of the Past in English Culture c. 1890–1914," *Past and Present* (2005): 147–199.

Such representations of the Inns of Court in print took on increasing weight because of the growing importance of public opinion to Victorian society, culture, and politics.[5] Public opinion and the distinct but related concept of the cultural imaginary are notoriously slippery to define, but even the Victorians acknowledged their importance. In 1905, renowned legal thinker A. V. Dicey published seminal texts on the relation between Victorian law and public opinion in which he described public opinion as the "wishes and ideas" of the "majority of those citizens who have at a given moment taken an effective part of public life." Dicey argued that "the development of the law" in nineteenth-century England (unlike other states or in other periods) had rightly been governed by public opinion, a testament to the successes of English democracy. For Dicey, a Benthamite liberal, the importance of public opinion lay in securing the freedoms of the individual rather than reflecting the view of the populace at large. Indeed, his definition restricted the public to the enfranchised subset of the population, which at the time of publication included neither women nor the lowest orders of the working classes.[6]

Despite Dicey's inegalitarian conception of the public, his work nevertheless spoke to a change in Victorian cultural and political life: thanks to Reform Acts across the century, polities and institutions that had once been private, elite, and/or aristocratic came under the scrutiny of an increasingly middle-class electorate. Indeed, historians have demonstrated that public opinion informed the activities not only of Victorian legislators but also of institutions ranging from medical schools to savings banks.[7] The nineteenth-century Inns of Court were no exception. Subsequent chapters of this book explore facets of the Inns' relationship to public opinion, ranging from calls for parliamentary reform of the legal profession to controversies over barristers' published editorials. This chapter examines the societies' relationship to the public via its relationship to the surrounding city, as well as the way that

---

[5] Raymond Cocks, *Foundation of the Modern Bar* (London: Sweet & Maxwell, 1983), 56–57. Lawrence Goldman, *Science, Reform, and Politics in Victorian Britain* (Cambridge: Cambridge University Press, 2002), 9; Jonathan Parry, *The Rise and Fall of Liberal Government in Victorian Britain* (London and New Haven, CT: Yale University Press, 1993), 245–246.

[6] A. V. Dicey, *Lectures on the Relation between Law and Public Opinion* (Indianapolis, IN: Liberty Fund, 2008), 9.

[7] Josephine Maltby, "'To Bind the Humbler to the More Influential and Wealthy Classes'. Reporting by Savings Banks in Nineteenth Century Britain," *Accounting History Review* 22 (2012): 200; D. G. Boyce, "Public Opinion and Historians," *History* 63 (1978): 214; Laurence Fenton, *Palmerston and the Times*: Foreign Policy, the Press and Public Opinion in Mid-Victorian Britain (London: IB Taurus, 2012), 2; W. John Morgan, *Law and Opinion in Twentieth-Century Britain and Ireland* (New York: Palgrave), 9–31.

relationship was upheld or critiqued in Victorian print, the de facto mouthpiece of public opinion.

The Inns of Court frequently appeared in Victorian newspapers, literary fiction, and topographic guidebooks, in which authors characterized the societies as cherished symbols of Old London or as antiquated institutions out of step with the changing world around them. Many authors, including Charles Dickens, regarded the Inns with both esteem and ridicule, often within the same works. Victorian literary fiction and topographic guidebooks also frequently characterized the Inns of Court in monastic terms, as places of rest and respite. After all, authors noted, buildings, walls, and gates separated the Inns from the surrounding city. Outside, choked arteries like Fleet Street and the Strand rang out with the noise of iron-shod horses and wheels, and their sidewalks teemed with pedestrians. Inside, writers claimed, the Inns experienced little more than the soft footfalls of barristers coming and going to court.

Despite their cloistered geography, however, the Victorian Inns were anything but disconnected from the rest of London. Rather than reserve their sanctuary for members only, the modern Inns opened their buildings and grounds to visiting tourists for leisure and spectatorship. The logic behind the decision to open their grounds is not explicitly stated in any of the societies' records. The Inns charged no entrance fees and thus did not directly profit from visitors. Yet successive generations of benchers kept the gates of the Inns open to the public. It is possible that the Inns desired the cachet attached to occupying a privileged place in the Victorian cultural imaginary. The societies tried to balance the mystery of the ancient Inns with a certain degree of visibility. As many scholars have noted, Victorians privileged vision above all other senses, leading to a variety of viewing-as-knowledge-formation practices: flâneurie, exhibitions, and tourism.[8] Aficionados of travel literature, and of Charles Dickens and other popular authors, understood the Inns of Court as an essential feature of literary London. Allowing tours of the societies' buildings and grounds extended the visibility of the Victorian Inns of Court beyond the pages of the narrative, newspaper, or novel, cementing the Inns as a fixture of the distilled, essentialized version of London created by tourism.

The Inns also sought cachet from a more contested form of public engagement: they opened their grounds not only to tourists but also to the largely working-class residents of the nearby parishes of

---

[8] Lynda Nead, *Victorian Babylon* (New Haven, CT: Yale University Press, 2000); Chris Otter, *The Victorian Eye* (Chicago: University of Chicago Press, 2008); Nancy Rose Marshall, *City of Gold and Mud* (New Haven, CT: Yale University Press, 2012).

St. Giles, St. Clement Danes, Covent Garden, Drury Lane, and St. Martin in the Fields. Admitting working-class neighbors sometimes proved unpopular with barristers, who complained about the noise while they were trying to work, and with middle-class locals, who complained about the immorality on display within plebian recreation. Nevertheless, the benchers insisted on opening the gardens. Why they did so is not explicitly stated in society records, though politicians and the Victorian press interpreted the decision as connected to concern for the public good. How so? In the early nineteenth century, sanitary science reapproached the problem of disease by attending to the physical environment: the triumph of health and virtue over pestilence and vice became contingent upon the success or failure of the sanitary city. Middle-class moral and sanitary reformers alike touted the benefits of parks, gardens, and other spaces for outdoor recreation. Central London lacked green spaces, and the Inns thus offered a salubrious environment for a population otherwise confined to overcrowded slums.[9] Significantly, the benchers seemed to have reached this conclusion of their own accord, without pressure from sanitary reformers.

That private, extra-parochial institutions without any legal or financial obligations to the neighboring poor voluntarily admitted the surrounding populace into their gardens was remarkable – one MP noted that the benchers were "the only persons in London who gave free admissions to their gardens."[10] That they did so is explained by the importance placed on philanthropy and its relationship to the dominant politics of much of the century. Philanthropy was a key marker of status in Victorian men's personal and professional lives – a means, as historian Peter Shapley argues, "of acquiring or reinforcing ... symbolic capital and social position."[11] When institutions engaged in philanthropic practices, it "reflect[ed] credit" on the trustees of these institutions.[12] Furthermore, Victorian culture increasingly understood the condition of urban neighborhoods overall as a reflection of the individuals and institutions contained therein. The prestige of the Inns was therefore tied to the health and orderliness of central London.

The Inns' philanthropic actions were also connected to political concerns, at once a means of checking working-class radicalism and

---

[9] Todd Longstaffe-Gowan, *The London Square* (New Haven, CT: Yale University Press, 2012); Hazel Conway, *People's Parks* (Cambridge: Cambridge University Press, 1991); Brent Elliot, *Victorian Gardens* (London: Batsford, 1986).

[10] HC Deb 4 July 1862 vol. 167 col. 1477.

[11] Peter Shapley, "Charity, Status and Leadership: Charitable Image and the Manchester Man," *Journal of Social History* 32 (1998): 157.

[12] Maltby, "To Bind the Humbler to the More Influential and Wealthy Classes," 207.

upholding the liberal principles that were becoming requisite for middle-class respectability. On the one hand, philanthropic practices were imagined to have established "links of gratitude" between interclass neighbors, links designed to deter working-class political radicalism.[13] Such ties were valued by many voluntary societies, but were particularly crucial for the Inns of Court, whose borders with working-class neighborhoods in central London offset social distance with geographic proximity. Significantly, philanthropic undertakings might target the material circumstances of the working classes, but they did so for the benefit of the middle classes and almost uniformly without conceding any political, cultural, or financial power to the lower social orders.

Voluntary philanthropic activities reflected the pervasiveness of liberal ideology in Victorian politics and culture. Here I mean liberalism as a broad category encompassing several loosely linked concepts, including reason, economy, utility, and efficiency, the valuation of which resulted in reform measures across the nineteenth century. Notably, this definition does not confine liberalism to the tenets or actions of the Liberal Party. Indeed, the drive for reform singularly undergirded no one Victorian party: both the Whigs and their Liberal successors *and* the Conservatives under Disraeli embraced several of these tenets and spearheaded reforms. Likewise, to describe the Inns as engaging in liberal projects is not to ascribe to the legal profession a particular political identity. Historians have noted that middle-class professionals constituted almost half of the Liberal Party, and until the 1880s, members of the bar who sat in parliament were mostly Liberals, but this does not mean that non-MP barristers were Liberals in the same proportion, nor does it account for prominent Conservative members of the bar, like Disraeli.[14] Rather than trying to parse the legal profession's fit within Victorian political parties, I want to think about the profession's relationship to the competing and sometimes incoherent principles within liberalism as an ideology.

Metropolitan liberalism centered on a paradox: the rationalized, centralized bureaucratic and infrastructural systems that could best secure individual freedom could only be put in place through government interventions that superseded local authority. Liberal reforms in the metropolis therefore required constant negotiation between factions that

---

[13] Ibid., 205.
[14] Barristers' Liberal affiliations were likely the result of their largely nonaristocratic social origins and the better chances for success that Liberal affiliation afforded. Duman, *The English and Colonial Bars*, 171–172; Vincent, *The Formation of the British Liberal Party* (New York: Scribner, 1967), 76–84.

favored centralization at the expense of local authority, and factions that
sought to preserve local authority even if it would hinder urban rationalization. Historians such as Ben Weinstein and Harold Perkin both
describe metropolitan professionals – including barristers – as being
squarely in the centralization camp, as such professionals imagined that
centralization would create bureaucratic positions to be filled by their
own expertise.[15] While centralization undoubtedly received visible and
vocal support from the medical profession, a close inspection of the
primary evidence reveals barristers to be at best divided.[16] Rank-and-file
members of the bar may have supported centralization and the opportunities it might create for them, but the benchers of the Inns
were reluctant to cede institutional authority. Indeed, at mid-century
the Inns clashed with newly created central metropolitan bodies
designed to override local authorities in an effort to unify and order the
sanitary city.

The legal profession's embrasure of sanitary reform while rejecting
centralization epitomizes the ways in which conservative institutions
selectively engaged with liberal principles. Historians of liberal reforms
tend to emphasize the rationality sought by reformers, from the merito-
cratization of the professions to the transformation of city infrastructure.[17] Rather than champion rationalization and the meritocratic
opportunities it would supposedly create, however, the benchers of the
Inns envisioned the legal profession as taking on a paternalist role,
replacing the *noblesse oblige* of the aristocracy with a middle-class obligation to the public good.[18] This version of reform was essentially a
defensive strategy, a way of meeting social need while preserving and
protecting institutional autonomy. Such a strategy allowed the Inns to
nominally address calls for improvement while ultimately maintaining
their status quo. The Inns serve as one of many reminders that the tide of
Victorian liberalism never swept away illiberal barriers but rather flowed

---

[15] Benjamin Weinstein, "Metropolitan Whiggery, 1832–1855," in *London Politics,
1760–1914*, ed. Matthew Cragoe and Anthony Taylor (New York: Palgrave, 2005),
65; Benjamin Weinstein, *Liberalism and Local Government in Early Victorian London*
(Suffolk: Boydell & Brewer, 2011), 145.

[16] *The First Report of the Metropolitan Sanitary Association* (London, 1850). While some of
the prominent voices in the report, such as R. A. Slaney, MP, and Charles Dickens, had
connections to the bar, none were practicing barristers, nor did any of the hundred-plus
members of the General Committee identify themselves as barristers or Queens
Counsels (QCs). Most were medical men, church men, or MPs. The makeup was
similar to the Health of London Association; see *Report of the Health of London
Association on the Sanitary Condition of the Metropolis* (Chapman, CA: Elcoate, 1847).

[17] Joyce, *The Rule of Freedom*.

[18] Perkin, *The Origins of Modern English Society* (London: Routledge, 2002), 264.

around them: by the 1850s, bodies like the Metropolitan Board of Works (MBW), supposedly created to rationalize the city, sacrificed the Chadwickean vision of metropolitan centralization to leave power in the hands of the local vestries; infrastructural improvements in one part of the city led to unforeseen blockages and damage to others; and piecemeal voluntary activity was left to meet the needs of the poor. The Victorian capital undertook rationalization in an extremely irrational way.

The Inns in the Cultural Imaginary

Why would something so parochial as legal societies attract the attention of tourists to the capital? The answer lies in the Inns' location and age. The Societies of the Inner and Middle Temple occupied grounds on the City of London's western border, just north of the Thames; Lincoln's Inn and Gray's Inn lay a short distance north in Holborn. The Inns were thus not only among the oldest professional societies in England, but they also occupied some of the most ancient – and, by extension, presti-gious – real estate in the capital. The vast majority of buildings at the Inns were barristers' chambers, brown-brick edifices constructed in the late seventeenth century to reduce the threat of fire.[19] Victorian topographic guides to London encouraged visitors to stop at the Inns not to view these prosaic structures but to marvel at a handful of remains of Old London: the rounded nave of the Temple Church, the elaborate wood interiors of the Middle Temple and Lincoln's Inn halls. Indeed, from the beginning of the nineteenth century, guides considered the Inns a requisite site to see.[20] In its plan for viewing London in eight days, for example, *Mogg's New Picture of London and Visitor's Guide to Its Sights* included Lincoln's Inn and the Temple Church and Gardens on day six. Similarly, Peter Cunningham's 1850 *Hand-book of London* recom-mended Temple Church under "Places Which a Stranger in London Must See," along with the Tower, Westminster Abbey, and St. Paul's.[21]

Touring the Inns was a relatively informal affair compared to other emerging historical sites with admission fees, like Westminster Abbey, or

---

[19] Geoffrey Tyack, "The Rebuilding of the Inns of Court, 1660–1700," in *The Intellectual and Cultural World of the Early Modern Inns of Court*, ed. Jayne Elisabeth Archer, Elizabeth Goldring, and Sara Knight (Manchester: Manchester University Press, 2011), 200–203.

[20] See, for example, John Feltham, *The Picture of London, for 1803* (London: Lewis, 1802).

[21] Edward Mogg, *Mogg's New Picture of London and Visitor's Guide to Its Sights* (London: E. Mogg, 1843); Peter Cunningham, *Hand-book of London* (London: John Murray, 1850); see also G. F. Cruchley, *Cruchley's London in 1865* (London, 1865); Robert Hunt, *Guide A Londres et a L'Exposition de 1862* (London: W. Jeffs, 1862); Élisée Reclus, *Londres Illustré Guide Spécial Pour L'Exposition de 1862* (Paris: Libraire de L. Hachette, 1862).

elaborately staged interiors, like Hampton Court Palace.[22] To visit the Inns, observers merely walked or drove through one of the societies' open gates. Organized groups might bring their own tour guide, and they could write to the societies in advance for permission to enter spaces like the Middle Temple Hall when not in use. Otherwise, visitors directed themselves with guidebooks and whatever outside knowledge of history and literature they possessed. Tourists viewed mostly exterior spaces – the gardens, the fountain, perhaps Goldsmith's tomb – though the societies opened the church to visitors several days per week as well as for services on Sunday.

Guides figured the Inns of Court as a physical manifestation of two particularly valued historical moments: the medieval and Elizabethan eras. The Victorian reverence for these periods pervaded literary and artistic movements of the time, from the Romanticism of Sir Walter Scott through the Arts and Crafts movement at the end of the century. Emphasizing material relics and architectural details, Victorian topographical guidebooks culled particular historical associations for the Inns and cemented the spaces as uncommonly old and quintessentially English. Notably, while emphasizing these periods, topographic guidebooks placed as much, if not more, importance on the Inns' extra-legal associations as home to crusading knights and literary figures such as Dr. Samuel Johnson, Oliver Goldsmith, and Charles Lamb. Indeed, guides almost never suggested that visitors could or would learn something about law or the legal system from their visit. The benefit of touring the Inns lay in their architectural history and the general *mise-en-scène* that had inspired (or so guides suggested) invaluable poems, essays, plays, and lexicography.

Of the four Inns, the Inner and Middle Temples held particular cachet. As historian Billie Melman argues, in addition to visions of an idealized Arcadian history, Victorian culture privileged narratives of an urban and grotesque-but-titillating past.[23] The Temple, with its compelling dark legends of the Knights Templar and its secluded green spaces, represented both tropes, providing the frisson of danger and the charm of "Merrie England." The *Hand-book of London*, for example, detailed the revels of the early-modern Inns, in which the benchers and judges "danced … round about the coal fire, according to the old ceremony," followed by an evening of plays, poems, and country dances. The guidebook also quoted Shakespeare's *Henry VI*, noting that "the red rose and

---

[22] Simon Thurley, *Hampton Court: A Social and Architectural History* (New Haven, CT: Yale University Press, 2003).

[23] Billie Melman, *The Culture of History* (New York: Oxford University Press, 2006).

the white," which would send "[a] thousand souls to death" in the War of the Roses, were plucked from Temple Gardens. Victorian visitors would find chrysanthemums rather than roses in the garden, the guidebook noted, as the latter could not survive "the smoke and foul air of London," but surely tourists could imagine the historic scene.[24]

Mid-century popular fiction intensified interest in the societies already stoked by topographic guidebooks. Stories, poems, and novels offered readers a virtual view of the Inns of Court, piquing their interest in visiting and providing a detailed imaginary landscape for those who could not. In fact, mid-Victorian works of literary fiction set in the Inns made the societies a must-see for tourists wishing to experience "Dickens' London."[25] In an 1855 short story, Herman Melville explicitly encouraged readers to visit the Inns in order to relive the protagonist's dreamy experiences in the Temple. "Take your pleasure, sip your leisure, in the garden," the narrator urged, "go linger in the ancient library; go worship in the sculptured chapel."[26]

None of the Victorian Inns of Court actively sought or encouraged tourism, nor did they profit from visitors' attendance in any financial sense. Indeed, unlike other newly emerging tourist sites, such as the Tower of London, the societies did not charge admission to their grounds or the Temple Church. Nevertheless, if the Inns did not want visitors, they had only to shut their gates, but they did not shut them. Permitting tourists to visit the Inns, after all, reinforced the trope of the societies as a valuable artifact of Old London. Emphasizing the Inns' ancient and aristocratic past drew attention away from the socially heterogenous Victorian Inns with their glut of barristers struggling to find work, and instead bolstered the status and prestige of the societies in British culture.

Furthermore, when renovating their buildings, the Victorian societies deliberately chose architectural forms that would reflect the grandeur of the Inns' past. The medieval and Elizabethan eras had been high points

---

[24] William Shakespeare, *Henry VI*, Act II, Scene 4, as quoted in Cunningham, *Hand-book of London*, 245, 486.

[25] Late in the century, authors published guides for this explicit purpose. These works invariably included the Temple. William Richard Hughes, *A Week's Tramp in Dickens-Land* (London: Chapman & Hall, 1891); Robert Allbut, *Rambles in Dickens' Land* (London: S. T. Freemantle, 1899); H. Snowden Ward and Catherine Weed Barnes Ward, *The Real Dickens Land* (London: Chapman & Hall, 1904).

[26] Herman Melville, "The Paradise of Bachelors and the Tartarus of Maids," in *The Piazza Tales and Other Prose Pieces*, ed. Harrison Hayford, Alma A. MacDougall, G. Thomas Tanselle, and Merton Sealts (Evanston, IL: Northwestern University Press, 1987), 316, 318.

Figure 2.1 Engraving of the Temple Church, 1750.
London Picture Archive.

for the Inns, and the societies embraced historicist architectural styles
that emphasized these moments. In 1842, for example, the benchers of
the Inner and Middle Temple collaborated to restore the Temple
Church to a medieval appearance.

Originally constructed in the twelfth century, the societies had remod-
eled the church in 1682 to conform to the hybrid classical and baroque
style (or English baroque) characteristic of Sir Christopher Wren, the
royal architect.[27] See Figure 2.1. The Victorian benchers rejected the
English baroque in favor of the gothic revival, which rose to prominence
for the construction of churches in the nineteenth century as it emphasized the long tradition and history of Christianity.[28] In an attempt
to realize a perfect medieval ideal, Sydney Smirke, the project's architect,

---

[27] Anthony Sutcliffe, *London: An Architectural History* (New Haven, CT: Yale University
Press, 2006), 36.
[28] The style also achieved secular popularity for similar reasons. For example, in
reconstructing the Palace of Westminster, it was decided that the gothic or Elizabethan
style should be used as it "expressed the strength of a great democratic and national
tradition going back to medieval times." Sutcliffe, *London*, 101, 106.

mercilessly removed all traces of Wren from the church.[29] Smirke laid a solid-colored floor and installed new stained-glass windows. He commissioned the colorful painting of the walls and ceiling.[30] Covered in bright images of the gospels and elaborate scrollwork, they stood in sharp contrast to the formerly imageless and muted walls. See Figure 2.2. The renovation received glowing praise from the press, which extolled the church's "pristine beauty," its "mystic and quaint devices." Newspapers wasted no ink mourning the former Wren fittings, instead devoting paragraphs to the restoration's colors, paintings, and stained glass. The Temple, papers contended, had done "all lovers of antiquity" a great service in restoring the church to an ancient appearance "unparalleled in modern days."[31]

Recurring articles in the local and national press, especially the illustrated papers, reported on changes to the material Inns, generating continued interest in the societies and opening up formerly privileged interior views to middle-class readers. The *Illustrated London News* – a steadfast watchdog over changes to London's topography – was sure to note major construction projects at the Inns, such as the renovation of the church or the building of the new library. A middle-class paper pandering to a respectable readership since the 1850s, the *ILN* had simultaneously extolled infrastructural improvements and mourned the destruction of historic buildings throughout the city, including those at the Temple.[32] In March 1869, for example, the paper featured an engraving showing the demolition of the old Inner Temple Hall, typical of the *ILN*'s renderings of the destruction/construction process: a tangle of splintered wooden beams occupied the center of the frame, with laborers at the edge much dwarfed by their physical surroundings. The article accompanying this ruinous scene traced the long history of the hall, noting that it replaced an original medieval version destroyed by a

---

[29] W. R. H. Essex and S. Smirke, *Illustrations of the Architectural Ornaments and Embellishments and Painted Glass of the Temple Church, London, with an Account of the Recent Restoration of the Church* (London: 1845), as quoted in Gerard Noel, *A Portrait of the Inner Temple* (Norwich: Michael Russell, 2002), 81.

[30] Karl Baedeker, *London and Its Environs: Handbook for Travellers* (Leipzig: Karl Baedeker, 1911), 86.

[31] "The Temple Church," *Morning Chronicle*, November 21, 1842; "The Temple Church," *Illustrated London News*, November 5, 1842; "The Temple Church," *Ipswich Journal*, October 29, 1842.

[32] Anne Baltz Rodrick, "'Only a Newspaper Metaphor:' Crime Reports, Class Conflict, and Social Criticism in Two Victorian Newspapers," *Victorian Periodicals Review* (Spring 1996): 8–10; Peter W. Sinnema, "Reading Nation and Class in the First Decade of the 'Illustrated London News,'" *Victorian Periodicals Review* (Summer 1995): 136–152; Nead, *Victorian Babylon*, 31, 40.

Figure 2.2 Interior view of the Temple Church, 1843.
London Picture Archive.

fire in the seventeenth century.[33] The broken wood's jarring angles and the haphazardly scattered debris, combined with the article's mournful tone, signaled the loss of a significant piece of London's history. At the same time, however, the image gave the viewer imagined access to a space normally reserved for elite eyes, the hall's disarrayed grandeur creating a sense of visual intimacy for the reader.

Admitting visitors allowed both men and women to view the Inns, but the degree of access they afforded varied in accordance with the privileged place of brotherhood at the all-male societies. The respectable male visitor, particularly if he had any London connections, might access aspects of the Inns' fraternal culture in a form of homosocial tourism. Herman Melville, for example, recorded two diary entries near the end of his 1849 trip to London about time spent in the Temple. On his penultimate day in the capital, Melville visited the Temple chambers of Mr. Cleaves, a "fine fellow" that he met dining in the Erechtheum Club, St. James's the night before. Melville's connections to London's elite male networks (he had been invited to the club by his publisher's cousin) granted him entry to the homosocial spaces of the West End, where he in turn gained contacts that led to privileged access at the Inns of Court. Mr. Cleaves treated Melville to a tour of the Inns that included spaces rarely seen by visitors, including the kitchen and the benchers' parliament chamber. Two days earlier, Melville dined at the Middle Temple chambers of another cousin of his publisher, noting the "glorious time" he had with a group of legal and artistic minds. It was, he noted in his diary, "The Paradise of Bachelors."[34] Ten years married and father of four, Melville did not in fact fit the profile of the confirmed bachelors who resided at the Inns. Yet his visit to the Temple allowed him to imagine, if only for a night or two, that he, like the Temple residents, "had no wives or children to give an anxious thought."[35]

Literary descriptions presented the Inns as masculine spaces, but well-to-do women regularly permeated this all-male preserve as tourists. During her 1839 trip to Europe with her extended family, for example, Massachusetts-native Harriette Story Paige recorded being "much pleased" with her visit to the Temple. She was particularly taken with the storied history of the hall, marveling at the idea of judges dancing in their wigs during the "revels ... held ... in the olden time." Paige also

[33] "Rebuilding of the Inner Temple Hall," *Illustrated London News*, March 6, 1869.
[34] Herman Melville, *The Melville Log* (New York: Gordian Press, 1969), 350–352; Harrison Hayford, Alma A. MacDougall, and G. Thomas Tanselle, "Notes on Individual Prose Pieces," in *The Piazza Tales and Other Prose Pieces*, 709–710.
[35] Herman Melville, "The Paradise of Bachelors and the Tartarus of Maids," in *The Piazza Tales and Other Prose Pieces*, 322.

echoed the cloister rhetoric with which fiction and guidebooks described the gardens, noting their "remarkable air of quiet, and seclusion, in the midst of so vast, and busy a city." Likewise, on her 1852 European tour, American author Sara Jane Lippincott recorded her pleasure at viewing the "curiously painted walls and roof" of the "rarely beautiful" Temple Church.[36]

Significantly, the Temple functioned as one of several emerging spaces in the city, including parks, exhibition halls, and department stores, in which women could be seen in public without being seen as public women.[37] Like these other sites, the Temple was open to the public, but not indiscriminately so. Warders at the gates kept out the disreputable, creating a bounded and protected space for respectable women's leisure. Women attended particular events at the Inns, such as the Inner Temple Chrysanthemum Show, with male escorts or without.[38] See Figure 2.3. The Temple also served as a site of relaxation for women unaccompanied by men. As photographs of the Inns' grounds attest, in mild weather, women visitors lounged on benches around the fountain or promenaded through the gardens.

Women visitors did not, however, experience the same degree of privileged access as male visitors like Melville. To be sure, the Inns did not shut women tourists out of masculine spaces completely: in addition to facades and fountains and flowers, both Paige and Lippincott viewed the Inn's fraternal inner sanctum, the hall. Well-educated women were meant to take an architectural, as well as historical, interest in the space. An 1870 engraving in the *ILN* marking the opening of the new Inner

---

[36] Diary of Harriette Story Paige, August 1839, in *Daniel Webster in England: Journal of Harriette Story Paige,* ed. Edward Gray (Boston: Houghton, Mifflin, 1917), 168; Diary of Sara Jane Lippincott, July 1852, in *Haps and Mishaps of a Tour of Europe* (Boston: Ticknor, 1854), 437; see also Diary of Emma Cullum Cortazzo, November 14, 1865, in *Emma Cullum Cortazzo, 1842–1918* (Meadville: Shartle, 1919), 34–47; Letter from Ellen Tucker Emerson to Ralph Waldo Emerson, December 6, 1867, in *The Letters of Ellen Tucker Emerson,* vol. 1, ed. Edith W. Gregg (Kent: Ohio State University Press, 1982), 452–453.

[37] Judith R. Walkowitz, "Going Public: Shopping, Street Harassment, and Streetwalking in Late Victorian London," *Representations* 62 (Spring 1998): 1–30; Deborah Nord, *Walking the Victorian Streets* (Ithaca, NY: Cornell University Press, 1995); Erika Rappaport, *Shopping for Pleasure* (Princeton: Princeton University Press, 2000); Anne Friedberg, *Window Shopping* (Berkeley: University of California Press, 1993).

[38] "Chrysanthemums in the Inner Temple Garden," *London Illustrated News,* November 18, 1854. Elite women's presence at such an event was consistent with their involvement in the flourishing Victorian interest in horticultural display and competition. Richard Middleton, "The Royal Horticultural Society's 1864 Botanical Competition," *Archives of Natural History* (2014): 25–44.

Figure 2.3 Chrysanthemum show in Middle Temple Gardens, from the *Graphic*, 1884.
Illustrated London News Ltd./Mary Evans.

Temple Hall depicted small groups of well-dressed women and men touring the hall's interior. See Figure 2.4. The ladies appeared as engrossed by the architectonic details as did their gentleman companions. Preceded by an opening ceremony conducted by Princess Louisa, the sixth child of Victoria and Albert, wealthy and well-born individuals toured the hall that day. Even for aristocratic women, however, their tour would have been one of the few occasions they would be permitted inside the hall. A telling illustration from the *Graphic* depicting the evening's dinner from the same occasion showed five long tables of seated gentlemen stretching the length of the hall. See Figure 2.5. The engraving's caption read, "THE PRINCESS LOUISE AT THE NEW INNER TEMPLE HALL," but the princess herself was impossible to spot amidst the rows of bewigged and bearded male diners.[39] Women might tour the hall to view its fine architectural features, but they remained excluded from the ancient homosocial rituals it housed.

[39] "The Princess Louise at the New Inner Temple Hall," *Graphic*, May 21, 1870.

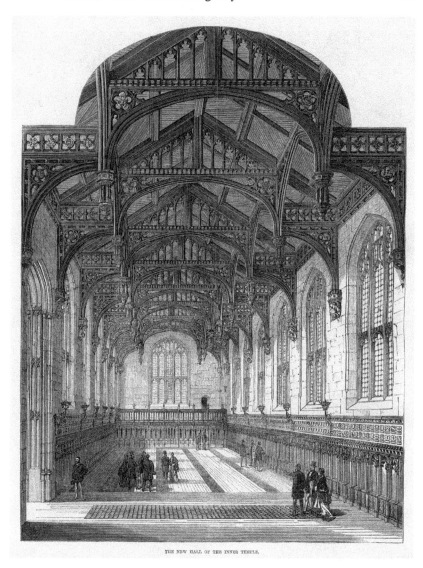

THE NEW HALL OF THE INNER TEMPLE.

Figure 2.4 "New Hall of the Inner Temple," *ILN*, 1870.
Illustrated London News Ltd./Mary Evans.

THE PRINCESS LOUISE AT THE NEW INNER TEMPLE HALL

Figure 2.5 "Princess Louise at the Inner Temple Hall," *Graphic*, 1870.
Illustrated London News Ltd./Mary Evans.

"Common People in the Temple Gardens"

In addition to permitting middle-class tourists, the Inns also received regular visits from local residents and were a notable haunt for children and their nursemaids. As one newspaper correspondent explained, throughout the entire year, the Inns gave permission to about two hundred families to walk in the garden at any time of day. Presumably of the better classes, one author explained that these "quiet and characterless" children gave the Inns "so little trouble that the vigilant beadles of the ground do not even care to watch them."[40] Neither the Inns nor the newspaper identified these children and their nursemaids or suggested where they lived. Some of them undoubtedly belonged to the small number of families residing at the Inns. Others were likely the progeny of respectable inhabitants on the eastern border of Bloomsbury, or perhaps particularly wealthy tradesmen and artisans in Holborn and the City. Wherever they came from, they were a regular-enough feature of the daytime landscape that, in 1834, the Inner Temple revoked one perverse barrister's use of the garden to prevent him from "expos[ing] his person to all the little Children and nursery-Girls."[41]

The Inns opened their grounds to children because their gardens were some of the few sizeable tracts of grass left in central London. Newspapers indicate that the Inns allowed ladies and gentlemen to walk in their gardens from at least the mid-eighteenth century on, though it is unclear if the Georgian societies extended this permission to children as well.[42] Of Georgian origin or not, the practice of admitting children to the gardens would have taken on increased significance in the nineteenth century, when the new public health emphasized the importance of light and air for both physical and moral benefits.[43] Parks played an essential part in the resultant emphasis on outdoor leisure, and as London expanded east and west, Parliament reserved large tracts of grass and trees for recreation in newly created spaces like Victoria and Battersea Parks. Central Londoners were left to find or create small green spaces in piecemeal fashion. Responding to civic pressure in the second half of the century, churches converted graveyards into public gardens and some of

---

[40] "Gray's-Inn-Gardens," *The Times*, July 6, 1858; "The Temple Gardens," *Freeman's Journal and Daily Commercial Advertiser*, July 6, 1872.

[41] IT DIS/1/L2 1849.

[42] "News," *London Evening Post*, June 18, 1767; "News," *Public Advertiser*, July 9, 1778; "News," *Gazetter and Daily Advertiser*, January 31, 1782.

[43] Conway, *People's Parks*; Helen Meller, *Leisure and the Changing City* (London: Routledge, 1976).

the formerly enclosed squares were opened to the public.[44] The Inner and Middle Temple Gardens occupied less than six acres combined, but they were still one of the largest spaces available for play (especially before Lincoln's Inn opened its gardens in the 1860s or 1870s). The societies were under no obligations to improve public welfare, but they acted out of the philanthropic impulses expected of wealthy men and the prestigious institutions to which they were attached.[45]

Indeed, by the 1850s these philanthropic impulses led the Inns to open their grounds not only to respectable children but also to impoverished youth from nearby neighborhoods.[46] None of the societies' records offer a rationale for their decision, but philanthropy was a requisite girder for elevated social status.[47] Societies keen to prove that their elite character had not been diluted by a growing middle-class membership may have embraced willingly their obligation to the public good. Furthermore, Victorian interlocutors increasingly judged individuals and institutions according to the state of the neighborhoods in which they were located. The prestige of the Inns was therefore tied to the reputation of central London.

Certainly, the contrast between the Inns of Court and the nearby abodes of the poor would have made a significant sensory impression on anyone who traveled between them. The neighborhoods surrounding the Temple were mixed areas, where the middle class and well-to-do lived on broad thoroughfares, while the impecunious crowded behind them in narrow alleys.[48] Despite such close quarters, the poor rarely made themselves visible in upper-class spaces: a visit to the Temple would have been a rare exception. A child coming from St. Martin's or Whitefriars would begin his or her journey in their tangled maze of back alleys. These warrens of rotting timber, infinitely subdivided and notoriously overcrowded, stank of refuse and human waste, both of which lined

---

[44] White, *London in the Nineteenth Century*, 61; Tim Brown, "The Making of Urban 'Healtheries:' Transformation of Cemeteries and Burial Grounds in East London," *Journal of Historical Geography* 42 (October 2013): 12–23.

[45] Seth Koven, *Slumming* (Princeton, NJ: Princeton University Press, 2004); Lara Kriegel, *Grand Designs* (Durham, NC: Duke University Press, 2007); Stanish Meacham, *Toynbee Hall and Social Reform 1880–1914* (New Haven, CT: Yale University Press, 1987).

[46] Both societies' records allude to this practice but never give an official start date. Newspapers first took an interest in commenting on the admission of poor children in the 1850s, but the papers never reported on whether this development was new or ongoing.

[47] Peter Shapley, "Charity, Status and Leadership: Charitable Image and the Manchester Man," *Journal of Social History* 32 (1998): 157; Maltby, "To Bind the Humbler to the More Influential and Wealthy Classes," 207.

[48] This was true even by the end of the century, after various slum clearance initiatives. See the LSE Charles Booth Archive Online, 1898–99 Poverty Map.

their courts and paths. Sunlight could not penetrate the built-out dwellings that overshadowed narrow walks: darkness prevailed by day and night. Paper-thin walls separated neighbors' bodies, but let through the shouts, grunts, cries, and clangs of daily life.[49]

Imagine, then, stepping from this world into the Temple: spacious, paved courts swept clean by porters; sunlit lawns trimmed with beds of vibrant chrysanthemums; ornate gothic windows pointing up to the crenellations and finials of majestic rooflines; the trickle of a fountain. Working-class visitors may not have commanded the extensive architectural vocabularies of learned tourists, but they would have readily recognized the wealth and privilege of the Inns, signaled by the scale of Temple buildings and grounds. They may not have understood the Inns in terms of English heritage and the English past, but they likely apprehended that the societies were both old and important, and that access to such spaces in their lives was rare and valuable.[50]

Wealthy children might occupy the gardens during the day, but in the summer months, between six and eight o'clock in the evening, the societies opened their gardens to the city children of Whitefriars. Their window of play was shorter than and segregated from their well-heeled peers, though it may have been well-timed for free hours after work. Approving newspaper articles explained the delight with which these children, otherwise condemned to "fashion mud-pies in the black alleys," greeted the open lawns of Temple Garden.[51] By the end of the century, the societies had even begun hosting special events for impoverished child visitors. See Figure 2.6. In 1887, Lincoln's Inn ordered a "Treat be given to not more than 600 children in the Garden." Events like these included food – tea, bread and butter, jam, cake, fruit – as well as toys, marionettes, and a *Punch and Judy* show. In 1893, Lincoln's Inn had to increase its guest lists, as well as its £77.7.3 budget. Through some mishap, the Inn's invitations had not reached "the poor Children who are the ordinary visitors to the gardens of the Society," and so the society extended welcome to an extra 250 invitees.[52]

---

[49] Mackay, *Respectability and the London Poor* (London: Pickering & Chatto, 2013), 72. For more on impoverished London, see Gareth Steadman Jones, *Outcast London* (London: Verso, 1971); Anthony Wohl, *The Eternal Slum* (Montreal: McGill-Queen's University Press, 1977).

[50] Later in the century, charitable organizations, like the Working Men's Club and the YMCA Rambling Club, sometimes brought groups of young men to tour these spaces, perhaps hoping to impress some of the finer points of the Inns' history and significance. MT MPA July 16, 1878; November 8, 1889; November 13, 1891.

[51] "Common People in the Temple Gardens," *Lloyd's Weekly Newspaper*, September 19, 1858.

[52] Black Books of Lincoln's Inn, 1887, 1893.

Figure 2.6 Photograph of children in the Inner Temple Gardens, 1902.
Illustrated London News Ltd./Mary Evans.

The press frequently described child visitors to the Inns with the negative and threatening language of swarms and hordes, but they also acknowledged the respect the children held for the Inns' property. The children's presence in the gardens, the papers concluded, resulted in no more damage than some trampled grass. One author praised the Temple's policy, asking, "If the prettiest ... pleasure-grounds in London can, without suffering any damage, ... minister to the health and happiness of the little people living in its neighborhood, why should not the experiment be tried with others of the open spaces adjoining the crowded districts out of reach of any of the parks?"[53] The societies, the papers suggested, set a charitable example for their peer institutions.

Individual members of the Inns, however, did not uniformly share the benchers' investment in philanthropy or the press's enthusiasm for opening the garden to children. As a space of contemplation, the occasional tourist did not disturb barristers at work, but young people coming to enjoy themselves upset the societies' cherished "clerkly monkish

[53] "The Children in the Temple Garden," *Pall Mall Gazette*, September 16, 1870.

atmosphere."[54] The benchers may have wished to contribute to public welfare by providing sunlight and fresh air to the central London populace, but individual barristers did not wish to improve salubrity at the expense of their comfort. Members of the Inns repeatedly complained of "the shouting of children." Noise was both a sign of disorderly society and a practical concern: most barristers practiced out of chambers at the Inns.[55] In 1861 even the society's gardener complained that he could not get *his* work done, as he was constantly distracted by having to keep "privileged Children & Nursemaids from making noises and climbing up the fences." That same year a barrister threatened to sue the Inner Temple after tripping over a wire in the gardens – a measure intended to keep children off the grass – and breaking his kneecap in the fall.[56]

Other petitioners feared that opening the Inns' gardens permitted the unrespectable poor to encroach on what should have been a thoroughly respectable space. Drawn to the Temple Gardens, residents complained, nearby slum-dwellers flaunted their raucous behavior and sexual impropriety along the way. Sunday evenings, they agreed, were the worst. In 1854, the rector of St. Dunstan in the West wrote to the Inner Temple asking if something could be done about the "very disgraceful scenes" that confronted his parishioners as they left his church. According to the rector, persons of "both sexes have come out of the [Temple] Gates ... in so disorderly a manner" that it upset many of his female congregants and stood "as a frequent source of temptation to Servants and other young persons." Whereas newspaper accounts typically rendered children in the gardens as "aged 12 and downwards," the rector's account implied these young people were postpubescent.[57] In 1861 a petition from twenty-five residents of Whitefriars complained of the disturbance from children seeking admission to the gardens, "the language and behavior is disgusting in the extreme, fighting and throwing stones is the rule." A resident of the Temple suggested, "I am quite aware that ... you are actuated solely by the supposed benefit to these poor people but ... it would be far better for them to be in the Streets where they must conduct themselves with some decency."[58] The poor, these writers suggested, were taking advantage of the opportunity for light and air, but they were hardly being improved by it. After the Middle Temple received an 1891 petition "on the subject of the inconvenience

[54] Dickens, *Barnaby Rudge*, 188.
[55] James H. Winter, *London's Teeming Streets: 1830–1914* (London: Routledge, 1993), 71.
[56] IT BEN November 22, 1861.
[57] "The Temple Gardens," *Freeman's Journal and Daily Commercial Advertiser*, July 6, 1872.
[58] IT BEN May 1, 1854; July 1, 1861; July 4, 1861.

caused by the Admission of Children to the Garden" signed by no fewer than 198 members, the benchers vowed to look into the matter. As a compromise, the benchers closed off portions of the garden closest to the common room and Garden Court, one of the residential buildings favored by the wealthiest members of the profession.[59] Overall, however, the societies adamantly kept the gardens open to children.

Naysayers objected not merely to children's presence at the Inns but also to outsiders in general, as hosting visitors created additional expenses and more work for the Inns, pulling resources away from the societies' primary purpose as legal institutions. The gardener, for example, complained of grass trampled by "the Rifle Gentlemen," members of the Inns of Court Rifle Volunteers (a mixture of members from all four societies), and the resultant "increase of labour," which caused "other things to be neglected."[60] In 1885 the benchers of the Middle Temple agreed to "abandon the Annual Show of Chrysanthemums on the grounds of economy, want of space, and the consequent additional labour involved."[61] That same year a correspondent of the *Pall Mall Gazette* critiqued the Inn's use, or rather misuse, of their funds by feigning indignation at the loss of the show. "Much as I admire the spending ... on flower shows, stately buildings, [and] ornamental services at the Temple Church, ... instead of on legal education, ... I protest against the action of these all too-mercenary Benchers." Such expenditures, the author argued, were hardly justifiable if the society increased the rents for chambers – pricing out all but the most successful barristers – in order to pay for them. The correspondent also derided the flower show's capacity for bringing women into the Temple, sarcastically mourning the loss of "the British matron, stout and energetic" and the "buxom, fresh-coloured daughter, with lawn-tennis shoulders." A self-described "constant Tory," the author implied that the Inns violated their own cherished culture and traditions in the name of frivolous and feminized pursuits.[62]

Members of the societies more actively intervened in the lives of London's poor by broadening their charitable impulses beyond the confines of the Inns, for example, by founding the Inns of Court Mission in 1897. The founding committee, led by the lord chancellor with the support of the attorney general, envisioned an organization that would "assist the clergy in religious, social and educational work" in a manner

[59] MT MPA June 12, 1891; June 19, 1891; July 2, 1891; May 6, 1892. The societies also allowed the committee to reserve at least two lawn tennis courts for members' exclusive use, which the Lawn Tennis Club later protested was insufficient for its thirty-five members. The benchers remained unmoved by the players' complaints.

[60] IT BEN November 20, 1861.   [61] MT MPA April 17, 1885.

[62] "Rebels in the Temple," *Pall Mall Gazette*, reprinted in *Law Times*, June 20, 1885.

not unlike existing public school and college settlements. Moved by the "strong and peculiar claim upon their assistance," the committee agreed to work in the area between Holborn and the Strand because of its mixed population of "respectable artisans" and "lower and poorer classes," as well as its connection to the spaces where the "majority of the members resided and practised."[63] With the approval of the Bishop of London, the committee chose the Rev. H. G. D. Latham to run the mission, with help from members of the bar. Funded primarily by contributions from members of the Inns of Court, in 1904 the Prince of Wales (an honorary member of the Middle Temple) presided over the opening of an £8,600 premises on Drury Lane.

Unlike its East End counterparts, the West End facility provided affordable housing for respectable, working-class young men and boys as well as the trappings of club life. It included a "large hall, coffee-bar, a billiard room, bagatelle-room, library, card-room, a committee-room, small club for boys ... three dressing-rooms and a caretaker's flat," as well as accommodation for up to 1,000 men and boys.[64] In addition to games and athletic undertakings like cricket, the mission became a major space of rational recreation, featuring a debating club, choral class, drama class, and a bank.[65] These amenities and activities were no doubt conveniently located for many participants, but the Drury Lane building also allowed the Inns to engage in philanthropy while keeping the poor at a safe remove from the societies' grounds.

That said, unlike the bar's other philanthropic undertakings, the Inns of Court Mission had the unique goal of promoting socialization and interactions between members of the Inns and nearby working-class Londoners. In declaring "the object of the mission" to foster association between barristers and "the large number of men and boys ... in the immediate neighbourhood," the Inns of Court Mission replicated the societies' values of fraternity in an interclass context and made Drury Lane a satellite of homosociality.[66] The lord chancellor framed the undertaking in humanitarian terms, declaring it the responsibility of

[63] "The Inns of Court Mission," *Times*, May 22, 1896; "The Inns of Court Mission," *Times*, April 1, 1897.
[64] "Building News," *British Architect*, November 25, 1904. At the time the mission had about 400 members; "The Inns of Court Mission," *Times*, November 21, 1904; Koven, *Slumming*, 243–244.
[65] "Inns of Court Mission," *Times*, May 23, 1925; Peter Bailey, *Leisure and Class in Victorian England* (London: Routledge, 1978).
[66] "Inns of Court Mission," *Times*, October 27, 1897. The mission did not, however, retain its purely masculine character. Fairly early on it enlisted ladies' help in raising funds, and by 1925 it instituted a program for women and girls to attend once-a-week meetings. "Inns of Court Mission," *Times*, May 23, 1925.

members of the legal profession to recognize the laborers of Drury Lane and the immediate vicinity as fellow "human creatures" for whom "the world should entertain sympathy and do what it could to make their lives brighter." Of course, the degree to which the mission succeeded in allowing "the rich ... to learn to understand the poor, and ... the poor ... to understand the rich" is debatable. Early in its founding, for example, members of the Inns of Court were more willing to donate their money than their time. In its first year the mission amassed over 250 members, but the Rev. Latham lamented that only six volunteers from the Inns regularly helped out at Drury Lane.[67] The mission continued its work into the 1980s, but gradually became the purview of the "ladies' section," formed after women were admitted to the bar in 1919.[68] This shift meant the Inns abandoned any pretense of cross-class homosociality as a goal of the mission and likewise let go of the attachment between philanthropic practice (rather than mere philanthropic giving) and gentlemanliness.[69]

The Inns and Outside Authorities

The Inns' flexibility in regard to whom they permitted to enter their gates was made possible by the certainty that, however popular or unpopular the decisions might be with members, the societies were fully in control over who entered and when. When faced with challenges to their independent authority and extra-parochial status, however, the Inns responded by forcefully reasserting their power over their grounds. The societies' relationship with the corporation of the City of London, for example, had been contentious for centuries, particularly for the Inner and Middle Temples, whose grounds abutted the City's border. The Temple was legally as well as physically separate from the City, and as one Victorian memoirist explained, "The gentlemen of the Temple have

---

[67] "The Inns of Court Mission," *Times*, May 16, 1902; "The Inns of Court Mission," *Law Times*, April 23, 1898.

[68] "Church News Letter," *Temple Church London*, November 6, 2020, 3.

[69] Philanthropy was understood as a respectable female occupation by the mid-nineteenth century, and by the early twentieth century, women were increasingly moving into leadership roles within philanthropic organizations. Frank Prochaska, *Women and Philanthropy in Nineteenth-Century England* (Oxford: Oxford University Press, 1980); Carrie Howse, "From Lady Bountiful to Lady Administrator: Women and the Administration of Rural Nursing in England, 1880–1925," *Women's History Review* 3 (2006): 423–441; Joyce Goodman and Sylvia Harrop, "'The Peculiar Preserve of the Male Kind': Women and the Education Inspectorate, 1893 to the Second World War," in *Women, Education Policy-Making and Administration in England: Authoritative Women since 1880*, ed. Joyce Goodman and Sylvia Harrop (London: Routledge, 2000), 137–155; Catherine Hindson, *London's West End Actresses and the Origins of Celebrity Charity, 1880–1920* (Iowa City: University of Iowa Press, 2016), 10, 94.

always been very jealous of their rights." For centuries, the lord mayor, officials of the ward of Farringdon Without, and the city surveyor tried but failed to exercise jurisdiction in the Temple. Early-modern attempts at exerting symbolic authority – such as the lord mayor carrying his sword and mace while on the premises – provoked violent reactions from students and inhabitants. By the nineteenth century, custom dictated that the mayor keep his sword down when in the Temple.[70] The Victorian Inns also performed symbolic acts of resistance, such as shutting their gates on Lord Mayor's Day, to "protect the rights of the Inn."[71] Furthermore, the societies countered the Corporation of London's legal efforts to encroach on the Temple with successful petitions to parliament in favor of the Inns' autonomy.[72] As an agglomeration of lawyers with close ties to powerful parliamentarians, the societies were formidable foes in any legal battle. Through these parliamentary petitions, the Inns ensured their exclusion from Acts encompassing everything from municipal elections to the maintenance of smallpox patients, and they would continue to use the same means to protect their autonomy throughout the twentieth century.[73]

The Temple successfully warded off City infringements, but by the mid-nineteenth century, new centralized metropolitan authorities confronted the societies with farther reaching powers and parliamentary backing. In 1855, as part of parliamentary attempts to centralize London's patchwork infrastructure, the Metropolis Management Act created the Metropolitan Board of Works, tasked with the "paving, cleansing, lighting, and Improvements" to London's notoriously dysfunctional sewerage and drainage systems.[74] The scope of its projects spanned across the metropolis, and its dictates would trump those of local authorities. The Inns of Court had never faced such a foe. To be sure, the City Corporation may have had centuries of countless privileges confirmed by innumerable royal charters; a complex hierarchy topped by the lord mayor and festooned with sheriffs, aldermen, and councils; and the immense prestige that accompanied this history and structure. But at the end of the day the griffin's talons extended only 1 square mile. The Inns stood up to the City so successfully because the City was an admittedly powerful but equally bounded local authority. The jurisdiction of the MBW, by contrast, covered the entire area designated "London" in the 1851 census.

---

[70] Stephen Coleridge, *Quiet Hours in the Temple* (London: Mills & Boon, 1924), 106.
[71] MT8 SRV Staff Records.   [72] LMA Petition to the House of Lords, 1907.
[73] IT BEN April 15, 1859; January 31, 1867; February 1, 1867.
[74] Metropolis Management Act, 1855, 18 & 19 Vict, c. 120.

Bodies like the MBW and its successor, the London County Council, which sought to standardize, rationalize, and consolidate the Victorian city, viewed the Inns of Court (to say nothing of the City Corporation) as stubborn anachronisms in the center of the metropolis. To be sure, the societies participated in the processes of improvement that dictated the terms of London's metropolitan modernity. But the Inns of Court preferred to pick and choose which infrastructure to integrate themselves into and which to undertake separately. As Patrick Joyce, Lynda Nead, and others remind us, improvements were often uneven and unresolved compromises between local government, private industry, competing vested interests, and traditional authorities.[75] The Temple, for example, accepted patrols from the city police in 1858, for example, and gave up their own fire engine in favor of the Metropolitan Fire Brigade in 1865. Yet they maintained their own separate sewer system, paved and cleaned their own streets, paid for the supply and upkeep of their own streetlights, collected their own garbage, and supported their own foundlings and paupers.[76] In return, they expected to be exempt from rates for these various municipal services and to remain outside the domain of any authority carrying them out.

In 1860, due to the efforts of the MBW, the Temple faced a startling exception to indemnity from the dictates of outside legislation, as well as changes to the Inns' topography of a magnitude hitherto wrought only by citywide fires.[77] The Temple's solicitors warned the societies of a scheme pushed by a select committee of the House of Commons and promoted by the Board of Works. It would lay a sewer not under Fleet Street and the Strand, as was first proposed, but along the northern banks of the Thames. If the undertaking went forward, the solicitors warned, the "viaduct for a public Road" included in the plans would be raised 10 or 15 feet above the Temple Gardens and "completely cut off the Gardens from the River." Hitherto the Temple's southern boundary ended where the Thames began. In fact, early-modern Templars had regularly traveled by boats launched from Temple dock. The Victorian

---

[75] Nead, *Victorian Babylon*; Joyce, *Rule of Freedom*; Gloria Clifton, *Professionalism, Patronage, and Public Service in Victorian London* (London: Athalone Press, 1982); David Owen, *The Government of Victorian London, 1855–1889* (Cambridge: Belknap Press, 1982).

[76] LMA Petition to the House of Lords, 1907.

[77] Three early-modern fires, including the Great Fire of 1666, destroyed significant portions of the Inns. The contemporary Inns' characteristic brick facades date back to the 1667 Rebuilding Act, which stipulated brick over timber to reduce fire risk. Geoffrey Tyack, "The Rebuilding of the Inns of Court, 1660–1700," in *The Intellectual and Cultural World of the Early Modern Inns of Court*, ed. Jayne Elisabeth Archer, Elizabeth Goldring, and Sara Knight (Manchester: Manchester University Press, 2011), 203.

societies did not pretend that direct access to the river was necessary for members' commutes (though they would later go to extremes to preserve their right to the dock), but the loss of a river view would diminish property values by destroying their "privacy and ... ornamental character."[78] The Inns' deference to the MBW thus signaled the societies' diminished authority, symbolic and literal, and raised questions of aesthetics and their translation into pounds, shillings, and pence.

Well before the board finalized plans for the project, the societies had to invent new ways of exerting some influence on the undertaking. Given that members of the board were nominated by the vestries rather than elected, the MBW had little reason to be swayed by either popular opinion or that of local authorities, including the Inns of Court.[79] The Middle Temple's engineer warned that the "Commissioners [of the board] are not disposed to regard private interests with much favour and therefore any detailed discussion with them as to the wishes of the Middle Temple Authorities had better be avoided." The Inner Temple solicitor agreed but suggested a different tack. He proposed that the society's surveyor explain to the committee that the Temple's shoreline, "one of the important features of London," would be deteriorated, if not destroyed, by the project. He also proposed that the Temple gardener testify as to "the thousands of persons who are in the habit of resorting to, and having the enjoyment of the Gardens."[80] No one was under any illusions that the societies' objections could much affect the works, but by mobilizing rhetoric about the Temple as a hallmark of Old London and as a space of benefit to the greater public, the benchers hoped that the committee might concede something in the societies' favor.

Framing the Inns as a space of public recreation and civic benefit proved a successful strategy for the societies to mitigate the effects of the construction along the Thames. In 1862, Parliament finally passed an act that empowered the MBW to build a sewer, subway, railway, and roadway along the north bank of the Thames by reclaiming land from the river.[81] The Victoria Embankment would stretch from Westminster to Blackfriars Bridge, and the Temple would no longer be a riverfront

---

[78] IT BEN June 1, 1860; MT MPA June 12, 1861.

[79] The structure of the board also gave it little reason to take into account popular opinion, making it ill-loved by Londoners whose rates paid for its workings. A series of scandals and charges of corruption did little to improve its reputation. See Owen, *The Government of Victorian London, 1855–1889*; Clifton, *Professionalism, Patronage and Public Service in Victorian London*.

[80] IT BEN June 1, 1860; MT MPA June 12, 1861.

[81] The MBW was in fact acting through the Thames Embankment Board, consisting of four members of the MBW, two of the City Corporation, and the chairman of the MBW.

property. The Inns, however, successfully petitioned the Office of Works for compensation in light of their diminished property values and struck a deal with the board. By the terms of the Thames Embankment Act 1862, the Inns would receive 120 feet of land reclaimed from the river to add to their gardens, with 18 inches of garden soil included at the project's expense. The board would also provide a gate for each society, as well as a gardener's lodge, though the Inns would never be permitted to build anything more permanent than this one-story structure on the property. The real estate offset the societies' losses, while the greenery, visible from the embankment and guaranteed to remain undeveloped, would provide an aesthetic benefit to the public and additional grounds for those enjoying the gardens.[82]

After a prolonged construction process, in which Temple tenants complained to benchers of noise and disruptions, benchers harassed the board about construction delays, and the board routinely blamed the Metropolitan District Railway for slowing their progress – the MBW finally completed the Victoria Embankment in 1870.[83] The project successfully diverted waste from flowing directly into the Thames, though not as efficiently or completely as its engineers had hoped.[84] Traffic noise replaced construction noise at the Inns' southern border, and members bemoaned the "dull wearying hum of trains" from the District Railway.[85] The embankment's promenade allowed pedestrians to peer into what had once been the societies' secluded gardens.[86] On the other hand, the new roadway and railway line provided an efficient means to travel to Westminster law courts. Of course, as one member complained, the Inner Temple stubbornly refused to open their southern gate to carriages, leaving drivers to either deposit their passengers on the embankment footway or drive them all the way around to the northern gate.[87] Furthermore, work on the new Royal Courts of Justice, an undertaking that relocated the High Court and Court of Appeal from

---

[82] LMA Report from the Select Committee on the Thames Embankment Bill 1862, as quoted in the LCC Architecture Department Memorandum March 14, 1898.

[83] IT BEN; MT MPA.

[84] The board faced a daunting series of obstacles along the way, including professional rivalries, bureaucratic obstructions, and parliamentary confusion. The completed project did not account for heavy rains, at which times storm valves opened to relieve pressure on sewers and shot waste directly into the Thames. White, *London in the Nineteenth Century*, 55.

[85] Arthur Munby, *Man of Two Worlds*, ed. Derek Hudson (Boston: Gambit, 1972), 175.

[86] Even so, a letter to the editor complained of the "massive iron screen as now marks the boundary and obscures the contemplation" of Temple Gardens. The Man on the Embankment, "The Templars and Their Gardens," *Pall Mall Gazette*, February 25, 1898.

[87] Plain Stuff, "The Embankment and the Temple," *Times*, June 14, 1875.

Westminster to the Strand – that is, almost directly across the street from the Middle Temple – began the same year the embankment was finished. Barristers were thus able to enjoy the benefits of swift travel to Westminster for about a decade before the new courts obviated the need for regular trips in that direction.

If anyone imagined that the end of the construction of the embankment would signal the end of the Inns' complaints about it, they were much mistaken. In subsequent decades the reclaimed land given to the societies by the Embankment Act became the source of conflicts regarding everything from rate assessment to the Temple's sole right to dock and launch boats from Temple Landing Place. Generally, the societies got their way by petitioning Parliament, as they did in contemporaneous conflicts with the City Corporation.[88] They were not above conducting symbolic acts of authority, however, even if it meant chartering a steamer for a river trip for no other purpose than asserting their right to the dock.[89]

In 1898, however, the Inner Temple found itself in a frustrating bind that neither petition nor performance of symbolic authority could resolve. Membership in the society had expanded at such a rate that it "urgently needed" to increase the number of chambers available for barristers to let. The Inn wished to solve this dilemma by extending King's Bench Walk, a row of buildings on its eastern border, onto a portion of the lands reclaimed from the Thames. The Embankment Act 1862, however, prohibited expansion on these lands; the societies had agreed to erect nothing larger or more permanent than the one-story gardener's lodge. Hoping to lift this restriction, in late February 1898 the society introduced a bill into Parliament to allow them to expand King's Bench Walk. The bill asked for about 80 feet of the reclaimed land on which they hoped to erect new chambers.

The local and national press universally denounced the bill, accusing the Inner Temple of acting for base reasons at the expense of the public good. As the *London Argus* explained, "Any scheme ... which aims at curtailing ... the area of the few open spaces left to London is sure to meet with severe criticism." Both the Conservative *Times* and the Liberal *Pall Mall Gazette* suggested that the greedy Inns were seeking to obtain "building land on the cheap," and that they should count themselves lucky the 1862 Embankment Act gave them land at all. The Inns would not, asserted the *Pall Mall Gazette*, "get such a nice little present in these days." Beyond this, the ultra-conservative *St James Gazette* suggested

---

[88] LMA Rating of Reclaimed Land Act 1920.
[89] MT MPA June 11, 1880; IT BEN May 29, 1934.

that the real motivation for construction was not to expand cramped chambers but to block the view of the soon-to-be-erected Employers' Liability Insurance building at the Temple's eastern boundary. "The Inner Temple desires to have its gardens overlooked by buildings of its own," the paper explained, "rather than by the back windows of its neighbours." The *Times* worried that for such a petty reason "the Temple-gardens, which add so much to the beauty of the embankment … will be shut out from public view." Similarly, the *Evening Standard* suggested that the public had a right to the gardens as they "teem with associations historic, regal, literary, and legal."[90] In so asserting, the paper used the familiar trope of the Inns as a site of English heritage to limit rather than bolster the society's authority over its grounds. For the *Standard*, it was the popular press, rather than the institution, that should arbitrate cultural heritage.

At the heart of this conflict lay a competition for the right to define public good and the best means of providing public benefit. In parliamentary review, opponents of the bill to extend King's Bench Walk concurred with the press. The MBW had turned the Temple Gardens into a public spectacle, giving promenaders the right of peering in whenever they desired, all in the name of the Temple's vaunted history and importance to British cultural heritage. The opposition to the bill asserted that metropolitan authorities had an obligation "to maintain in its integrity any bargain made with the public."[91] The Inner Temple, by contrast, suggested that it deserved public consideration for its expansion project on the grounds that it had for so long voluntarily aided public welfare, "throw[ing] open the gardens, at no small expense, every evening during the summer months." The society did not dispute the importance of the public good, but it demanded the right to control its landscape and restore the balance of mystery and proximity it so prized. Unfortunately for the Inn, the subcommittee of the House of Lords was not persuaded by this argument. They decided "that it is not expedient to proceed further with the Bill." In so doing the Lords privileged centralized over local authority and affirmed the Temple's status as a sight of permanent display.

If the Inner Temple decidedly lost the battle over expanding King's Bench Walk, it is important to remember that the 1898 Bill was one skirmish in a much longer conflict between the Inns and outside

---

[90] "The Temple Gardens," *Times*, February 23, 1898; "The Templars and Their Gardens," *Pall Mall Gazette*, February 23, 1898; LMA Clippings from London County Council Architect's Department B.A. 13125.

[91] "King's Bench Walk," *Daily News*, March 19, 1898.

authorities. The Inns' relationship to the board and the capital overall remind us that the processes of rationalization were contingent, uneven, and never divorced from a deep valuation of London's history. At the same time, the building of the Victoria Embankment and subsequent related controversies were only one of a variety of parliamentary interventions the Inns had to navigate in the nineteenth and early twentieth centuries.

Conclusion

This chapter has established the Inns of Court as physically separated from the rest of the capital but bound to London's visitors and residents via tourism and philanthropy, undertakings uniquely necessary for the Victorian Inns to maintain their status as elite institutions. The Inns, like many other Victorian institutions, were increasingly beholden to public opinion and the values of liberal ideology. Yet as the final section of this chapter has shown, competing and incoherent strains within liberalism demanded that elite institutions engage in philanthropy and reform in ways that could both solidify and destabilize institutional authority. The societies did their best to respond to these demands to their advantage and, on the whole, were successful in retaining their autonomy. Nevertheless, new metropolitan authorities and the growing weight of public opinion meant that the societies could not work around all constraints and caused divisions between rank-and-file members and the leadership of the benchers. As subsequent chapters explore, these divisions were exacerbated by the growing variety of differences between members of the bar and led to a reemphasis on fraternity within legal culture to counter the effects of growing heterogeneity.

3 The Culture of the Bar

In 1843, both the *Illustrated London News* (*ILN*) and the humor magazine *Punch* featured articles and images depicting goings-on at the Temple, two of London's four Inns of Court. The respectively reverent and satirical depictions were emblematic of the publications in which they originated, but they also encapsulated mid-Victorian understandings of the Inns as at once enduring but fusty institutions. In November 1843, the *ILN* ran a half-page feature celebrating the ancient origin and ongoing practices of the Inns. See Figure 3.1. An engraving in the center of the page, dwarfing the accompanying text, depicted the interior of the Middle Temple's Elizabethan hall during a formal dinner. In the image, the curved arches of the hall's elaborate double-hammer beam ceiling framed straight lines of staid barristers and benchers, each in their black gown. The cavernous architecture impressed its obvious age and size; the men engaged in sober ceremony.[1] The *ILN*'s image figured the Inns as dignified repositories of venerable rituals and highlighted the masculine nature of the legal profession.

Yet six months before the *ILN* ran its feature, the humor magazine *Punch* included an article on the dowager Queen Adelaide's visit to the Temple, an occasion also marked by antiquated ceremony. See Figure 3.2. Unlike the dining rituals in the *ILN*, in *Punch*'s account, Queen Adelaide's visit lacked dignity. Off to an inauspicious start, her cortège arrived at successive Temple gates to find footpaths instead of carriage roads. When the entourage finally made it to the hall, it was greeted by a deputation of benchers out of breath from chasing the cortège. Thence followed a ludicrous procession, detailed as well as illustrated by *Punch*: porters waving sticks; charwomen "carrying the venerable ashes of the grate in order to mingle them with the dust of surrounding Templars;" a treasure chest-like wig-box "supported by" clerks; a junior barrister "not supported by anything, but ... endeavouring

---

[1] "Dining in the Middle Temple Hall," *ILN*, November 4, 1843.

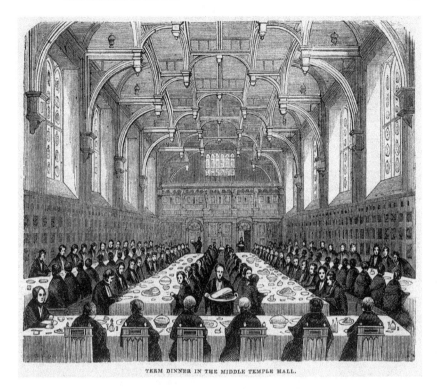

TERM DINNER IN THE MIDDLE TEMPLE HALL.

Figure 3.1 "Dining in the Middle Temple Hall," *ILN*, 1843.
Illustrated London News Ltd./Mary Evans.

to support himself;" and the queen surrounded by the benchers. Her majesty received a fourpenny lunch on a table propped up by a city directory, followed by a tour in which Pump Court lacked a pump; Fig Tree Court a fig tree; and Fountain Court a functioning fountain.[2] *Punch* reduced the ancient grounds of the Inns to obstacles to comfort and convenience and dismissed their historic artifacts as nothing more than shoddy furniture. The inhabitants were dusty and equally outmoded or, as in the case of the junior barrister, comically unsuccessful in the modern world.

These two contrasting views of the Inns reflect ways in which the mid-Victorian legal profession was at something of a crossroads. As discussed in Chapter 1, the societies derived prestige from their ancient roots but

---

[2] Adelaide, widow of King William IV, survived her husband by twelve years. "Queen Adelaide's Visit to the Temple," *Punch*, May 27, 1843.

PORTERS WEARING THEIR TICKETS,
(*walking partially backwards, and beating off the boys,*)

THE LAUNDRESS OF THE HALL STAIRCASE,
(*carrying the venerable ashes of the grate in order to mingle them with the dust of surrounding Templars,*)

THE SIX CLERKS OF THE HALL STAIRCASE,
(*bearing the bags of brieflessness,*)

MR. THESIGER'S WIG-BOX,
(*supported by his clerks,*)

A JUNIOR BARRISTER,
(*not supported by anything, but vigorously endeavouring to support himself,*)

Her Majesty Queen Adelaide,
(*surrounded by the deputation of Benchers, and followed by the royal footmen, &c. &c.*)

Figure 3.2 "Queen Adelaide's visit to the Temple," *Punch*, 1843.
Punch Cartoon Library.

were also forced to contend with the needs of modernity. The benchers eventually resolved this tension in the physical spaces of the Inn through architectural historicism, outfitting new buildings that looked old with cutting-edge amenities. But the societies also derived prestige from the social status of their membership. In the early-modern period, members of the Inns overwhelmingly hailed from the aristocracy, but patrician membership waned across the eighteenth century. By the mid-nineteenth century, the Inns had instated a variety of measures to keep the profession exclusive to the well-educated and financially sound, such as requiring a £100 deposit for admission. Successful members of Britain's expanding middle class, however, were increasingly able to meet these requirements and catapult their sons up the socioeconomic ladder into the position of barrister.[3] This meant that the bar at mid-century was not only more socially heterogenous than ever before, it also had a glut of members. The massive increase in the number of practicing barristers resulted in heavy competition and not enough work to go around. It created both a wider variance between the social backgrounds of barristers and a financial gulf between the bar's most successful members and those desperate for work.

In the face of these demographic changes, inculcating members with a particular set of priorities and values became essential to ensuring the gentlemanly character of the bar. The societies relied on embodied ritual and affective ties to instill these values. As historians and literary critics argue, whether manifested in the Hellenistic friendships of Oxbridge aesthetes or in the robust comradeship of martial activities, idealized male affect occupied a privileged place in Victorian society.[4] At the Inns, the societies relied on fraternization with older generations, rather than codified rules, to inculcate new members with the priorities of the legal profession. Law thus differed from other gentlemanly professions in that it relied almost exclusively on cultural and affective rather than formal, structural processes to forge its members.[5] In letters, diaries, and memoirs, barristers defined legal culture as one in which men

---

[3] Daniel Duman, *The English and Colonial Bars* (London: Croom Helm, 1983); Leonore Davidoff and Catherine Hall, *Family Fortunes* (London: Hutchinson, 1987).

[4] Eve Kosofsky Sedgwick, *Between Men* (New York: Columbia University Press, 1985), and *Epistemology of the Closet* (Berkeley: University of California Press, 1990); Linda Dowling, *Hellenism and Homosexuality in Victorian Oxford* (Ithaca, NY: Cornell University Press, 1994); Christopher Lane, *The Burdens of Intimacy* (Chicago: University of Chicago Press, 1999); Paul Deslandes, *Oxbridge Men* (Bloomington: Indiana University Press, 2005).

[5] Douglas Melvin Haynes, *Fit to Practice: Empire, Race, Gender, and the Making of British Medicine, 1850–1980* (Rochester, NY: University of Rochester Press, 2017), M. J. D. Roberts, "The Politics of Professionalization: MPs, Medical Men, and the 1858 Medical Act," *Medical History* 53 (2009): 37–65.

studied together in the library, chatted in the common room, drilled with the Volunteer Rifle Corps in the garden, and, most importantly, dined together in the hall. This latter practice attempted to instill a sense of brotherhood in members by enacting a series of formal rituals of medieval or early-modern origin revived or reemphasized by the Victorian societies.[6] The Inns' material environs thus not only housed but also actively contributed to the historic and historicist rituals at the center of the Inns' fraternal culture, inducting members of the bar into a pertinaciously English, masculine sociability.[7]

Significantly, the Inns also fostered their fraternal atmosphere outside the pageantry of formal ritual in residential chambers shared by single men. Bachelor domesticity at the Inns, as elsewhere in the city, removed the feminized center of Victorian domestic ideology, but nevertheless retained essential features of the home such as seclusion, comfort, and emotional warmth. Little explicit evidence of queer practices survives, but male intimacy in chambers allowed for blurred boundaries between social bonding and homoerotic desire. While actual residence at the Inns declined across the Victorian period, in the late nineteenth and early twentieth centuries, members of the societies idealized literary depictions of mid-century bachelor domesticity.

In both quotidian intimacies and in institutional rituals, the Inns epitomized a homosocial culture of affective same-sex bonds.[8] The fraternal world of the Inns would have been familiar to most members, who cross-populated other homosocial spaces such as sports teams, the universities, and clubland.[9] Yet the Inns differed from other homosocial spaces in several regards: unlike cloistered Oxbridge or the Royal College of Physicians in Pall Mall, the Inns were located in central London, near the poverty of decaying rookeries, the pleasures of Soho, and the oddities of bohemian culture; they gave men unmonitored social and sexual freedoms; they were not connected to a particular life stage, but spanned all adulthood; they served both professional and domestic functions. Legal culture and life at the Inns – concentrated, enduring, and pertinaciously masculine – thus stands as an example par excellence of the

---

[6] For similar practices in other contexts, see Eric Hobsbawm, "Introduction," in *The Invention of Tradition* (New York: Cambridge University Press, 1983), 1–14; David Cannadine, "The Context, Performance and Meaning of Ritual: The British Monarchy and the 'Invention of Tradition,'" c. 1820–1977," in *The Invention of Tradition*, 101–164.

[7] Henri Lefebvre, *The Production of Space* (Cambridge: Blackwell, 1991); Edward Soja, *Postmodern Geographies* (New York: Verso, 1989).

[8] Sedgwick, *Between Men.*

[9] Paul Deslandes, *Oxbridge Men* (Bloomington: Indiana University Press, 2005); Elaine Showalter, *Sexual Anarchy* (New York: Viking, 1990); Amy Milne-Smith, *London Clubland* (New York: Palgrave Macmillan, 2011).

gendered operations of Victorian professional life and the ways in which entrenched masculinity shaped professional success or failure.

Indeed, despite the rhetoric of brotherhood at the Inns, this chapter also explores the limitations of sociability. Sara Ahmed has shown how social groups can deploy affective rhetoric and praxis not only to create insiders but also to mark outsiders.[10] For the increasingly heterogeneous population of the Inns, historic rituals could highlight differences in background, status, and success that made it harder for some men to fit in. The hall served as a site of friendship and connection, but it also functioned as a stage on which to dramatize enmity. Barristers expressed their personal or professional squabbles with one another during meals in hall in informal attempts to shame opponents. Members also brought grievances to the attention of the benchers in hopes of securing formal censure against other barristers.

The failures of sociability between men highlighted the instability of the category of "gentleman" and competing visions over what gentlemanliness did or did not entail. As historians such as David Castronovo and Penny Corfield have argued, in the early-modern period, the term "gentleman" exclusively referred to men of wealth and status, but by the nineteenth century, elites whose respectability was tied to land, leisure, and classical learning increasingly coexisted with those who made fortunes via commercial or speculative capitalism. The meaning behind "gentleman" grew until it was capacious enough to include even middle-class men and led to debates as to whether a gentleman was born or made.[11] While there was never consensus on this question, Victorians began to use the term gentlemanliness to describe a certain kind of masculine respectability, one that many middle-class men believed they possessed, even as they feared their social betters – or, worse, inferiors – might not recognize it as such.[12] This gray penumbra around what had once been a black-and-white category meant that appropriate behavior became a more important benchmark for measuring gentlemanliness than ever before. Even then, what counted as appropriate behavior was both debated and increasingly subject to middle-class values. For example, one aspect of gentlemanliness was undoubtedly about a set of relationships and, especially in the case of the bar, how a man related to other men. The abilities to get on with one's fellows and to be both

---

[10] Sara Ahmed, *The Cultural Politics of Emotion* (Edinburgh: Edinburgh University Press, 2014), 2.

[11] David Castronovo, *The English Gentleman: Images and Ideals in Literature and Society* (New York: Ungar, 1987), 7, 14, 19, 31, 45, 52; Penny Corfield, "The Democratic History of the English Gentleman," *History Today* 42 (December 1992): 45.

[12] Milne-Smith, *London Clubland*, 61.

honest and respectful were all important qualities for the gentlemanly professional. Yet Victorian law students and barristers faced questions about the appropriate way to treat someone whose status outside the bar, due to age or rank, did not match their level of professional success. They were also faced with ambiguity about recourse or redress when not treated with the respect they were due.

The ambiguities of who could be considered a gentlemanly professional became all the more fraught as developments in the late nineteenth and early twentieth centuries forced the societies to respond and adapt to the growth of the capital and concurrent cultural shifts. The Inns maintained an ambivalent relationship, for example, to the blossoming of the nearby West End into an urban pleasure zone. Throughout the nineteenth century, the narrow streets and crowded rookeries of central London were slowly shaped into a district in which the middle and upper middle classes could enjoy new restaurants, theaters, clubs, and shops. A variety of spaces still offered men the comforts of all-male company, but an increasing number of heterosocial spaces – music and dance halls, theaters, and eventually cinemas – helped change the expectation that men and women would socialize apart.[13] In tracing the development of the West End, Judith R. Walkowitz asserts that nineteenth- and early twentieth-century cosmopolitanism was characterized by the double valences of pleasure and danger associated with the transnational.[14] The rapid material changes to the face of the West End and the influx of nonnative businesses and residents brought with them the excitement of new entertainments, services, and visual and tactile pleasures, but also fears of sexual danger and licentiousness, shifting cultural identities, and the loss of the familiar. Members of the Inns embraced the pleasures of the West End while simultaneously casting the Inns of Court as bulwarks against an unstable central London. This buttressing was also spurred by a crisis in the profession regarding the demands of Britain's expanding empire, the disruptions to sociability brought about by the Great War, and the encroachment of the female white-collar worker on male professional spaces.

In the face of these changes, the trope of the Inns of Court, their occupants, and their rituals as stalwart remainders of Old London endured and gained force in the twentieth century, as writers figured

---

[13] Judith R. Walkowitz, *City of Dreadful Delight* (Chicago: University of Chicago Press, 1992), and *Nights Out* (New Haven, CT: Yale University Press, 2012); Peter Bailey, *Leisure and Class in Victorian England* (London: Routledge and Kegan Paul, 1978); Anthony Sutcliffe (ed.), *Metropolis 1890–1940* (Chicago: University of Chicago Press, 1984); Lynda Nead, *Victorian Babylon* (New Haven, CT: Yale University Press, 2000).

[14] Walkowitz, *Nights Out.*

the societies as bastions of continuity with the past. This chapter thus contests the views of scholars who argue that the rapid pace of change in the early twentieth century swept the past from its privileged place in British culture.[15] Beginning in the 1890s and reaching its peak after the First World War, members of the societies published histories of legal London entirely devoted to the Inns of Court. Drawing on mid-Victorian literary depictions, these works were steeped with nostalgia for pleasingly deteriorated environs. Rather than the fragmented and fraught relations between men depicted in modernist literary works, members of the Inns emphasized a rosier, more Victorian notion of idealized friendship.[16] The books ignored or dismissed male outsiders to this world, particularly colonial subjects. They prized and reaffirmed the value of friendship between men and propagated a culture deeply resistant to women.

The Materiality of Legal London

Law was a uniquely metropolitan profession. Unlike doctors or clergy-men who lived and worked throughout the UK, most barristers practiced in the 2 square miles surrounding the Inns of Court. This concentration of lawyers in London stemmed in part from the centripetal nature of training at the Inns, and in part from the nature of England's court system. Barristers made twice-yearly pilgrimages to serve provincial legal needs via the circuit courts, but the bulk of litigation took place in the capital. As a response to overcrowding in the profession, a small but growing number of barristers made a living in larger provincial cities or colonial outposts, but these options were viewed as inferior to practice in legal London. The exception came in the form of law students from the empire, the majority of whom returned to practice in their countries of origin.[17]

The societies' location in the heart of central London significantly shaped the Inns' topography. After a number of timber-framed buildings succumbed to citywide fires in the second half of the seventeenth

---

[15] Peter Mandler, *The Rise and Fall of the Stately Home* (New Haven, CT: Yale University Press, 1997); José Harris, *Private Lives, Public Spirit* (New York: Penguin Books, 1994); Raymond Chapman, *The Sense of the Past in Victorian Literature* (New York: St. Martin's Press, 1986); P. B. M. Blaas, *Continuity and Anachronism* (Boston: M. Nijhoff, 1978); David Lowenthal, *The Past Is a Foreign Country* (New York: Cambridge University Press, 1985). For a compelling argument for the continued importance of the past, see Paul Readman, "The Place of the Past in English Culture, c. 1890–1914," *Past and Present* (2005).

[16] Sarah Cole, *Modernism, Male Friendship, and the First World War* (Cambridge: Cambridge University Press, 2003).

[17] Duman, *The English and Colonial Bars*, 1, 85, 122–123.

century, the Inns set about erecting brick edifices with somber brown facades designed for barristers' and law students' business and residential purposes.[18] Elsewhere in London the Georgians erected gleaming white buildings, which the Victorians replaced with red brick. But the Inns of Court had no investment in such aesthetic updates. By the mid-nineteenth century, the buildings and grounds of the Inns included gardens, libraries, halls, and churches, but the majority of buildings were these same brown-brick chambers.

Chambers primarily provided barristers and law students with offices and residences, making the Inns a majority-male enclave. Renting a set of chambers was not compulsory, but as the Inns were considered the center of the legal profession, a successful barrister was likely to have business chambers at his Inn. A basic set included four rooms that could be flexibly arranged, though members might expand their sets to suit their purposes and pockets. At the beginning of the nineteenth century, a barrister was likely to rent a full set for his practice alone, but by the 1850s, barristers began to split sets of business chambers with one or two colleagues to reduce costs. This newly emerging professional practice caused the Inns to worry about decreasing rental rates. In 1855, for example, the Inner Temple fixed its rents at 10 percent below market value to make renting them more attractive. The treasurer explained that the Inn was making less of a profit on sets of business chambers, as barristers found it more "convenient and more economical, for two or three to take a set of Chambers" rather than to each rent their own. Such a strategy may have been necessary for the members of a profession whose numbers at mid-century exceeded the demand for practitioners. Significantly the trend of sharing not only chambers but also secretaries, clerks, and cases grew to become standard practice for barristers by the twentieth century. As Raymond Cocks argues, practicing together presented senior barristers with new means of regulating the conduct of young men and gave junior barristers greater impetus for seeking the approval of senior members.[19]

If members of the profession retained chambers as offices, albeit in new ways, they increasingly declined to rent chambers as dwellings. Residence in the Inns decreased dramatically throughout the nineteenth century: for example, the Temple's 867 residents in 1801 had diminished

---

[18] Geoffrey Tyack, "The Rebuilding of the Inns of Court, 1660–1700," in *The Intellectual and Cultural World of the Early Modern Inns of Court,* ed. Jayne Elisabeth Archer, Elizabeth Goldring, and Sara Knight (Manchester: Manchester University Press, 2011), 200–203.
[19] Duman, *The English and Colonial Bars,* 4; Raymond Cocks, *Foundations of the Modern Bar* (London: Sweet & Maxwell, 1983), 9.

to 251 by 1881.[20] The remaining population of the Inns included barristers and law students, a number of clerks, a few tradesmen, some civil servants, and house servants, known as laundresses. Families were not unknown, but residents were overwhelmingly bachelors or widowers, able to enjoy the fellowship of other single men unrestrained by the tenets of conventional domesticity. Single women in residence tended to be servants or widows, or their daughters.[21]

The mid-Victorian Inns experienced a decline in their residential rentals for a variety of reasons, including the cultural obsession with rationalizing space. More than any of their forbearers, Victorians demanded both domestic and professional buildings be subdivided into rooms for discrete purposes. During the first half of the nineteenth century, the law courts, for instance, were almost uniformly rebuilt or renovated to create separate entrances for legal officials and the public, restricted areas for judges, and designated retiring rooms for jurors, witnesses, prisoners, and barristers.[22] At the Inns, Victorian members of the profession were no longer content to let one property as domicile and office alike. Indeed, historians have outlined the growing spatial separation between home and work for middle-class professionals.[23] As part of this trend, chambers at the Inns increasingly came to be used by barristers for professional purposes only.

Another factor that accounts for the Inns' decrease in residents was the growing popularity of living outside the city center among the elite and middle classes. According to the 1855 Inner Temple treasurer, "professional gentlemen" had begun to set up homes or practices in "the neighborhood of London, where the railways take them," rather than in

---

[20] The population of both Inns had been steadily decreasing since the beginning of the century. In 1801 the Inner Temple had 485 residents and the Middle Temple 382; in 1841 the Inner Temple had 278 residents and the Middle Temple 229; and by 1881 the Inner Temple had 156 residents and the Middle Temple 95. Census of Great Britain, 1851; Census of England and Wales, 1881: preliminary report and tables of the population and houses enumerated in England and Wales; Census of England and Wales, 1891.

[21] "The factor which counted most in determining many men to buckle to and devote themselves seriously to the profession was marriage. So long as they remained single they could jog along comfortably, but with the advent of a wife and children they found that the income … must be supplemented by professional fees." Gilchrist Alexander, "The Modern Outlook at the Bar," *Law Times*, October 20, 1950; Census of Great Britain, 1851, 1861, 1871, 1881.

[22] Clare Graham, *Ordering Law: The Architectural and Social History of the English Law Court to 1914* (London: Routledge, 2003), 123.

[23] Davidoff and Hall, *Family Fortunes*; John Tosh, *A Man's Place* (New Haven, CT: Yale University Press, 2007).

the city itself.[24] As London expanded in all directions, suburbs afforded the pleasures of country-living merely a few miles from the heart of the metropolis. Neighborhoods like Islington to the north, Brixton to the south, and Kensington, Knightsbridge, and Belgravia to the west offered larger houses with modern amenities, a greater degree of privacy, and a pleasant front garden.[25] The benchers had to work hard to make chambers more appealing than a semi-detached house in Chelsea. The Inns also faced a competitive threat in a new form of housing, the mansion flat. Particularly concentrated in Kensington and Westminster, mansion flats gained prominence in the 1880s and continued to be popular well into the new century, especially among bachelors.[26]

The Inns' steady decline in inhabitants also came about because of the disastrous state of the societies' dwellings in the mid-century. The societies' descriptions of these dilapidated wooden buildings conjured up images closer to the ramshackle housing stock of the city's poor than the homes and offices of the professional elite. In 1854, the Middle Temple treasurer described the Inns' chambers as in "a very wretched condition," in need of being pulled down and rebuilt. The society's surveyor agreed, particularly for Elm Court, which was "entirely constructed of timber ... of prior date to the Great Fire."[27] In 1857, the Inner Temple surveyor cautioned that No. 4 Temple Lane existed "in a state of great and manifest danger." A person standing in the attic of the latter could "see through various cracks in the wall which [was] bulging outwards many inches."[28] An 1864 Chambers Committee at Lincoln's Inn concluded that a "drain nuisance" in four Old Buildings had caused a tenant to suffer from "alarming illness."[29] Such ruinous housing stock could hardly compete with newly constructed, up-to-date dwellings.

Writing to the benchers, mid-century residents confirmed this bleak picture and chafed at the attendant discomforts of life at the Inns. In January 1853, Charles H. Station asked the Inner Temple for a

---

[24] William Whateley, Esq., QC, Inner Temple Treasurer, *Report of the Commissioners Appointed to Inquire into the Arrangements in the Inns of Court* (London: George Edward Eyre and William Spottiswoode, 1855).

[25] Jerry White, *London in the Nineteenth Century* (London: Jonathan Cape, 2007), 77–90.

[26] Chris Hamnett and Bill Randolph, *Cities, Housing and Profits* (London: Taylor & Francis, 1988), 17–20. For the British love of semi-detached houses, see Davidoff and Hall, *Family Fortunes*, 357–397; Sharon Marcus, *Apartment Stories: City and Home in Nineteenth-Century Paris and London* (Berkeley: University of California Press, 1999), 83–134. For a description of public transit, see White, *London in the Nineteenth Century*, 37–48.

[27] *Report of the Commissioners Appointed to Inquire into the Arrangements in the Inns of Court*, 1855; MT MPA Surveyor's Report, 1858.

[28] IT BEN May 29, 1857.   [29] Black Books of Lincoln's Inn, 1864.

reduction in his rent of eighty pounds per annum. "My Chambers are [on] the third floor," he explained, "up a flight of 72 steps consisting of one sitting room and three smaller ones, of which the latter one only is large enough to make an ordinarily convenient bedroom." Other members, he argued, paid lower rents for more commodious chambers. Similarly, in 1857 Cadogan Morgan explained that "in June 1854 when No 3 Plowden Building became so ruinous and unsafe for habitation" he had removed his "furniture and books ... to a place of safety." He had not since occupied the chambers, but had paid "more than £800 for the rent of them as well as about £40 for their repair and the fixtures in them." He asked that the Middle Temple remit at least some of the money. Even fixed at 10 percent below market rate, these men implied, Temple rents were not so low as to offset the inconveniences and indignities brought about by antique housing stock. The Inner Temple benchers informed the unfortunate Station that they did "not feel at liberty to enter into the question," but the Middle Temple benchers agreed to return Morgan's most recent quarterly payment.[30]

Members also complained of physical discomforts in the common areas of the Inns, decrying the failure of material interventions to ensure the uninterrupted mental labor of the middle-class professional. Barristers concerned themselves, for example, with the insalubrious effects of improper heating and ventilation. In 1855, George W. Hastings claimed that he had suffered a serious illness from a cold caught in the Middle Temple Library, "a cold and draughty room." This illness hampered his work on antiquities, his purpose for frequenting the library in the first place. Two years earlier, the Inner Temple made efforts to increase the temperature of its library from "53° to 60°" by installing hot water pipes.[31] Men of learning, members charged, could not carry out their ponderous tasks in rooms that failed to provide for their basic bodily requirements.

Similarly, Victorians increasingly viewed running water as a necessity for maintaining bourgeois respectability, in terms of both bodily hygiene and social status. At the Inns, older buildings without "lavatory accommodation," such as Lincoln's Inn Hall, received critiques for their "extremely primitive" arrangements.[32] As the societies renovated buildings, they provided washrooms with running water for occupants in common. Nevertheless, plumbing, or the lack thereof, remained a

---

[30] IT BEN January 25, 1853.
[31] *Report of the Commissioners Appointed to Inquire into the Arrangements in the Inns of Court,* 1885; IT BEN December 8, 1853.
[32] Black Books of Lincoln's Inn, March 21, 1899.

frequent bone of contention between members and the benchers, as the societies left it to renters to carry the expense of installing plumbing in individual chambers. Members expressed indignation at the societies' indifference to such "a necessity of life." In 1857 Samuel Carter, an irate resident, upbraided the Middle Temple benchers, declaring their refusal to supply him with water "illiberal and unworthy of the proprietors of [such] exorbitantly rented houses." Premises on Fleet Street or the Strand, he asserted, surely had water.[33] For Carter and other residents, not only did the societies jeopardize their health and comfort by refusing to install modern conveniences, the Inns did so at a price that could not justify such hardships.

Aware that their buildings were both insalubrious and unappealing to tenants, the societies undertook a great number of renovations and expansions between the 1850s and 1890s. In 1843, Lincoln's Inn rebuilt its hall and library "on a scale commensurate with the requirements of the age," enlarging this new library again in 1870.[34] In 1857, the Middle Temple began plans for a new library of their own on the western bounds of their property.[35] Tom Taylor penned the 1859 poem "Ten, Crown Office Row" as a farewell to that eponymous building, anticipating the erection of "statelier chambers," with "airy bed-rooms" and "wider panes" than the "narrow and dark" rooms he had inhabited.[36] In 1870, the Inner Temple completely gutted and renovated its hall. It extended its library in 1880 and rebuilt Hare Court in 1892. All of this is to name but a few of the societies' improvements.

If, as discussed in Chapter 2, the aesthetic choices of these renovations were decidedly historicist, the Victorian Inns nevertheless stressed fitting their new buildings with modern amenities. In an 1861 contract to renovate the Middle Temple's Church Yard Court, the Lucas Brothers Builders agreed to "fit up the several water closets ... with 1 inch Honduras Mahogany seat[s] French polished ... The front and seat to be made to lift so as to get at the apparatuses with ease."[37] When the Inner Temple replaced its 1678 hall with a neogothic building in 1870, the society ensured that the structure was fitted with lavatories, gaslight,

[33] MT MPA July 10, 1857.

[34] William Holden Spilsbury, *Lincoln's Inn: Its Ancient and Modern Buildings: With an Account of the Library* (London: Reeves and Turner, 1873), 99; Black Books of Lincoln's Inn, 1870.

[35] MT MPA January 14, 1857; April 30, 1858.

[36] "Ten, Crown Office Row. A Templar's Tribute," *Punch*, February 26, 1859.

[37] MT6 RBW, Agreement between Charles Thomas Lucas and Thomas Lucas and Thomas Henry Dakyns, Under Treasurer, 1861.

steam heat, and the "latest modern appliances" in the kitchen.[38] The cost of modern amenities marked wealth and status for the societies and their members, and materials like mahogany represented the luxury of exotic imports. Equally important, these features rationalized the bourgeois interior, allowing for the greater subdivision of spaces according to their function and the removal or rapid elimination of waste and dirt from the body, workplace, and home.[39]

Legal Sociability: Fraternity

What was life like for the denizens of this world of drab brick facades and mahogany toilet seats? In three memoirs recounting his life as a young barrister at the Inns, Gilchrist Alexander recalled days spent almost exclusively in the company of other men. He shared residential chambers in the Middle Temple with his flatmate Jimmy Gray. Recently called to the bar and lacking briefs of his own, Alexander prepared briefs for his mentor, the successful barrister Willes Chitty. He gave finished notes to Arthur Smith, his amiable junior clerk. At the end of the workday, Alexander found friends smoking cigars, chatting, or reading newspapers in the common room. They indulged in a game of bowls or lawn tennis in fine weather, a game of chess in foul. Eventually they sallied forth to one of the taverns on Fleet Street for dinner, then retired to somebody's chambers to drink and smoke before heading off to bed. As Alexander noted, the only "feminine element" they encountered were laundresses, "elderly women, weighed down ... by odd bags and bundles," easily dismissed as *personas non grata*.[40] Otherwise, from waking to after-dinner cigars, Alexander's life as a young barrister revolved around his links to other men in the profession: his flatmate, his mentor, his clerk, his friends.

All of the relationships Alexander described were deliberately culti-vated by the Inns of Court. After all, the purpose of these professional societies was not to instruct students in the technicalities of law, nor to hone essential legal skills like oratory; the Inns expected members to acquire legal precepts through self-directed study and to have already developed skills like public speaking at the public schools or Oxbridge. The societies instead understood their role as instilling in students

---

[38] "New Hall of the Inner Temple," *ILN*, February 12, 1870.

[39] Davidoff and Hall, *Family Fortunes*, 382–383; Judith Flanders, *Inside the Victorian Home* (New York: Norton, 2003), 324–340.

[40] Gilchrist Alexander, *Middle Temple to the South Seas* (London: John Murray, 1927), *The Temple of the Nineties* (London: William Hodge, 1938), and *After Court Hours* (London: Butterworth, 1950), 6.

Figure 3.3 Barristers called to bar, 1870.
Mary Evans Picture Library.

the values and attitudes appropriate to British barristers.[41] A shared
professional outlook could not be gained through textbooks; it
required common professional practices that linked new and established
members. The Inns built a culture of fraternity by encouraging members
to take part in dining rituals, socialization in common spaces, and volunteer drill corps. Sociability and embodied ritual provided all members
with shared experiences across generations, bringing together junior and
senior members and allowing newcomers to undertake what previous
cohorts had already undertaken. See Figure 3.3. Most law students
would have been familiar with similar practices at other homosocial
institutions to which they belonged, particularly the universities.
Gilchrist Alexander, for example, sometimes dined with his chum John
Buchan, whom he first met as a student at Glasgow University. Friends
Arthur Munby and William Ralston knew each other from their time at
Trinity College, Cambridge, the same college that a full quarter of the
Inns' Oxbridge members had attended.[42]

For the decreasing number of men who lived at the Inns, chambers
provided the fellowship of other single men unrestrained by the tenets of
domesticity – and from the Inns, it was a short walk to the pleasures of
Soho and the West End. As Alexander noted fondly, "In those days there
were few married men among the Temple residents."[43] The societies'
residents shared many features with those of the Victorian and
Edwardian bachelors identified by historians John Tosh, Matt Cook,
and others. These authors describe bachelorhood as most often a
transitional feature between adolescence and paterfamilial duties, when

[41] Duman, *The English and Colonial Bars*; Cocks, *Foundations of the Modern Bar*.
[42] From 1835 and 1885 samples in Duman, *English and Colonial Bars*, 24; Alexander, *After
Court Hours*, 65; Arthur Munby, *Munby, Man of Two Worlds*, ed. Derek Hudson (Boston:
Gambit, 1972), 10.
[43] Alexander, *After Court Hours*, 67.

men – who either could not afford to or did not wish to take up the burdens of a family – enjoyed the freedoms of the city.[44] Similarly, some members of the bar treated residential chambers as a steppingstone between university and domesticity, an extension of bachelordom, but not an outright rejection of marriage. Alexander, for example, lived in chambers for more than ten years, then accepted a judicial position in Tanganyika before returning to England to marry. Other members rejected domesticity altogether out of the desire for a "gay" life or, in the case of Arthur Munby, the freedom to travel. Munby's friend and fellow resident of Figtree Court, the Russian scholar William Ralston, preferred intellectual male company.[45]

Even if most members of the bar no longer lived at the Inns, they participated in a variety of activities that forged homosocial relationships – informal common-room chats, chess, lawn tennis, the debating and musical societies, and, most importantly, dining in hall. In the mid-nineteenth century, the only requirement for students to be called to the bar was to "keep term" by dining in the societies' halls at least three times each quarter. For some social commentators, this practice was a source of derision. In 1862, Henry Mayhew and John Binny wryly wrote, "The lawyerlings 'qualify' for the bar by eating so many dinners, and become at length – gastronomically – learned in the law."[46] Quips from popular authors were unlikely to perturb the Inns, but as Chapter 4 details, in the mid-nineteenth-century, parliamentary investigative committees also questioned the logic of the Inns' practices and requirements. In response, mid-Victorian legal authorities defended the dining requirement on the grounds that it built intergenerational professional connections. Some of the highest-ranking members of the bar, including the vice-chancellor, insisted that "dining together not unfrequently [sic] in Hall" gave students the "considerable advantage" of "social intercourse." Such opportunities were all the more important, he contended, given that "members of the Inns of Court have ... ceased to reside in their precincts or vicinity."[47] Dining in commons, legal luminaries argued, allowed students and young barristers to liaise with older and more established members of the profession, even if those members had taken residence in some of London's new suburbs.

---

[44] Tosh, *A Man's Place*, 172–187. For similar instances in the American Gilded Age, see Howard Chudacoff, *The Age of the Bachelor: Creating an American Subculture* (Princeton: Princeton University Press, 1999).

[45] Alexander, *Temple of the Nineties*, 244; Munby, *Munby*, 12–13.

[46] Henry Mayhew and John Binny, *The Criminal Prisons of London and Scenes of London Life* (London: Griffin, Bohn, 1862), 72.

[47] *Report of the Commissioners Appointed to Inquire into the Arrangements in the Inns of Court*, 1855.

Other professional authorities maintained that commons functioned as a conversational space for students to reinforce what they had learned from their law books and tutors. William Lloyd Birkbeck, the 1854 reader on equity, explained, "It is impossible to fix a subject of such extent as Law upon [students'] memory without that sort of repetition which is induced by conversation." The Middle Temple treasurer likewise emphasized the importance of association for learning "professional conduct."[48] In encouraging conversations about law and professional practice, the Inns of Court significantly differed from counterparts like the gentlemen's clubs of the West End. Membership at the Inns of Court overlapped with that of London clubland, but clubs strictly removed professional life from fraternization. Whereas clubs prohibited all talk of "business," socialization at the Inns – by design – forged professional solidarity.[49]

The Inns differed from clubland in other essential ways. Located in the heart of the fashionable West End, gentlemen's clubs were designed for the social elite, whether distinguished by wealth, title, or accomplishment. Men who lacked these distinctions might visit, but it was unusual for guests – tellingly referred to as "strangers" – to enjoy the same privileges as members.[50] The Inns of Court were hardly egalitarian institutions, but as long as a man could pay his deposit, he could join regardless of his other accomplishments and without fear of being blackballed. The clubs of Pall Mall and St. James' also made no pretense of serving the interests of anything but their membership, whether that was associated with a particular political party or nonpartisan intelligentsia. The Inns understood themselves to be the institutional home of the law, and thus as fundamentally tied – perhaps even obligated – to the nation. This difference was built into the philanthropic practices of the Inns, discussed in the previous chapter, but also the food served, and quite literally into the very architecture. Compare, for example, the plate-glass windows of the Eccentric Club or the Grecian frieze of the Athenaeum to the leaded stained-glass windows and gothic ribs and spandrels of the Middle Temple Hall. The neoclassical and neo-Palladian facades of the majority of Piccadilly clubs contrasted with the Inns' neo-Tudor and neogothic buildings. While the Tudor and gothic styles looked back to particular moments in a national past, the fashionable edifices of clubland espoused a style that combined modern elements with a distinctly continental historicism.[51]

---

[48] Ibid.   [49] Milne-Smith, London Clubland, 13.

[50] Ibid., 31. An exception to this was the Cosmopolitan Club; Munby, Munby, 24–25, 121.

[51] Anthony Sutcliffe, London: An Architectural History (New Haven, CT: Yale University Press, 2006), 132; Milne-Smith, London Clubland, 27.

If legal culture was distinct from that of other homosocial spaces in London, it was nevertheless not fully restricted to the Inns of Court. Members of the bar carried their *esprit de corps* outside the Inns through jokes and horseplay in court retiring rooms, at bacchanalian dinners while on circuit, and while congregating for the cheap but hardy fare of Fleet Street taverns. The latter were not officially legal spaces, but establishments like the Cock and the Cheshire Cheese had maintained centuries-long connections with the bar. They were particularly important spaces for those early in their careers, for whom tight finances could be a bond. Alexander described the taverns as populated by "a coterie of young barristers ... united by the common tie of paucity of means and alertness of intellect."[52] Particularly at mid-century, available legal work was often disproportionately scarce to available practitioners. One common way for impecunious lawyers to subsidize their income was by writing for newspapers. The Inns thus maintained a long-standing geographic and economic link with not only Fleet Street taverns but also Fleet Street presses. In his 1853 *Saunterings in and about London*, Max Schlesinger stated that of the *Times*' staff of twelve to sixteen parliamentary reporters, the "majority are young barristers, whom the connexion with the great journal enables to follow up their legal career."[53] According to Alexander, many young barristers also acted as correspondents for provincial papers. He joked, "The London correspondent knows everything ... But ... much of the information which is vouched for as being from the highest authority has been gleaned at Fleet Street bars."[54] Alexander's humorous insight suggests that sociability could connect law students and young barristers with leads or information to subsidize struggling legal careers.

Importantly, the extension of legal sociability outside the Inns to Fleet Street and the Strand meant that the locus of legal culture overlapped with the center of London's sex trade. In the mid-nineteenth century, Fleet Street and the Strand catered to men's pleasures, hosting the cigar divans and brothels that were the center of prostitution. The connection between prostitution and the Strand was regularly touted in the sporting press, such as in an 1860 account of "a showily-dressed prostitute, named Susan Williams," who attempted to steal a gentleman's watch in front of an oyster shop in the Strand.[55] A sex worker interviewed by Henry Mayhew in 1862 described the Inns of Court as infamous among

---

[52] Alexander, *Temple of the Nineties*, 57.
[53] Max Schlesinger, *Saunterings in and about London* (London: Nathaniel Cook, 1853), 244.
[54] Alexander, *Temple of the Nineties*, 75.
[55] "Latest Intelligence," *Bell's Life in London and Sporting Chronicle*, October 14, 1860.

prostitutes as "the ruin of many a girl." Lawyers were known both for dollymopping (soliciting young women who had not previously sold themselves) and bilking (cheating women out of their money). Mayhew's interviewee continued, "There is not a good woman in London who'd go with a man to the Temple, not one. You ... take a woman out, put her in a cab, and say you were going to take her to either of the Temples ... and she'd cry off directly."[56] Removed from the surrounding city and populated by experts in legal manipulation, the Inns made sex workers extra vulnerable to exploitation; for these same reasons, they were also ideal locations for men to buy sex. Peter Cunningham's well-known 1850 *Hand-book of London* even included the bawdy popular verse:

> Inner Temple rich,
> Middle Temple poor
> Lincoln's Inn for gentlemen,
> And Gray's Inn for a whore.

That a guidebook targeting a respectable middle-class audience included the rhyme suggests that the verse was so familiar to readers as to be considered unobjectionable.[57]

Many of the factors that made the Inns of Court ideal for purchasing heterosexual sex would have made them likewise ideal for homosexual encounters. They had an exclusively male membership and almost exclusively male residents, including a subpopulation of confirmed bachelors; they encouraged male affect; they were outside the jurisdiction or patrol of the Metropolitan Police until 1858, and chamber interiors were never subject to any kind of surveilling authority. In these regards, they resembled other homosocial institutions noted for homosexual liaisons and, in fact, may have provided an even safer environment for both sexual encounters and ongoing relationships than places like the universities, which were both transitional and subject to scrutiny.[58] But while literary depictions of the Inns were often laced with homoeroticism, I have found no concrete evidence of homosexuality among the societies – not even rumors. The *least* likely reason for not finding this evidence is that homosexual relationships did not happen at the Inns. More likely,

---

[56] Henry Mayhew, *London Labour and the London Poor*, ed. Lee Jackson (London: Griffin, Bohn, 1862), www.victorianlondon.org/crime1/pros-08.htm (accessed December 11, 2023).

[57] Cunningham, *Hand-book of London*, www.victorianlondon.org/legal/innsofcourt.htm (accessed December 11, 2023); a less ribald version was "Gray's Inn for Walks/ Lincoln's Inn for a Wall/Inner Temple for a Garden/And the Middle for a Hall;" Alexander, *Temple of the Nineties*, 267.

[58] Deslandes, *Oxbridge Men*, 111.

homosexual relationships were successfully concealed or, if revealed, dealt with privately and off the record. (The Inns' records, particularly when it comes to disciplinary cases, are fragmentary and incomplete. It is easy to imagine the strategic nonrecording or deletion of references to an unspeakable act.) It is logical that there is no evidence of prosecution of any members of the Inns for sodomy: if sex was most likely to happen between residents of the Inns, their population was greatest at mid-century, when there was less fervent prosecution of homosexuality. By the late 1880s and 1890s, during a frenzy of sodomy prosecutions, the population of the Inns had dwindled. Likewise, it is logical that there would not have been cultural preoccupations about the sex lives of men at the Inns the way there were for young men at school and university. For one thing, law students and barristers had access to heterosexual sex in a way that public school boys and university students did not, meaning that those otherwise inclined toward heterosexuality had no reason to turn to homosexual behavior. There was also not a coterie of concerned parents and moralists worrying about the proper development of the nation's elite youth. Reformers might question the efficacy of legal education, but they were unconcerned with the private lives of barristers and whatever other eccentric bohemians might populate the Inns. Lastly, we know that the history of homosexuality overlaps greatly with the history of prostitution, and that spaces home to illicit sex between men and women were often the same spaces that hosted illicit sex between men.[59]

The benchers of the Inns never explicitly referenced concerns about the connection between the societies and London's sex trade, but neither could they have been unaware of cultural tropes of barristers as carousing philanderers. Countering such images was perhaps one of many reasons that the societies enthusiastically supported the formation and activity of the Inns of Court Volunteer Rifle Corps (ICRV), known as the "Devil's Own."[60] According to a recruiting pamphlet, the corps had first been formed in 1584 to fight at Tilbury – a suspiciously grand beginning – and, over the centuries, had traditionally disbanded and reassembled as necessary.[61] The Victorian corps re-formed in 1859 as part of the then-popular Volunteer Movement and was in keeping with values of stoicism

---

[59] Frank Mort, *Dangerous Sexualities* (London: Routledge, 2000), 122.
[60] Graham, *Ordering Law*, 128–129.
[61] The nickname "Devil's Own" purportedly came from George III. "As they marched past at a review the king asked of what class that fine body of men was composed. 'Lawyers,' said Lord Erskine. 'Lawyers, all of them?' asked the king. 'Yes, your majesty,' Lord Erskine replied. 'Then,' said the king, 'call them the Devil's Own.'" "The Inns of Court Volunteers," *Law Journal*, December 14, 1895; LMA, "Inns of Court Officers Training Corps," undated, likely 1915.

and strenuousness that had come to define middle-class masculinity in opposition to the respective indolence and intemperance of the aristocratic and working classes.[62] The corps remained in existence until its transformation into an Officers' Training Corps early in the First World War.[63] Less than a year after its re-formation, the ICRV had upwards of 260 members.[64] Featuring patriotic displays of robust masculinity, participation in the corps signaled the vitality of both its members and the nation. The societies supported the corps, allowing them to drill in the gardens and dine later than usual in hall on the days of marches. They hung Devil's Own banners from the reign of George III, preserved in the Inner Temple archive, in the Inner and Middle Temple Halls in alternating years. The Inns sponsored trophies for shooting matches and hosted the corps' balls and events.

While many other volunteer corps hoped to improve class relations and elevate working-class members, the Inns of Court volunteers held no such pretenses. The Devil's Own remained one of the wealthiest and most exclusive units in the movement.[65] Members of the corps recalled with fondness the oddity of a military group composed entirely of barristers and law students – figures associated with mental rather than physical labor. Colonel Errington, the commander of E Company, described summer training as a "somewhat dilettante affair." W. Valentine Ball, king's remembrancer, recalled, "One delightful man ... once appeared [at inspection] at the last moment with evening shoes on his feet, his shoulder straps hanging down his back, and his overcoat hung on his arm!" In Ball's account, evening attire represented both wealth and frivolity, characteristics equally out of place in the field. Despite the gulf between barristers' professional and social obligations and their voluntary activities, however, memoirists insisted that the Inns of Court Rifle Volunteers earned the respect of army officers, even if they were "d ... d lawyers."[66]

Part of the appeal of joining the Devil's Own was deeply related to the rituals and pageantry of high Victorian monarchy and empire. After all, barristers generally occupied the professional class that most fervently

[62] Stefan Collini, *Public Moralists: Political Thought and Intellectual Life in Britain 1850–1930* (Oxford: Clarendon Press, 1991), 189.

[63] John Cordy Jeaffreson, "A Book about Lawyers," *London Quarterly Review* 28 (April and July 1867); LMA, Notes from Colonel Errington's Anecdote Book, 1928/29.

[64] "The Volunteers," *Bell's Life in London and Sporting Chronicle*, May 13, 1860.

[65] Hugh Cunningham, *The Volunteer Force* (Hamden: Archon Books, 1975), 5–15; Ian F. W. Beckett, *Riflemen Form* (Barnsley: Pen & Sword Books, 1982), 60.

[66] LMA, Notes from Colonel Errington's Anecdote Book, 1928/29; "Memories of the 'Devil's Own' by W. Valentine Ball O.B.E."

supported the imperial project. Even diarists who kept the most minimal entries noted being measured for uniforms. Sir Frank Douglas MacKinnon, a High Court judge, recalled an inspecting officer from the War Office who noted the quality of the brigade's boots. In 1860, William Grantham, then a first-year student at the Inner Temple, penned one of his longest diary entries – nine sentences – to detail the events of the Grand Volunteer Review and Parade. After a "capital lunch" given by the Middle Temple benchers, the five hundred members of the corps marched to Hyde Park. There they "had good view of Queen. P. Albert. D. of Cambridge. K. of Belgians &c. &.c &c." The event, which he estimated as having between 200,000 and 300,000 spectators, was "all over at 6.15 when Queen left after a hearty cheer which had wonderful effect from between 20 & 30,000 Volunteers."[67] According to David Cannadine, such rituals generated popular support for the queen and helped imperial cohesion by creating a sense of inclusion in the empire.[68] The ICRV, however, did not permit students from India or the dominions to join the Devil's Own.[69] The corps was not intended to promote imperial cohesion, but rather to underscore the Inns as institutions distinctly and importantly English.

Drilling with the corps, "a delightful brotherhood within the brotherhood of lawyers," also reimagined legal fraternity as common physical exertion beyond the borders of the Inns.[70] Though the volunteers sometimes drilled in the Temple or Lincoln's Inn, they most frequently gathered at the Deer Park in Richmond, far beyond London's bounds. William Grantham recorded frequent shooting practices with friends there and noted seeing "several fellows of my Company" at the Epsom Derby. Lord Justice Paul Ogden Lawrence, then a young man at the bar, recalled rowing away from camp with a friend or two to fish and drink beer. Drill could also be an important place to make connections with more advanced members of the profession, especially as "distinctions of ranks were not observed." Lawrence fondly recalled a lunch with the corps at which he was "frightfully thrilled that a Lord Justice ... should be

---

[67] LMA, "The Devil's Own by F. D. Mackinnon;" 1859–1864 Extracts from the Diary of W. W. Grantham, later Mr. Justice Grantham; 1900–1901 Scrapbooks, compiled by Pte L. Green Wilkinson or Pte R. Wason who served with the Inns of Court Cyclist Section.

[68] David Cannadine, "The Context, Performance and Meaning of Ritual: The British Monarchy and the 'Invention of Tradition,' c. 1820–1977," in *The Invention of Tradition*, ed. Eric Hobsbawm and Terrence Ranger (Cambridge: Cambridge University Press, 1983), 101–164; David Cannadine, *Ornamentalism* (London: Allen Lane, 2001).

[69] IT BEN March 2, 1897; MT MPA January 22, 1897.

[70] For the growing emphasis on a more robust masculinity, see Deslandes, *Oxbridge Men*; Brent Shannon, *The Cut of His Coat* (Athens: Ohio University Press, 2006).

handing me (a young law student) potatoes." Equally important for promoting this fraternal atmosphere was time spent roughing it in the outdoors. Grantham described a "splendid day" as one in which he had to "skirmish through a forest of juniper bushes" and ended up "covered with mud if not with glory." Errington recalled 18- or 20-mile marches and "sleeping in barns or other uncomfortable places." Yet almost every diarist or memoirist recorded singing together in the evening, noting favorite songs or vocalists.[71]

The Limits of Legal Sociability

The relationships between the members of the profession described above were in many ways the bar's ideal: senior members dining with junior to impart wisdom, men of all ages dropping honorifics to parade for queen and country. No doubt, as the evidence above indicates, such amity characterized the experiences of some law students and barristers. Not all members of the bar embraced the culture of the Inns, however, or eagerly participated in its rituals and social organizations. For some, practices like dining in hall were something to be endured rather than enjoyed. Charles Dickens, erstwhile member of the Middle Temple, described "preparing for the Bar" as a matter of "having a frayed old gown put on ... and, so decorated, bolting a bad dinner in a party of four, whereof each individual mistrusts the other three."[72] In emphasizing the shabbiness of the gown, Dickens suggested that the Inns' traditions were not venerable so much as worn-out; their dinners not simple, hearty fare but simply "bad;" and their members not brothers so much as competitors. Even Gilchrist Alexander, who loved legal culture enough to write three separate memoirs about it, admitted that "there were those who despised the Temple and all its antiquated ways." Alexander dismissed these figures as fleeing to the suburbs at the end of the workday, leaving "the Temple and Fleet Street" to those enamored of the Inns' fraternal rituals.[73] While it is true that well-established barristers could leave the Inns after hours if they so wished, law students keeping term and early-career barristers seeking briefs were less able to opt out of dinners in hall, even if they found dining rituals (or fare) not to their taste.

That these two authors felt so differently reflects not only their divergent tastes and values but also the temporal distance between them.

---

[71] LMA, "Memories of the 'Devil's Own' by W. Valentine Ball O.B.E.;" 1859–1864 Extracts from the diary of W. W. Grantham, later Mr. Justice Grantham; Extracts from the Diaries of Sir Paul O. Lawrence, 1878–1882.
[72] Dickens, *Uncommercial Traveller.*   [73] Alexander, *After Court Hours*, 63.

Dickens was a member of the early Victorian Inns, when the societies were in their most physically decayed state and a glut of barristers made jobs scarce. He abandoned his pursuit of law in favor of literature and likely found the requirements of the Inns an unnecessary tedium while he was trying to launch the latter.[74] Alexander, by contrast, began his studentship in the late Victorian period, after the Inns had undertaken a number of renovations and when the profession had ceased to be so overcrowded. His memoirs, published in the interwar and postwar periods, are steeped with nostalgia for youth and for a prewar world.

Several other factors accounted for whether members felt particularly enthusiastic about the Inns. In terms of residents, younger men who would someday marry seemed to enjoy a prolonged adolescence at the societies, whereas older, confirmed bachelors could, at least from outside descriptions, be lonely. Likewise, those just beginning careers might accept some degree of financial hardship, but those who continued to struggle later in their careers might resent ongoing privation. Some rank-and-file members of the Inns denounced the wealth and power of the benchers. In 1885, as a response to the honorary induction of Prince Edward to the Middle Temple, an anonymous barrister submitted an editorial in the *Pall Mall Gazette*, later reproduced in the *Law Times*. The author complained of the disconnect between the wealthy benchers, "men who have a large balance in the bank and to whom old port is grateful and comforting," and young barristers struggling to make ends meet. He accused the benchers of spending lavishly on "eating and drinking, on flower shows, stately buildings, ornamental services at the Temple Church" and other frivolities, noting bitterly that the festivities for the prince were paid for by money collected from arrears. The article's author insisted that while renovating chambers, the benchers had erected "mansions and palaces" that junior barristers could not afford, and chafed that the Inns had collected on the debts of junior barristers barely scraping by to fund the prince's feast.[75] For this author, the pageantry of the Inns and the rhetoric of brotherhood were perverse in the face of substantial inequalities between the bar's most and least successful. Indeed, members of the Middle Temple who shared similar sentiments protested the Inn's spending on the dinner by refusing to attend, instead convening at the Holborn Restaurant.[76] Their act of dissent was rewarded with a single sentence in the *Law Times*, and the prince's dinner was popular enough that, even after the hall had been

[74] MT MPA, April 20, 1855.
[75] "The Rebels in the Temple. By an Outer Barrister," *Law Times*, June 20, 1885, 144.
[76] "At Length the members ...," *Law Times*, June 20, 1885, 129.

outfitted with "narrow modern tables" to increase its capacity, tickets for the feast had to be awarded by ballot.[77]

Amicable bonds were predicated on meeting social expectations associated with members' age, status, and life stage. When these expectations were not met, the resulting conflicts emphasized the limits of "the brotherly feeling which should reign among all members of the bar, from humblest to most exalted."[78] Take the example of barrister Thomas Chisholm Anstey. In 1867, at the age of fifty-one, Anstey had just returned to Britain from appointments in Hong Kong and Bombay (from which he had been removed due to his vocal critiques of other government officials). He was trying – and failing – to start a practice in London. Over the next two years, Anstey penned a series of letters to the benchers of the Middle Temple remonstrating against various wrongs done to him. As a parliamentarian and imperial legal official, Anstey was no stranger to passionate composition. But unlike six-hour speeches calling for the prime minister's impeachment, these particular letters – though no less passionate in tone – called attention to incidents far smaller in scope.[79] In 1867, Anstey raged that a porter had directed him to step out of the way of a senior member of the bar on the steps of the society's hall. Two years later, he contended that another barrister had publicly insulted him while dining in hall, "indulging in vituperative expressions & in language which one gentlemen would not ... address to another in any decent society."[80]

Anstey's indignant letters implied that he had not been dealt with in the manner his membership of the bar demanded and expressed a sense of impugned honor. Anstey was a gentleman, but had not been treated as one. Take, for instance, Anstey's encounter on the steps of the hall. Porters policed public visitors, but were viewed by barristers as servants of the Inn. When the porter directed Anstey to step out of the way, he behaved as if Anstey were a member of the public rather than a member of the society. Indeed, Anstey interpreted the man's behavior as "a very offensive piece of misconduct." Anstey noted that he was wearing his bar gown at the time, making it impossible for the porter to have taken him for anything but a barrister. By asking him to move, the porter also implied that Anstey and the colleague to which he was speaking should defer to a senior barrister – another violation of the norms of the

[77] "Prince Edward at the Temple," *Law Times*, June 13, 1885, 122.
[78] "On This Fact ...," *Law Times*, November 2, 1895, 2.
[79] C. C. Macrae, "The Late Mr. Chisholm Anstey," *Standard*, September 10, 1873; Sydney Lee and K. D. Reynolds, "Anstey, Thomas Chisholm," *Oxford Dictionary of National Biography*, September 23, 2004.
[80] MT MPA June 14, 1867; December 6, 1867; June 25, 1869.

bar. "I am not aware," Anstey explained, "that two Gentlemen of the Bar and Members of the Society, though not of the Bench, are bound to do more for another Gentleman of the same Bar who happens to be on the Bench."[81] The bar was by no means a horizontal organization: those who governed the Inns held a great deal of arbitrary power, and distinctions of rank were observable via wig, gown, and barrister bands, to say nothing of unofficial sartorial trappings of success. But law student or QC, legal culture dictated that, at least within informal social interactions, members of the bar treat each other as equals. Anstey, perhaps especially because he was senior in years if not in rank, bristled at not being accorded the respect he was due.

Insults and injuries that took place in the hall had a public and sometimes performative character, making the wounds they inflicted deeper than words exchanged in private. When writing to the benchers about being insulted by the porter, Anstey concluded by assuring them that he wrote not to seek "reparation," but because he had a duty to "Gentlemen present in the Hall ... who have had reason themselves to complain."[82] Perhaps Anstey truly felt called to right wrongs against other barristers, but the fact that these gentlemen witnessed the porter's disrespect toward Anstey undoubtedly made his indignity all the greater. The benchers themselves noted that indecorous behavior in hall set a poor example for younger members of the bar. When mediating Anstey's complaint about being insulted while dining, the benchers admonished the offending party that "if the junior members the students in this Hall are not ... as reticent & as decorous as they were in old times," then senior members indulging in indecent language would only increase those faults. (Perhaps losing patience with the imperious Anstey, the benchers assured his adversary that they were certain his inappropriate expressions were not without provocation.[83])

The public nature of insults in hall could leave men without a clear recourse for addressing attacks against their honor. In 1857, Edward Lambert sent a letter of complaint to the Inner Temple benchers against another barrister of that society, Charles Wordsworth. According to Lambert, though the two "had not been on speaking terms for some time past," while dining in hall with the senior mess in 1855, Wordsworth took the opportunity to make "an offensive comment" about Lambert. When Lambert remarked on his rudeness, Wordsworth responded by denying he had spoken to Lambert, asserting, "I never condescend to speak to you, because you are not a gentleman." After

[81] MT MPA June 14, 1867.   [82] Ibid.   [83] MT MPA June 25, 1869.

heated words, Wordsworth declared before all present, "Mr. Lambert you have called me a liar twice & if you do not retract the words I will pull your nose." This threat escalated into violence on the entrance stairs, a "disgraceful scene" that only ended when the gardener and another servant intervened.[84]

In their words exchanged in hall, each man had clearly impugned the other's honor – Wordsworth by directly questioning Lambert's gentle-manliness, and Lambert by calling into question Wordsworth's honesty, which was the equivalent. That Wordsworth threatened violence against Lambert's nose is also significant. As Kenneth Greenberg argues in his article on nose-pulling in the antebellum south, "a man's character was expressed in what could be publicly displayed, not what was hidden under clothes or skin."[85] The nose, as the most prominent feature of a man's face, thus represented his character, and a nasal assault was the physicalization of a character assault. The nose may also have been a stand-in for another masculine organ unmentionable by gentlemen in public. In the eighteenth century, due to its association with the anus and with syphilitic infection, violence directed at the nose carried sexual meaning.[86] This sexual connotation may have continued across subsequent centuries; James Samuel Van Teslaar's 1922 *Sex and the Senses* contended that "there has always been" an association between the nose and the male reproductive organ.[87] Wordsworth's declaration that he would pull Lambert's nose was, then, a public attack on Lambert's masculinity, whether in the form of his character or his penis.

The two men's divergent responses to this incident, engaging in inter-personal violence versus writing to the Inn to demand redress, reflected what Margery Masterson describes as "competing models of gentlemanly masculinity" in mid-nineteenth-century Britain. If it was clear that each man had undermined the other's honor, for mid-Victorian gentlemen, the question of what to do about it remained murky. In centuries past, calling someone a liar had been a cause for dueling (and still was in certain parts of the continent or United States).[88] But concerted anti-dueling campaigns in England in the 1840s meant that in the

---

[84] IT BEN July 2, 1857.

[85] Kenneth S. Greenberg, "The Nose, the Lie, and the Duel in the Antebellum South," *American Historical Review* (1990): 68.

[86] Shoemaker, Robert Brink. *The London Mob: Violence and Disorder in Eighteenth Century England*. New York: Hambledon Continuum, 2007, 57.

[87] Van Teslaar substantiated this claim with scientific research that demonstrated a "sympathetic influence" between genital and olfactory mucous membranes. Van Teslaar, *Sex and the Senses* (Boston, MA: Gorham Press, 1922), 293–298.

[88] Robert Baldick, *The Duel: A History of Dueling* (London, 1965), 33; Greenberg, "The Nose, the Lie, and the Duel in the Antebellum South," 63.

subsequent decade, many considered duels outmoded. Historians of masculinity, such as John Tosh, point to this shift away from interpersonal violence as the result of the rise of a middle-class masculinity based on character and self-restraint supplanting an aristocratic masculinity based on external validations of honor. As Margery Masterson convincingly argues, however, the need to maintain social status and defend against defamation left gentlemen without a clear course of action when their honor had been challenged. Pursing legal action in the courts could draw out and publicize incidents that could be more quickly resolved and forgotten by dueling, meaning that the rejection of interpersonal violence as a tool for defending a man's honor was uneven at best.[89] Lambert, injured by the violence between them, described Wordsworth's actions not as one gentleman challenging another but as "the part of a Ruffian" attacking a victim. He described Wordsworth as "a more powerful man than myself," a description designed not to complement his foe's physique but to suggest that it was brutish of the other man to engage him in physical struggle.[90] The benchers of the Inner Temple, however, did not respond to Lambert's missive. Their lack of action seems as likely born out of indifference to a petty squabble as a sanction of interpersonal violence, but it also reinforced the notion that physical violence guaranteed a resolution to conflict, whereas appealing to an intermediary could leave conflict unresolved.

Literary Representation of Legal Sociability

The question of who could be considered a gentlemanly professional and how such a person should behave took on a new dimension in the flurry of changes to society and culture in the late nineteenth and early twentieth centuries. In response to the dislocations of the Boer War and especially the Great War, the increasingly cosmopolitan character of central London, the atomization of professional life, and the rise of the New Woman, members of the bar began to publish works devoted to the societies steeped with nostalgia for fusty Victorian days. These works began to appear as early as the 1890s, but they were published with increasing frequency after the First World War. Authors most often categorized their works as histories of the Inns, though in reality the books spanned genres, incorporating aspects of antiquarianism, memoir,

---

[89] John Tosh, "Masculinities in an Industrializing Society: Britain, 1800–1914," *Journal of British Studies* 44 (2005): 334; Margery Masterson, "Dueling, Conflicting Masculinities, and the Victorian Gentleman," *Journal of British Studies* 56 (2017): 608.
[90] IT BEN July 2, 1857.

and topographic guidebook. Like tourist guides, histories of legal London highlighted landmarks, legends, and literary references of interest to visitors, but they fused this content with authors' memories of the prewar Inns, musings on the present-day societies, and short pieces of fiction. Unpreoccupied by accuracy or authenticity, the works connected the Inns to eminent political, literary, and artistic moments and figures in Britain's past to claim prestige for the societies. They emphasized references and practices that figured the Inns as homosocial bastions of brotherly love.

Members of the bar writing about the Inns and the legal profession was nothing new; indeed, the combination of mid-century resident literati and briefless barristers desperate for a side hustle produced a spate of Victorian literature that featured the societies. Sociability at the ruinous Inns became a popular literary trope. Authors like Tom Taylor and William Makepeace Thackeray composed poetry and prose fiction that transformed drafty chambers into the ideal backdrop for warm friendships. In an 1859 poem that first appeared in *Punch*, Tom Taylor described Inner Temple chambers (based on those he had shared with Thackeray) as "grimy, dull, and grim." Likewise, Thackeray, in his own contribution to *Punch*, characterized chamber furnishings as "cheap treasures." Yet in detailing the "old armour, prints, pictures, pipes, china (all crack'd)" of a semi-fictitious Temple household, rather than a bleak picture, Thackeray portrayed a room full of curiosities and fantastic objects characteristic of a middle-class home, albeit in somewhat deteriorated condition.[91] Thackeray's chambers thus exemplified Victorian bachelor domesticity, selectively borrowed from conventional domestic ideologies to create an unrefined, but nevertheless recognizable, version of the bourgeois interior.[92] This homey, unpretentious setting fostered male affect. The narrator in Taylor's poem recalled "merry Sunday breakfasts" with his roommate, with whom he "chummed years without a single fight."[93] Similarly, in Thackeray's 1848–50 *Pendennis*, fictional roommates Pen and Warrington lived "almost as much in common as the Knights of the Temple, riding upon one horse" in their shared chambers in Lamb Building.[94] Here Thackeray referenced the medieval seal of the Knights Templar, in which two knights shared the same mount.

---

[91] Deborah Cohen, *Household Gods* (New Haven, CT: Yale University Press, 2006), 13, 89, 122.

[92] Snyder, *Bachelors, Manhood, and the Novel, 1850–1925*, 35.

[93] "Ten, Crown Office Row. A Templar's Tribute," *Punch*, February 26, 1859; "Love Songs by the Fat Contributor," *Punch*, March 27, 1847.

[94] William Makepeace Thackeray, *The History of Pendennis* (New York: Start, 2013), 1017.

Even more numerous and complex portraits of the Inns appeared in the many works of Charles Dickens, who invoked the age, mystery, and seclusion of the societies to describe them as at once reassuring and dangerous. On the one hand, for Dickens the Inns' "clerkly monkish atmosphere" could be a comfort and a buttress against the outside world. In *Great Expectations*, after an anxious encounter with the convict Provis, Pip returned to his shared chambers in Garden Court, declaring of his roommate, "Herbert received me with open arms, and I had never felt before so blessedly what it is to have a friend." Yet life in the opiate Temple was not entirely pleasurable. Pip described the Temple overall as "lonely," disconnected from the rest of the city and exposed to the river and the rain. In *Bleak House*, the secretive Mr. Tulkinghorn pondered over "that one bachelor friend of his," who one day conceived "an impression that [his life] was too monotonous ... and walked leisurely home to the Temple, and hanged himself." *Martin Chuzzlewit's* Tom found the Inns to have a "haunted air," even though dust "was the only thing in the place that had any motion about it." For Dickens, the species native to the decrepit societies was "the shabby-genteel" resident, a figure dressed in formerly smart attire now worn and threadbare. *Sketches by Boz* traced the gradual decay of one such man, as one by one the buttons disappeared from his waistcoat, then his coat, until "the man himself disappeared, and we thought he was dead."[95]

Novels such as Dickens' *Our Mutual Friend* and Mary Elizabeth Braddon's *Lady Audley's Secret* also imbued intimate friendships at the Inns with potentially homoerotic dimensions. Serialized between 1862 and 1865, both of these sensation novels featured bachelor barristers in residence at the Temple, unenthusiastic about beginning their careers. They were wasters, and as Sedgwick notes, "waste and wastage" were clear Victorian markers of a homosexual "type."[96] More languid than profligate, the protagonists nevertheless clearly squandered their time, familial resources, and education. Braddon's Robert Audley idled his hours away smoking and reading, until he chanced upon George Talboys, an old Eton friend. To his own surprise, Talboys' suspicious disappearance motivated Audley to spend his days sleuthing after the culprit rather than in repose at the Inns. "To think," Audley reflected after a long day obsessing over Talboys, "that it is possible to care so

---

[95] Regardless of the date of their publication, Dickens' novels seem to be set prior to Temple renovations, as the narrator makes clear in *Great Expectations*, 340, 311; *Bleak House*, 216; *Martin Chuzzlewit*, 612; *Sketches by Boz Illustrative of Every-Day Life and Every-Day People*, 142.

[96] Sedgwick, *Between Men*, 174–175.

much for a fellow!"[97] In *Our Mutual Friend*, the barrister Eugene Wrayburn passed his days with Mortimer Lightwood, his close friend and a likewise unemployed solicitor. One quiet evening in Temple chambers, the pair fantasized about life together in a deserted lighthouse, cut off from the rest of the world.[98] The two men later joked about their musing, but their laughter did not dispel or undermine the fact that they had vocalized a romance of running away together, a fantasy usually reserved for heterosexual partners.

Late nineteenth- and early twentieth-century histories of legal London deleted the ambivalence of mid-Victorian literary depictions, instead invoking romanticized images of serenity and decay by cherry-picking from earlier representations of the Inns and their environs. Later authors regularly quoted poems by roommates William Makepeace Thackeray and Tom Taylor to cast the societies as a homey refuge of fraternity inhabited by impoverished literary bohemians. An even greater number of these histories referred to Charles Dickens' description of Fountain Court in *Martin Chuzzlewit*, "Merrily the Fountain leaped and danced."[99] Such animated language lent the Inns a warm and spirited atmosphere. Significantly, authors omitted Dickens' more equivocal references to the societies in his other works, or even within *Martin Chuzzlewit*, which described the Inns as lonely, decaying, or haunted. Authors also ignored the quote's context. In Dickens' novel, the motion of the fountain echoed John Westlock's excitement at encountering his future bride, representing the thrill of heterosexual courtship. By refusing to situate the passage in the broader story, histories of legal London capitalized on the cultural cachet of Dickens without sacrificing the image of the Inns as a homosocial stronghold.

Histories of legal London also ignored the modern amenities added to the Inns and conflated Victorian historicist renovations with surviving medieval and Elizabethan architecture. In his 1914 *The Temple*, Hugh

---

[97] Mary Elizabeth Braddon, *Lady Audley's Secret* (Peterborough: Broadview Press, 2003), 71, 123.

[98] Charles Dickens, *Our Mutual Friend* (Oxford: Oxford World Classics, 2008), 145–147.

[99] Coleridge, *Quiet Hours in the Temple*, 17; C. P. Hawkes, *Chambers in the Temple* (London: Methuen, 1930), 4; Marjorie Bowen, *The Story of the Temple and Its Associations* (London: Griffin Press, 1928); Colonel Robert J. Blackham, *Wig and Gown: The Story of the Temple Gray's and Lincoln's Inn* (London: Low, Marston, 1932); Hyacinthe Ringrose, *The Inns of Court: An Historical Description of the Inns of Court and Chancery of England* (Oxford: R. L. Williams, 1909); W. J. Loftie, *The Inns of Court and Chancery* (Hampshire: Ashford Press, 1893); W. Marshall Freeman, *A Pleasant Hour in the Temple* (London: M. Hughes & Clarke, 1932); Hugh Bellot, *The Inner and Middle Temple, Legal, Literary and Historic Associations* (London: Methuen, 1902); Hugh Bellot, *The Temple* (London: Methuen, 1914).

Bellot imaginatively positioned Temple Church as a backdrop for recounting mysterious medieval legends and secrets, even though its appearance was of 1840s origin.[100] Similarly, interwar histories obsessed over the Inns' Elizabethan moment, a period marked by monarchical favor, the high point of legal instruction, and a resident population of fashionable gentlemen dilettantes.[101] The Elizabethan period tied the Inns to legends, events, and figures that formed part of a British national heritage and identity. Histories of legal London lauded the Elizabethan Inns for their revels, festivals, and plays, including the first performance of *Twelfth Night*.[102] Connecting Shakespeare to the Inns was one way that authors catapulted the societies from the local to the national, collective British past. Using material artifacts to attach Elizabeth I to the Inns also tied the societies to a national heritage. Many authors declared the benchers' table in Middle Temple Hall to be made of wood from Drake's *Golden Hinde*, referencing a triumph of Elizabethan imperial navigation.[103] These authors amalgamated archival research and oral or written legend, including stories without historical evidence, in their works, so long as their connection to the Inns was long-standing.

Placing new value on longevity and connection with the past, authors linked the Inns' ancient architectural spaces to the historic practices they housed, especially dining to keep term. While mid-Victorian members emphasized the practicalities of this custom, late nineteenth- and early twentieth-century authors defended keeping term as a historic ritual. For Edwardian and interwar members of the Inns, the societies and their rituals represented physical and embodied manifestations of valued pasts.[104] Histories detailed the Elizabethan features of the Middle Temple Hall, especially the dark wood paneling, elaborately carved screen, and double-hammer beam roof, to impress the hall's great age on readers. At the Middle Temple, authors noted, dinner began with the sounding of a medieval summoning horn. A 1919 article in the *Globe* proudly described this as "London's Oldest Custom." Whether or not this was true, the article substantiated its claim by referencing William George Thorpe's 1895 *Middle Temple Table Talk*, itself a mixture of archival research and oral legend. According to the *Globe*, before the start of the meal, an usher in purple gown knocked twice on the floor

---

[100] Hugh Bellot, *The Temple*, 38.   [101] Ibid., 28.

[102] E. A. P. Hart, *The Hall of the Inner Temple* (London: Sweet & Maxwell, 1952), 8; see also Adrian Poole, *Shakespeare and the Victorians* (London: Arden Shakespeare, 2004).

[103] See Bellot, *The Temple*, 146; Coleridge, *Quiet Hours*, 42; Freeman, *A Pleasant Hour in the Temple*, 10.

[104] Eric Hobsbawm, "Introduction," in *The Invention of Tradition* (New York: Cambridge University Press, 1983).

with his staff. The seated barristers and students, in black gowns, rose and "'dress[ed]' shoulder to shoulder, in military fashion." The benchers then processed into the hall, led by a ceremonial mace-bearer. While the Inner Temple had let such formalities go, the article lauded the Middle Temple for "scrupulously" preserving the Inn's ancient rituals.[105]

Authors celebrated the Inns' historic rituals because they anchored legal culture in ideas of brotherhood even as the texture of professional life was changing. More than ever before, barristers and law students lived in suburbs rather than at the Inns, limiting their opportunities for casual socialization in chambers. Social interactions beyond the societies' borders also began to decline. As Raymond Cocks argues, after the 1883 relocation of the law courts to the Strand, barristers no longer consorted via walks to Westminster. Railways made it so that barristers did not have to stay overnight while on circuit, resulting in a decline of circuit mess sociability. In light of these changes, the Inns relied upon dining rituals to buoy the corporate life of the societies.[106]

Histories of legal London celebrated one enduring extension of professional fraternity – the practice of eating together at nearby Fleet Street taverns, an informal but long-standing tradition at the Inns. Authors emphasized the historic associations of establishments like the Cock, Nando's Coffee-house, the Cheshire Cheese, or the Devil's Tavern, particularly as haunts of Dr. Samuel Johnson and Ben Jonson and his Apollo Club. One writer described the Cheshire Cheese as "still the dirty-fronted, low-browed tavern, with stone flasks in the window, that it was even before Johnson's time."[107] Authors emphasized how the same locales that had served Elizabethan and Georgian residents continued to serve nineteenth- and twentieth-century lawyers. The tradition of Fleet Street tavern patronage, these authors claimed, often led to a familiarity between members of the Inns and tavern waitstaff. Gilchrist Alexander recalled his relationship to the Cock Tavern, "We dined in one of the pew-like enclosures attended by Arthur, a very long-established waiter. After a few years in the tropics I went back ... to be greeted by the remark: 'Haven't seen you lately, sir.'"[108] In recounting the remark, Alexander figured the Fleet Street taverns as spaces of continuity with both the distant and more recent past, his years between visits mere

---

[105] "London's Oldest Custom. Middle Temple's Ox-Horn Summons to Dinner, Romantic Relic of 1184," *Globe*, June 14, 1919; see also C. P. Hawkes, *Chambers in the Temple: Comments and Conceits "In Camera"* (London: Methuen, 1930), 145–147.

[106] Raymond Cocks, "The Middle Temple in the Nineteenth Century," in *History of the Middle Temple*, ed. Richard O Havery (Portland, OR: Hart, 2011), 324.

[107] Arthur Ransome, *Bohemia in London* (New York: Dodd, Mead, 1907), 164.

[108] Alexander, *The Temple of the Nineties*, 51.

ellipses for the ever-present Arthur. Even law student Tom Wintringham, a member of the Communist International, extolled these alehouses of Albion. In 1926, Wintringham counted the Cheshire Cheese among the places he most wanted to visit after being released from his six-month imprisonment for sedition.[109]

In emphasizing these establishments' history as Elizabethan and Georgian haunts, authors highlighted the Englishness of the Fleet Street taverns relative to newer foreign – and feminized – restaurants along the Strand and in the West End. The food critic Lieutenant Colonel Newnham-Davis contrasted his account of eating *truite meunière* with Miss Dainty and her poodle at Romano's with his experience at the Cheshire Cheese. By 1899, Romano's, located on the Strand and formerly popular with a bohemian crowd, had become the domain of dining couples, with a menu entirely in French and a waiter named Antonelli. Conversely, Newnham-Davis described the Cheshire Cheese, a Fleet Street favorite, as the perfect place to go for a man who was not dressed for dinner anywhere else. There the host, Mr. Moore, dished out pudding and brought him a pint of beer and stewed cheese. Newnham-Davis then struck up a conversation with a nearby diner and shared with him a glass of Cheshire Cheese punch.[110] The food consumed was decidedly English, and the mood decidedly one of masculine sociability.

The same historic rituals and traditions that marked insider status for the British members of legal London, however, equally denoted outsider status for foreign members of the Inns, a fact glossed over by most interwar authors. As early as 1885, 12 percent of barristers and an even greater number of law students hailed from overseas, and their numbers only grew in the early twentieth century.[111] Yet writers described overseas students at the Inns as exotic others, not quite unwelcome but decidedly separate. Gilchrist Alexander, for example, noted the diversity of the Middle Temple, populated by "English, Scottish, Irish, Welsh, Colonial and others, with hundreds from India's coral strands and Afric's sunny fountains." Alexander treated overseas members as a curiosity, recounting their "wooly heads" in rows at the library as he might describe animals at the zoo.[112] Few authors described much socialization between Anglo-British and overseas students, barristers, or residents. Some writers contended that while dining in hall, men of all backgrounds ate with one another, but self-interest motivated these interactions. Diners in

---

[109] Liddell Hart Military Archives, Wintringham 9/5.
[110] Lieut.-Col. Newnham-Davis, *Dinners and Diners: Where and How to Dine in London* (London: Office of the Pall Mall Publications, 1899), 9–12, 22–29.
[111] Duman, *English and Colonial Bars*, 10.   [112] Alexander, *Temple of the Nineties*, 66, 78.

hall were divided into "messes" of four people, each mess allotted a certain portion of wine. As one author quipped, "For this reason a Mohammedan … is welcomed eagerly in any mess, for his unconsumed portion goes to augment the never sufficient allotment of the other members."[113] As histories of legal London made clear, Anglo-British and international students did not dine together to share in cultural exchange. In fact, the hegemony of English rituals at the Inns robbed transnationalism of any of the dangerous valences identified by historian Judith Walkowitz.[114] Foreign cuisine could be safely sampled in West End establishments, with the knowledge that fare at the Inns would consist of "soup or fish, a joint with potatoes and vegetables, apple or gooseberry tart, cheese, bread, and butter."[115] Despite their international population, the societies' culture and cuisine remained solidly English.

Like their Victorian predecessors, twentieth-century authors highlighted the homoerotic dimensions of male intimacy by absenting women from their narratives and placing men in typically feminine roles. Blending recollection, fiction, and legend, C. P. Hawkes offered a number of accounts of life at the Inns that blurred the lines of friendship, romance, aesthetic pleasure, and desire. Hawkes recounted the tale of two hallmates (perhaps fictitious, perhaps not) who despised one another, until they accidentally swapped headgear at a West End party, finishing with "a happy ending, in a union of hearts – and hats." Here, by joining "hearts," Hawkes echoed the language of heterosexual romance and marriage. In the subsequent story, the narrator became transfixed by the song of an ethereal "rich-toned tenor" voice issuing unseen from the Inner Temple. The narrator imagined himself as *The Tempest*'s Ferdinand and the singer as Ariel, until a policeman rounded the corner, revealing the source of the song and breaking the spell.[116] Hawkes's characterization of the enchanting voice as Ariel is significant, as this spirit was written with male pronouns but, until the 1930s, was typically played by a woman. Thus, Hawkes offered an account of blurred boundaries, in which the male narrator was enchanted by a male voice aligned with feminine qualities, which ultimately belonged to a robust and male-bodied individual.

Histories of legal London also contrasted their enduring, all-male professional world with caricatures of new female white-collar employees elsewhere in London. In the first two decades of the twentieth century,

---

[113] Hawkes, *Chambers in the Temple*, 146–147.   [114] Walkowitz, *Nights Out*, 17–43.

[115] Alexander, *After Court Hours*, 73.

[116] Hawkes, *Chambers in the Temple*, 91, 99–100; Anne Button, "Ariel," in *The Oxford Companion to Shakespeare*, ed. Michael Dobson and Stanley Wells (Oxford: Oxford Reference Online, 2001).

women made inroads into the business sector as secretaries and stenographers, but they remained shut out of work at the Inns. Authors like C. P. Hawkes compared "the shingled 'lady-stenographer' with her long French heels and her wide English simper" with the "Barrister's clerk, discreet, omniscient, and with an air of well-deserved responsibility."[117] Hawkes set stereotypes of the frivolous New Woman against the contained body of the responsible, male clerk. Hawkes also reaffirmed existent professional relationships and power dynamics between barristers and barristers' clerks. A good clerk knew how to win the best cases from solicitors for his barrister. In return he was paid a varying percentage (between 2.5 and 5 percent) of the barrister's fees. Thus, the success or failure of a barrister and a barrister's clerk was mutual. As a result, successive generations of barristers and clerks from the same families often had close ties and working relationships.[118] Men outside the legal profession might cultivate tenuous professional relationships with women, but histories of legal London celebrated the bar's perpetuation of a time-tested, thoroughly masculine work environment.

Authors of these histories uniformly ignored the most significant change in women's professional presence at the societies, the admission of women to the Inns of Court in 1919. Almost none of the histories of legal London written in the 1920s or 1930s acknowledged women barristers and law students at the Inns, despite women's highly publicized presence in the press. As challenges to both precedent and the Inns' homosocial culture, female members disrupted the continuous traditions that authors intended their works to convey. Hawkes alone included an ambivalent section on "Portia," in which he pondered whether women could adjust to the "masculine *religion d'avocat* of the English Bar." For Hawkes, women's integration into professional life was not impossible, but it required "time and mutual understanding" to "solve the difficulties of comradeship of men and women on circuit and in chambers." Tellingly, Hawkes concluded his section by paraphrasing *The Merchant of Venice*, "Portia may confidently trust that 'The four winds blow in renownèd suitors' (perhaps not only in the legal sense of the word) 'in plenty to her chambers.'"[119] By invoking a Shakespearean female lawyer, Hawkes reminded readers of the connection between the bard and the Inns and subtly indicated that women barristers were not entirely unprecedented. His parenthetical

---

[117] Hawkes, *Chambers in the Temple*, 10.
[118] Charles Booth, *Life and Labour of the People in London, Volume IV Part I* (New York: AMS Press, 1970), 38.
[119] Hawkes, *Chambers in the Temple*, 74.

interjection about nonlegal suitors, however, conveyed his hope that women barristers would find husbands, presumably to carry them safely back to the domestic realm.

Histories of legal London ignored or denigrated women's presence in the profession, but letters and diaries reveal that many members of the societies took advantage of the increased facility of interacting with women, in their personal if not professional lives. Gradually relaxed norms for heterosexual courtship, for example, changed the nature of intimacy between men and women at the Inns. When Hannah Cullwick stayed the night at Arthur Munby's chambers in the 1860s – a night Munby insisted they spend in separate bedrooms – she had to hide under a bed so as not to be seen by the housekeeper.[120] In her letters in the early 1920s, by contrast, medical student Elizabeth Arkwright joked about the Temple porters recognizing her from having spent so many nights in her fiancé Tom Wintringham's chambers. Her letters made explicit, as well, that these were not similarly chaste evenings.[121]

Even the ICRV – that brotherhood within a brotherhood – offered a variety of new heterosocial activities that encouraged interactions between men and women. When members of the mid-Victorian corps mentioned women at all, it was usually on those occasions when women materialized to admire men in uniform. In 1860, for example, William Grantham marveled at his "good luck to win a lady's ticket ... to see [the] Volunteer Review." Sir Paul Ogden Lawrence's 1878–82 diary mentioned several occasions on which lady friends came down to Richmond to watch drills on "ladies day." Lawrence discreetly edited out their names, perhaps because such an activity lay at the outer bounds of respectability. By the end of the century, however, the ICRV sponsored annual concerts, dinners, balls, and perhaps the most whimsical of heterosocial events, the yearly Gymkhana. In addition to regular jumping competitions, this event included horse races forcing riders to dress in drag, collect potatoes, or smoke cigars. Certain races required competitors to partner with a lady who would have to draw an animal, or guess a whistled tune, before the rider could finish the race.[122] Unlike the solemn volunteer review, at the Gymkhana, women could laugh at the antics of their male peers or even participate in the comedy themselves.

---

[120] Munby, *Man of Two Worlds,* 136.
[121] Liddell Hart Military Archive, Wintringham 9/3.
[122] LMA; Extracts from the Diary of W. W. Grantham, Later Mr. Justice Grantham, 1859–1864; Extracts from the Diaries of Sir Paul O. Lawrence, 1878–1882; 1896–1937 Miscellaneous Papers.

Conclusion

In many ways the bar does not match the narratives of professionalization or pathways of rationalization found in medicine, the civil service, or the army, but like these other professions, the Inns of Court had to contend with a swelling middle-class membership in the mid-nineteenth century. The societies responded to this middle-class membership by doubling down on the idea of barristers as gentlemanly professionals. They relied on the material environment of the Inns of Court to foster a culture of homosociality whose affective dimensions were essential for inducting members of the bar with the appropriate values and attitudes. Yet even as the Inns were determined their members should be gentlemen, the ideas of what exactly made a gentleman and who could qualify as one were in contest. Such ambiguities could leave barristers in confusion as to whether they and their fellows were behaving – or being treated – appropriately.

This chapter has focused on sociability and the ways in which it was intended to both forge and unite members of the bar. The two chapters that follow examine different instances in which sociability was understood to have failed, firstly via disciplinary cases in which barristers violated legal etiquette, and secondly in the case of Indian law students and their integration into the Inns. As both chapters contend, in many of these instances, the specific tenets or concerns were not explicitly about masculinity, but time and again, in cases ranging from fraud to sedition, or in discussions over the effective integration of students of color, the Inns came back to the gentlemanly character of members in question. Masculinity, in particular gentlemanliness and fraternal sociability, became benchmarks against which to measure a variety of political offenses.

4   Gentlemanliness, Etiquette, and Discipline

In 1868, the benchers of the Inner Temple called William Gill before a disciplinary committee to decide whether or not to disbar him. The year before, the society received a letter from a Scottish woman named Mary Dodd detailing "the facts" of her "unmitigated swindling" by Gill, who had reduced her "to a state of perfect destitution." According to Dodd, Gill seduced her, defrauded her, then left her and their child in "a state of starvation." He was not, Dodd felt assured, "a fit member of your Honourable Court."[1] Sixty years later, in 1928, another member of the Inner Temple, William Stafford Levinson, failed to appear at his own disciplinary hearing. Levinson also stood accused of defrauding a woman, in this case in the foreign outpost of Shanghai. Worse than that, it seemed Levinson had falsified various official documents for admission to practice in the British Supreme Court in Shanghai. By the time the acting judge discovered these fabrications, Levinson had already defrauded his widowed client, closed his bank accounts, and fled Shanghai on a Russian emergency passport. Not only was Levinson not the British subject he had claimed to be, but his travel patterns suggested he might be a Bolshevik.[2]

If, as Chapter 3 argues, ideals of gentlemanliness were predicated on a set of relationships between men at the bar, these ideals were limited to neither homosocial nor professional relationships alone. In fact, the behaviors and values cultivated by the Inns were meant to guide both how a barrister interacted with solicitors and clients, and his general conduct. In this regard, gentlemanliness was an essential component of legal etiquette, a term that encompassed inherited practices, unspoken understandings, and, after the 1864 Consolidated Regulations (but, significantly, not before), written rules. Members of the bar who violated legal etiquette – codified or not – could face disciplinary consequences ranging from censure to disbarment.

---

[1] IT BEN November 5, 1867.   [2] IT DIS/1/L1.

The disciplinary cases of Gill and Levinson, which bookend this chapter, exemplify the ways that the etiquette of the Victorian Inns of Court was transformed by the geopolitical context of the early twentieth century. To a certain degree, offenses that resulted in disbarment carried through from the mid-nineteenth century. The societies almost always disbarred members who committed illegal actions, such as defrauding a client. Furthermore, both Gill's and Levinson's exploitation of vulnerable women, and their duplicity, violated the bar's gentlemanly standards of honor and forthrightness. In Gill's case, however unusual it was for the Inns to comb through the details of a barrister's soured romance, the issues of fraud and disreputable behavior were familiar enough to the Victorian societies. Other barristers had swindled their clients and acted in ungentlemanly manners, if under somewhat less salacious circumstances. Levinson, however, compounded these familiar infractions with radical political actions disloyal to Britain and its empire. As one of several newly controversial figures arising out of the massive social and political transformations of the early twentieth century, he represented both political extremism and foreign danger. Communists, along with conscientious objectors and Indian nationalists at the Inns, forced the societies to consider a series of ethico-political questions regarding national loyalties, issues with which the Victorian societies had not had to contend. The questions surrounding these cases might still involve issues of legal etiquette and gentlemanliness, but they more firmly rested on the tensions between British citizenship, radical political expression, and membership in orthodox institutions deeply entrenched in the established order.

Gill and Levinson were subject to a series of rules and historical precedents, unwritten until the 1864 Consolidated Regulations, that delineated acceptable and unacceptable behaviors for members of the Inns. Legal etiquette defined the parameters of professional practice and the relationship between barrister and solicitor, and barrister and client. Its tenets also helped ensure the gentlemanly character of the bar. As we saw in Chapter 3, customs and rituals existed to imbue the barrister "with a reverence for the rules of his profession."[3] When members of the Inns violated these norms, various forces intervened. Jurist A. V. Dicey argued that professional opinion, rather than formal penalties, was the strongest force regulating barristers' actions. After all, a barrister with a bad reputation would not secure briefs. The circuit messes also had powers, such as expulsion from the mess, to discipline practice and

---

[3] A. V. Dicey, "Legal Etiquette," *Fortnightly Review* 2 (1867): 175.

behavior in court or while on circuit. This chapter is primarily concerned, however, with the role played by the benchers of the Inns, in
whose hands professional membership ultimately rested. It therefore
focuses on both barristers' professional practices and personal politics –
from fraud to Bolshevism – that did not accord with the Inns'
gentlemanly standards.

Legal etiquette had long been flexible or, as critics would put it, poorly
defined. Even the 1864 Consolidated Regulations did not capture and
codify every aspect of etiquette, nor did subsequent iterations. Members
of the profession could therefore dispute which aspects of legal etiquette
were to be strictly followed and which were customary but not inviolable.
Determining what constituted ungentlemanly behavior similarly created
gray areas. Exactly how much leeway did a member of the Inns have in
his conduct before he was deemed to have behaved in a manner
unworthy of a barrister? Disciplinary procedure called for the benchers
of the Inns to interpret barristers' actions based on precedent set
by earlier disciplinary cases, but the benchers' approach was hardly
systematic. Instead, the Inns judged cases on an ad hoc basis, giving
greater or lesser weight to standards and precedents depending on
their investment in a particular case's outcome. Like other Victorian
disciplinary institutions, such as the police, the Inns lacked a centralized
method of professional oversight: the societies disciplined members
brought to the societies' attention by outside parties, be they court and
government officials or members of the public.[4]

The flexibility of etiquette, coupled with the policing function of
professional opinion and the absence of an overarching supervisory
mechanism, meant that out of the thousands of practicing barristers,
perhaps fewer than one or two per year came before the Inns for disciplinary hearings.[5] The exact number of these cases is difficult to quantify,
however, as the societies kept only haphazard records of the proceedings.
As documented within existing archival materials, the four Inns combined disbarred only ten barristers between 1800 and 1860.[6] In the
eighty years following, I have encountered at least eighteen disciplinary
cases (fourteen disbarred) from the Middle Temple, fourteen cases

---

[4] Stefan Petrow, *The Metropolitan Police and the Home Office in London, 1870–1914* (Oxford:
Oxford University Press, 1994); Phillip Thurmond Smith, *Policing Victorian London*
(Westport, CT: Greenwood Press, 1985); Terry Standford, *The Metropolitan Police,
1850–1940* (PhD thesis, University of Huddersfield, 2007).
[5] In 1885, for example, the Law List included 7,250 barristers. Daniel Duman, *The English
and Colonial Bars* (London: Croom Helm, 1983), 50.
[6] David Woolley, "The Inn as a Disciplinary Body," in *A History of the Middle Temple*, ed.
Richard O. Havery (Portland, OR: Hart, 2011), 357–372.

(ten disbarred) from the Inner, and nine cases (eight disbarred) from Lincoln's Inn. Even if these forty cases were doubled or tripled, a very small fraction of the profession ever faced direct disciplinary action from the Inns, and an even smaller fraction were expelled from the societies.

Notably, disciplinary cases at the Inns occurred in temporal clusters, in part fueled by newspaper publicity. The societies disciplined more members during moments of heightened external scrutiny, such as during the convergence of parliamentary calls for reform and media scandals surrounding high-ranking members of the bar in the 1860s.[7] The societies also disciplined more members during periods of newsworthy political tumult, like the early decades of the twentieth century. The press devoted uneven attention to barristers' professional misconduct. Fleet Street did not waste ink on barristers who violated obscure tenets of legal etiquette of little interest to the public. Papers did, however, report on offending members of the profession already in the public eye from their participation in contested, high-profile court cases, such as Edward Kenealy, defense for the 1873–4 Tichborne claimant. The press also followed the disciplinary cases of members of the bar whose infractions originated in print, for example, barrister Shyamji Krishnavarma, who published anti-British editorials in 1909.[8] Newspapers thus brought barristers' misdeeds to the Inns' attention and also put pressure on the societies to censure offenders and reassure the public they could keep their members in check.

If few in number, disciplinary cases nevertheless reveal the societies' changing interpretation of standards required for barristers to fulfill their duty as advocates, as well as the Inns' shifting understanding of the role of legal institutions within Britain and its empire. The vague parameters of legal etiquette allowed the societies to emphasize or minimize various portions of their tenets. Disciplinary cases highlight the societies' particular preoccupations, revealing the gradual politicization of those

---

[7] It may have been fewer than one barrister per year called before the benchers. W. Wesley Pue, "Moral Panic at the English Bar," *Law & Social Inquiry* (Winter 1990): 56.

[8] On Kenealy's disbarment, see "Notes from Our London," *York Herald*, March 18, 1874; "From Our London Correspondent," *York Herald*, May 15, 1874; "From Our London Correspondent," *York Herald*, June 29, 1874; "Dr. Kenealy Disbenched," *Lincoln, Rutland and Stamford Mercury*, August 7, 1874; "Stray Notes," *Preston Guardian*, August 8, 1874; "Our London Correspondent," *Morpeth Herald*, August 15, 1874; "London Sayings and Doings," *Wrexham Advertiser*, August 15, 1874; "The Tichborne Mania," *Penny Illustrated Paper*, November 14, 1874; "Latest News," *Freeman's Journal and Daily Commercial Advertiser*, November 20, 1874; "The Benchers and Dr. Kenealy," *Birmingham Daily Post*, November 24, 1874; "Letter from London," *Cheltenham Chronicle*, November 24, 1874; "Dr. Kenealy Was on Wednesday Disbarred," *Star*, December 5, 1874. On Krishnavarma, see "Disbarring an Indian Agitator," *Manchester Guardian*, April 1, 1909; "Editorial," *Courier and Argus*, April 21, 1909; "The Indian Budget," *Times*, August 6, 1909.

aspects of legal etiquette most fiercely regulated by the Inns. The cases thus illuminate how the societies responded and adapted to social and political pressures from outside the Inns, from demands for rational reform to contestations over the best means of imperial governance. The cases expose tensions and disagreements within the societies, particularly regarding questions of political commitments and personal conscience. They remind us that, rather than monolithic institutions, the Inns were composed of a variety of members whose politics and priorities did not always align.

Counterintuitive though it may seem, the disciplinary process for practitioners of law was an extrajudicial one. Barristers or law students who came under the benchers' scrutiny generally received letters from their Inns calling them to account for offending actions. They or a representative party could then defend their deeds at a gathering of whichever benchers felt compelled to attend, generally held in the evening after dinner. For a disciplinary hearing that stretched across multiple meetings, nothing guaranteed that the same benchers who had attended the first would attend subsequent sessions, and vice versa. At the hearing, much was left to the benchers' interpretation and discretion, as they acted as prosecution, judge, and jury. If a barrister or student wished to challenge a decision, he could petition the judges of the High Court to sit as a tribunal of appeal. If the judges agreed to do so, their decision overrode that of the benchers, though only rarely did the conclusions diverge.

The infrequency of formal disciplinary measures, coupled with the tenets of legal etiquette itself, allowed the Inns to maintain the elite character of the bar with minimal interventions by the societies. To be sure, the Inns sought to actively shape the makeup of the profession. The societies' prohibitions against engaging in trade or advertising in newspapers, or their granting of privileges for those with university educations, courted the well-to-do. At the same time, however, the societies opposed standards such as qualifying examinations that would winnow the students eventually called to the bar. Instead, the Inns espoused a sink-or-swim attitude toward professional practice, believing that a combination of inborn intellect (perhaps cultivated by an Oxbridge education) and self-application, rather than examination and prescribed academic regimen, should determine success at the bar. As far as the Inns were concerned, the dictates of legal etiquette, combined with self-directed legal learning, sufficed to keep the profession stocked with high-quality barristers.

In contrast to this continuing hands-off approach to legal education and discipline, outside the Inns the same civic-minded social impulses that drove transformations to the city likewise inspired Whig and Liberal MPs to push for law reform for the public good. Henry Brougham, Whig politician and soon-to-be lord chancellor, ignited the fires of reform with an 1828 speech on sixty-two defects of the law and legal profession. Brougham and other reform-minded Whig and Liberal politicians insisted the law should be cheaper and more accessible to the public. They questioned the unbridled powers of the Inns of Court, institutions "whose functions are not of a public and responsible kind."[9] Spurred by the efforts of Richard Bethell (later Lord Westbury), an advocate of legal education, Parliament established three committees between 1834 and 1854 to investigate the state of the legal profession.[10] Reformers like Bethell demanded qualifying examinations, systematized legal education, and an outside body to monitor the workings of the legal profession. MP reformers argued that as advocates for the public, barristers needed to be accountable to the public. They remained unconvinced that calls to the bar without proper training and preparation could ensure the character and competence of members of the profession. The societies defended themselves from assaults on the privileges of the bar by initiating self-directed reforms that simultaneously met some reformers' demands for rationalization while reasserting the authority of the Inns. Furthermore, despite the zeal of certain individual reformers, Parliament overall had little motivation to reshape institutions that, if imperfectly meritocratic, were more or less functional.[11] The societies' ad hoc method of governance thus endured long after Victorian reformers gave up their efforts.

Victorian debates over the governance of the Inns of Court, like the tensions with the Board of Works in the second chapter, represented a conflict between the Inns' ancient, independent authority and Liberals' attempts to consolidate and order the nation's professions, institutions, and bureaucracies. The societies held the primary regulatory power over the profession, and each society's authority over its own Inn was nearly absolute. With decisions fragmented between four bodies, the Inns did not match the models of Victorian professionalization outlined by historian Harold Perkin.[12] The Inns of Court therefore provided an alternate model of professional modernity, in contrast to the army, civil service,

---

[9] Brian Abel-Smith and Robert Bocking Stevens, *Lawyers and the Courts* (London: Heineman, 1967), 29; *Sixth Report of Common Law Commissioners* (1834), as quoted in Abel-Smith and Stevens, *Lawyers and the Courts*, 64.
[10] Duman, *The English and Colonial Bars*, 55.   [11] Ibid., 65.
[12] William Joseph Reader, *Professional Men* (New York: Basic Books, 1966); Harold Perkin, *The Rise of Professional Society* (London: Routledge, 1989).

and other respectable professions, in which long-held values triumphed over meritocratic reform.

The endurance of older forms of organization did not shield the Inns from the currents of liberal values completely, however. Most notably, the Victorian societies embraced liberal religious toleration. A 1791 Act of Parliament had opened the bar to Catholics, and by 1833, Francis Goldsmid of Lincoln's Inn became the first Jew to be called to the bar.[13] In the second half of the century, when a growing number of Hindus, Muslims, Sikhs, and other non-Christians applied to the Inns, they faced no religious disabilities. Toleration was not acceptance, and the food, dress, and rituals at the Inns still presupposed Christian members. But the notion of at least surface-level respect for religious difference became an implicitly understood prerequisite of gentlemanliness, so that a slur based on religion was considered misconduct.

By the early twentieth century, the Inns no longer feared direct parliamentary intervention into the governance of the bar. Instead, they worried about whether and how to accommodate a growing number of dissident members within their ranks. The shifting global political context challenged the Inns with an increasing number of disciplinary cases in which members' actions fell outside established categories of permitted and proscribed behavior altogether. Anti-imperialism, world war, and Bolshevik revolutions forced the Inns to reinterpret their regulations, sometimes in order to defend or disbar particular violators. Ideological issues involving questions of free speech, political association, and action became bound up in the policing of gentlemanly conduct and challenged the limits of liberal toleration at the Inns, just as parliamentary legislation that curtailed freedoms of speech and association reined in liberalism more broadly. Could an Indian nationalist be disbarred merely for his written opinions? Had a student convicted of sedition really behaved in an ungentlemanly manner if he acted according to conscience? At what point did a political statement become a betrayal of British subjecthood and nation, and what role should the bar play in policing such distinctions? As they always had, the Inns deliberated over and judged these cases in an ad hoc fashion, their conclusions reflecting changing notions of foreign danger and a narrowing of the societies' willingness to accept ideological difference rather than mutually agreed-upon norms of professional etiquette and practice.

---

[13] John Cooper, *Pride versus Prejudice: Jewish Doctors and Lawyers in England, 1890–1990* (Cambridge: Cambridge University Press, 2019), 93.

Legal Etiquette and the Character of the Bar

Throughout the nineteenth century and into the twentieth, law became an increasingly stratified and heterogeneous profession. Members of an upwardly mobile middle class joined the sons of successful merchants and a core of aristocratic elites at the bar. Due in part to the efforts of the lower branch of law to professionalize, the distinction in prestige between barristers and solicitors shrank at the same time that the number of barristers at the bar surged. A growing colonial element added further diversity, as natives of Britain's colonies joined Anglo-British civil servants at the Inns in the hopes of inserting themselves into colonial bureaucracies.[14] As Chapter 3 argues, in the face of these changes, the Inns emphasized sociability to ensure the gentlemanly character of the bar, but they did not rely on sociability alone.

The Inns also policed the sharp distinction between engaging in a profession and engaging in trade. A barrister did not earn wages, but was paid an honorarium by the solicitor in the case. The lack of direct financial relationship between barrister and client maintained the barrister's position as an independent professional.[15] The Inns emphasized the difference between barristers and solicitors and roundly opposed any proposals that would blur the two sides of the legal profession. If a solicitor wished to become a barrister, he had to have been struck from the roll of solicitors for at least three years prior to his call to the bar.[16] Over the course of the nineteenth century, commerce became an increasingly acceptable source of wealth for members of the British elite, but legal etiquette prohibited law students and barristers from pursuing any trade while they remained members of the Inns.[17] Entrepreneurial barristers faced the censure of the benchers for offenses such as running manufactories or cinema companies. Members of the bar who were uncertain whether their pursuits violated etiquette could write to the benchers of their Inn to find out.[18]

Legal etiquette not only proscribed barristers from engaging in trade, it also prohibited practices or behaviors associated with trade, such as the

---

[14] Duman, *The English and Colonial Bars*; Raymond Cocks, *Foundations of the Modern Bar* (London: Sweet & Maxwell, 1983).

[15] The honorarium meant that barristers did not have the right to sue for nonpayment of fees, but also that clients could not prosecute barristers for nonappearance in court or negligence in conducting a case. See court decision *Kennedy v. Brown* 1863; Duman, *The English and Colonial Bars*, 43.

[16] IT BEN March 30, 1875.

[17] Charles Shaw, *The Inns of Court Calendar* (London: Butterworths, 1878).

[18] IT BEN December 21, 1866; April 20, 1915.

use of advertisements. For the Inns, advertisement could mean courting publicity in a newspaper. In 1899, for example, the Middle Temple issued a warning to the attorney general of the Leeward Islands who had advertised in the local papers there, reminding him that such practices were "most objectionable."[19] Advertising could also mean courting solicitors, a violation of the maxim Dicey playfully shorthanded, "thou shalt not hug attorneys."[20] In 1894, the Middle Temple admonished Laurence Ginnell for writing "to various Solicitors requesting them to send him business," deeming the solicitations a "grave Breach of the Professional etiquette of the Bar."[21] Solicitors were meant to seek out barristers based on their reputations. Ginnell, like others beginning their careers, faced the inevitable dilemma that the only way to establish a reputation was by holding briefs and the only way to hold briefs was by establishing a reputation. He nevertheless expressed "unqualified regret for his conduct" and was censured but not disbarred.

In addition to violating tenets particular to legal etiquette, barristers in the courts and common spaces of the Inns could find themselves subject to disciplinary action if they failed to conduct themselves in a gentlemanly fashion. In 1913, student Major W. A. Adam accused barrister Emanuel Wright of deliberately stealing his umbrella from the library cloakroom. Wright insisted that he had unwittingly substituted the umbrella for his own, but when he tried to return the umbrella to Major Adam, a heated correspondence ensued. Major Adam, unconvinced that Wright had taken his umbrella by mistake, threatened to "place the matter in the hands of the police." Wright, offended by the accusation of the umbrella's "fire-eating proprietor," "invite[d] him to go to hell." Eventually this dispute landed both parties before a disciplinary committee of benchers, and the two men, perhaps equally embarrassed, apologized and shook hands.[22] In cases such as this, the benchers objected not so much to the insults themselves – though they disapproved of foul language – as to the loss of reason and self-control such defamations implied. Similarly, it did not matter that the stolen article in question was an easily replaceable accessory. To knowingly take something that belonged to someone else was dishonest and dishonorable, an action unworthy of a barrister.

For the Inns of Court, gentlemanliness and legal etiquette were enough to ensure the proper functioning of the bar, but in the

---

[19] MT MPA January 15, 1910.   [20] Dicey, "Legal Etiquette," 175.
[21] Raymond Cocks, "The Middle Temple in the Nineteenth Century," in *A History of the Middle Temple*, 328; MT MPA January 12, 1894.
[22] IT BEN May 27, 1913.

mid-nineteenth century, the societies, like the other elite professions, faced heightened external scrutiny from reform-minded MPs and members of the bar. Utilitarian reformers, looking to centralized continental and American models of legal education and professional organization, objected to the many-headed structure of the bar's authority. They did not find the societies' medieval origins compelling justification for their continued existence.[23] Liberal politicians like Richard Bethell challenged the Inns' independence, contending that the societies should not be treated as exclusively private institutions, given that they routed men to public positions. In 1854, with Bethell's support, Sir Joseph Napier (a Tory MP, but one who valued education) secured the appointment of a parliamentary committee to investigate the efficacy of legal education.[24] This committee cast barristers as potential public officials who were thus accountable to the public. Barristers, the commissioners argued, enjoyed certain privileges: indemnities against charges of negligence; the sole right to plead for others in the Superior Courts of Westminster; exclusive eligibility for appointments of the offices of recorder, judge of a County Court, and police magistrate, as well as for numerous colonial judicial appointments. The committee reasoned that "the community is surely entitled to require some guarantee – first, for the personal character, and next for the professional qualifications of the individuals called to the Bar." Though the Inns did an adequate job regulating the former, the committee felt that only by instating entrance and qualifying examinations could the societies properly assess the intellectual capabilities of their members.[25]

The debates over the adequacy of legal education raised questions about the nature of professional training and whether it should look like older models of apprenticeship, or newer modes of university education. In 1846, for example, a parliamentary Committee on Legal Education (initiated by Bethell) encouraged the Inns to resurrect moots and other teaching practices that had died out after the civil war.[26] Such practices

---

[23] Reader, *Professional Men*; Perkin, *The Rise of Professional Society*; Cocks, "The Middle Temple in the Nineteenth Century," in *A History of the Middle Temple*, 303; Christopher W. Brooks, "The Decline and Rise of the English Legal Profession, 1700–1850," in *Lawyers, Litigation, & English Society since 1450*, ed. Christopher Brooks and Michael Lobban (London: Hambledon Press, 1998), 129–149.

[24] Abel-Smith and Stevens, *Lawyers and the Courts*, 66.

[25] The committee included some of the highest-ranking legal personages of the day, including the vice-chancellor, justices of the Court of Queen's Bench, and the attorney and solicitor generals. *Report of the Commissioners Appointed to Inquire into the Arrangements in the Inns of Court* (London: George Edward Eyre and William Spottiswoode, 1855).

[26] M. H. Hoeflich, "The Americanization of British Legal Education in the Nineteenth Century," *Journal of Legal History* 8: 3 (1987): 248–249.

required the Inns to take a more active role in legal education, but also accorded with the societies' historical customs. Reviving moots and other educational traditions would not interfere with the independence of the Inns. Other individuals who gave evidence before commissions, however, suggested that the Inns use their financial resources to transform the societies into a law university.[27] Such a transformation would dramatically alter the Inns' relationship to the bar, making them responsible for professional education rather than professional governance.

In debating measures like entrance examinations, high-ranking members of the bar expressed divergent visions of the individual who could or should succeed in the profession. Several law lecturers contended that a classical education denoted gentlemanliness, not inherently necessary for learning law, but highly desirable for members of a professional association. If the Inns were to instate an entrance examination, it would impede only "those who have not been so educated," implying that the latter were in any case undesirable candidates. Charles Howard Whitehurst, QC, then treasurer of the Middle Temple, vociferously argued against this position. Although Whitehurst was himself an Oxford graduate, he defined gentlemanliness as stemming from internal qualities and potentialities combined with professional training, rather than from academic and social pedigree. "Why should a man who never opened a Greek or Latin book not be a Lawyer?" asked Whitehurst. For Whitehurst, markers of status were irrelevant. "If [a barrister] is not qualified, he will get no business, and if he is qualified, he will get business."[28] In their sink-or-swim attitude, Whitehurst's opinions were closely in line with those who defended the self-directed learning of the public schools, as well as those who desired to maintain the status quo at the Inns.

Following the 1846 and 1855 Commissions, subsequent decades saw several more aggressive but ultimately impotent parliamentary interventions into the regulation of the Inns. Several times in the 1860s, Sir George Bowyer, a constitutional lawyer and Catholic convert, introduced bills to democratize the arbitrary powers of the benchers by

---

[27] Christopher Brooks, "The Decline and Rise of the English Legal Profession, 1700–1850," in *Lawyers, Litigation, and English Society*, 144.

[28] *Report of the Commissioners Appointed to Inquire into the Arrangements in the Inns of Court.* Like those who began to question the classical curricula of the public schools and universities at mid-century, Whitehurst dismissed a liberal education as "highly proper" but an unnecessary burden on men and their families. R. L. Archer, *Secondary Education in the XIX Century* (Cambridge: Cambridge University Press, 1921); John Chandos, *Boys Together* (London: Hutchinson, 1984). Whitehurst received his BA from Wadham in 1819. *The Registers of Wadham College, Oxford (Part II): From 1719 to 1871*, ed. Robert Barlow Gardiner (London: George Bell and Sons, 1895).

establishing a separate judicial body that would try all cases of professional misconduct. Bowyer's first bill even proposed to enfranchise the rank and file of the bar, making them responsible for the election of half of the benchers of their Inn. Bowyer's efforts met not so much opposition as indifference to changing what was, for most parliamentarians, a more or less functional system. When Roundell Palmer, Baron Selborne, then lord chancellor, proposed replacing the Inns of Court with a general school of law in the 1870s, his schemes met with more interest, but still could not win a majority. In 1875–6, Liberal MP Charles Norwood proposed a bill to abolish the barrister's honorarium, allowing barristers to sue for their fees, and clients to sue for barristers' nonappearance in court. Opponents argued that such a bill jeopardized the unique status of the bar and that of the barrister as advocate for rather than agent of his client. Certainly, Norwood's proposal would have restricted the hitherto unlimited autonomy and authority of the bar. The proposal lost 130 to 237 votes.[29]

Why was parliament content to leave the bar as it was? It was not because any significant number of barrister MPs blocked legislation. Only 20 percent of all MPs had been called to the bar, and the majority of this number did not actively practice law. According to Daniel Duman, respect for the long tradition of professional independence helped maintain the status quo, but in the end it was lack of agitation outside of Parliament, among the public or the members of the profession, that deprived reforms of force and momentum. Newspapers, even those with a decidedly reformist bent, reported on Bowyer's bill with apathy. Senior barristers had little desire to institute changes, and successful junior barristers likely looked forward to comfortable futures under the current system. Solicitors may not have been able to attain the same prestigious heights as barristers, but the divisions of the system ensured them a lucrative monopoly over their half of the legal profession. Only unsuccessful members of the junior bar would have had an impetus to mobilize, and they were likely too busy scratching out a living to do so.[30] Furthermore, Raymond Cocks notes that by the 1880s, general attitudes toward the Inns of Court had shifted away from criticizing the institutions. Like the ancient buildings themselves, the traditional workings of the Inns gained new prestige. Works like A. V. Dicey's *Law of the Constitution* equated commitment to the common law with of-the-moment jurisprudence. Rather than expensive and inefficient anachronisms, the Inns of Court, "home of the common law," regained their status as valuable legacies from the past.[31]

---

[29] Duman, *The English and Colonial Bars*, 56–66.   [30] Ibid., 64–65.
[31] Cocks, "The Middle Temple in the Nineteenth Century," in *A History of the Middle Temple*, 323.

Recognizing the need for at least limited changes, however, the Inns of Court undertook small, self-directed reforms in the second half of the nineteenth century. As an acknowledgment of the need for educational reform rather than a reform measure in and of itself, the societies created the somewhat toothless Council of Legal Education in 1851.[32] They likewise instated optional classes. In order to attract more college graduates, the societies gradually extended the privilege of call to the bar in three years rather than five from the Oxbridge elite alone to members of institutions such as the Universities of Dublin, London, Durham, Liverpool, Manchester, Leeds, Sheffield, Birmingham, Bristol, St. Andrew's, Aberdeen, Glasgow, and Edinburgh.[33] In 1864, they drafted the Consolidated Regulations of the Inns of Court to illuminate at least some of their rules and periodically updated these regulations in subsequent decades.[34] In 1872 the societies introduced compulsory qualifying examinations "to ascertain that [students] possessed a competent knowledge of Law."[35] They reserved the right to make exceptions, however, and frequently exempted foreign students from the examination.[36] The Inns gave the General Council of the Bar, formed in 1894, the power to establish and codify rules of professional etiquette and to speak as the voice of the profession in parliamentary committees and in the press. The Bar Council was composed of representatives from each society, however, and its decisions were not binding. The right to discipline barristers was left to the Inns. Formal rules, examinations, and councils may have been in keeping with the rationalization of other professions, but given that each Inn had the power to circumvent inconvenient regulations, by the end of the nineteenth century, the societies had conceded very little, if any, of their authority over the bar.

---

[32] Ibid., 305.

[33] MT MPA, "Deposits and Bonds for Admission as Students," April 22, 1920. These privileges originally dated back to the Georgian benchers. As early as 1762, the benchers noticed the decline of elite members and passed regulations allowing Oxford or Cambridge graduates to be called to the bar after three years rather than five. Duman, *The English and Colonial Bars,* 20.

[34] "The Jurist," *Jurist,* January 30, 1864.   [35] IT BEN June 7, 1898.

[36] MT MPA, Petition of Thomas Morris Chester of Monrovia, Liberia, June 7, 1867. See also Petition of Kettir Mohun Dutt, a native of Bengal, to be excused Latin; Tárak Náth Pálit, a native of Bengal, to be excused Latin; Peter Benemy, of Burmah, to be excused Latin; IT BEN Petition of Mr. Khoon Lipikorn, a native of Siam, to be excused Latin; Mr. M. E. Hussain, a native of India, to be excused Latin; Mr. Ali Ahmed, a native of India, to be excused Latin; Mr. B. H. Khoo, of India, to be excused Latin; Mr. M. A. Razak, a native of India, to be excused Latin; Mr. M. L. Khand, of India, to be excused Latin; Mr. R. O. Seneviratne, Mr. M. Walinthug, Mr. S. A. Hosain, and Min. G. Talpur, natives of Ceylon and India, to be excused Latin.

The only exception to the Inns' unchecked authority over their societies lay with the judges, who acted as the highest and only court of appeals for barristers who wished to dispute the benchers' actions in regard to disciplinary measures. This long-standing arrangement began when it was customary for the judges to leave their Inns and become members of Serjeants' Inn, making them theoretically impartial outsiders. Appeals to the judges continued, however, long after the abolition of Serjeants' Inn in 1873. The judges were under no obligation to review the disciplinary cases of disgruntled barristers, and more often than not, they refused to do so. When they did agree to hear them, their conclusions rarely diverged from those of benchers of the Inns, from whose ranks, after all, the judges originated.

The case of William Gill, which opens this chapter, was one of the few in which a barrister successfully appealed to the judges to reverse a decision of the benchers. Gill's was a case as much about honor and propriety as about criminal activity. Despite the fact that the Bow Street Police Court dismissed all charges against him in 1867, the benchers of the Inner Temple still decided to investigate Mary Dodd's complaints against Gill in November of that year. In a letter to the benchers, Dodd used the language and familiar narrative tropes of masculine exploitation to cast herself in a sympathetic, if fallen, position. An orphan, she had lived in Edinburgh with her two brothers until, she claimed, Gill took advantage of her while staying in their home. After seducing her, he convinced her to come to London and pursue litigation to wrest money due from her brothers. Dodd maintained that she wanted to leave, but Gill persuaded her that it would be bad for their case. She gave birth to a daughter. Gill won the suit against her brothers and, according to Dodd, induced her to invest the money in a slate quarry that would guarantee £400 per annum. He forced her to "write letters at his dictation and sign documents without understanding their purport" or else be "subjected to the most gross ill usage." When she received only a fraction of the promised annuity, Dodd filed a suit against Gill, claiming that he "lives in the lap of luxury at the Langham Hotel while my child and self have been ... in a state of starvation." Unfortunately for Dodd, key documents appeared in her handwriting rather than Gill's, and the Police Court dismissed the case. Dodd pleaded with the benchers, "I charge Mr. Gill with having dishonoured his position as a Barrister by the most unprofessional and dishonourable conduct" and asked them to inquire into the matter.

Significantly, rather than ignoring Dodd's complaint, a strategy usually favored by the benchers for dealing with cases already resolved by the courts, the society began a seven-month inquiry into the matter.

It appears that Dodd's plea moved the benchers; theirs was an investigation of dishonorable masculine behavior as much as of professional fraudulence. When called upon by the benchers to account for his actions, Gill dismissed Dodd's letter as "a tissue of falsehood and malice." He claimed that "witnesses and documentary evidence ... prove that I neither seduced nor deserted the complainant; that I never 'tempted her from her home'; never advised her to sue her relation." After receiving multiple accusatory letters sent to the benchers by both parties, in May of 1868 the benchers reviewed the case against Gill and decided to disbar him. The records left by the benchers do not indicate whether or not they were convinced that Gill was guilty of fraud or merely of dishonorable conduct toward Dodd. When in July 1868 Gill requested to know "the grounds" on which he had been disbarred, the Inner Temple treasurer responded tersely, "on the ground that the charges made against you had been proved."[37] Gill decided to appeal his case to the judges, with Sir Roundell Palmer – former attorney general, soon-to-be lord chancellor, and would-be reformer of the Inns' unchecked authority – serving as his counsel.

The benchers of the Inner Temple understood professional practice as deeply intertwined with personal honor, but in February 1869, the judges returned a decision that separated Gill's actions as a barrister from those as a lover, absolving him from any misdeeds in his capacity as the former. The judges outlined two charges against Gill: one of professional misconduct and one of "conduct inconsistent with honor and good faith such as should actuate a member of an honorable profession." Was it wrong for Gill, acting as Dodd's counsel, to borrow money from her and promise repayment from the interest of his investment in the slate quarry? The judges ruled that it was not, as they believed that the "transaction in question arose not out of the relations of Counsel and Client, but out of the domestic relations existing between the parties." The judges also dismissed the second charge, that Gill had behaved in a manner "imprudent and inconsistent with the character of a man of honor and a Gentleman." They did not believe that Gill "had any intention of deceiving Miss Dodd and appropriating her money to his use." Rather, they claimed, the loan was the result of Dodd putting "pressure upon the Appellant ... to allow her a far larger amount than his means would admit of, and ... from the desire of Mr. Gill to make provision for her, and to put an end to the connection." For the judges, it

---

[37] IT BEN. Pue suggests that the benchers may have kept the wording of their decisions ambiguous so as to make room for policy differences among them. Pue, "Moral Panic," 93.

was not Gill who had coerced Dodd, but the other way around. Her greed forced him to act even though "the hazardous nature of the security was fully made known to her." Despite their exoneration of Gill, the judges did express regret that the manner "in which the parties were placed relatively to one another was so much open to question."[38] The benchers had sympathized with the pitiable state of Mary Dodd; the tangled nature of Dodd and Gill's romantic and financial affairs likely influenced their decision against Gill. The judges' decision, by contrast, firmly limited potentially dishonorable behavior to dishonesty and deceit. Sexual impropriety they condemned, but they did not cast it as inherently ungentlemanly or abhorrent to the profession.

Following the judges' decision, Gill demanded reparation, as eighteen months out of practice had resulted in disastrous financial consequences. In July 1869 he filed for bankruptcy. The cause, he explained, was "from having been disbarred by the benchers of the Inner Temple and precluded from following his profession."[39] In £14,698 of debt, Gill would likely have faced bankruptcy even without his temporary disbarment. Nevertheless, he wrote the benchers twice that year demanding reparation "for the grievous injuries which you have inflicted upon me and my family by your erroneous order." When the benchers ignored his demands, Gill threatened to sue the Inner Temple. Such a threat was unlikely to intimidate a body composed of the most senior and successful barristers in the profession. The unflappable benchers directed Gill to their solicitors and heard no more from him again.[40]

Unlike Gill, the other barristers disbarred from the Inns faced the harsh reality of a career permanently stopped in its tracks. In June 1893, the Inner Temple disbarred Augustus Mirams, who had received six months' hard labor at the London County Sessions for intent to defraud. Mirams had given his landlord a check for £5 from an account so far overdrawn that the bank had ordered him to close it. In early 1897, Mirams began a twenty-six-year process of appeals to the Inner Temple to be reinstated at the bar. Mirams claimed that he had evidence to prove that he had "reasonable grounds for believing there would be funds" in his account on which to draw the check. He argued that his original conviction had been secured through the improper admission of evidence. In 1898 he asserted that he was "not guilty ... of any conduct unbecoming a member of the Bar or a gentleman." In 1901 he protested that the prosecuting counsel had treated him in

---

[38] IT BEN February 12, 1869.
[39] "Summary of This Morning's News," *Pall Mall Gazette*, July 31, 1869.
[40] IT BEN February 26, 1869; April 20, 1869.

"a most scandalous manner." He pleaded that he could not provide his family "with sufficient food and clothing," and that he suffered from "the mental agony which at times is enough to destroy one's reason." In 1902 he begged "as a Christian" to be allowed to clear his name. In 1910 Mirams appealed to the judges, but in vain. Mirams made further unsuccessful attempts to be reinstated in 1915, 1916, 1917, and 1923. Now 73 years old and in poor health, he asked that the Inns "make it possible for [him] to die in peace." They declined.[41]

Mirams's decades-long attempt to be reinstated as a barrister evidenced – even more dramatically than Gill's case – the high stakes of the Inns' censure and the degree to which barristers were at the mercy of the benchers. As Mirams pointed out in several of his letters, disbarment swept away his livelihood. For a man in his mid-forties at the time of conviction, it would be difficult to start over in a new career. On top of this, he had at least four dependent daughters. The vehemence with which Mirams attempted to be reinstated, however, reveals as much about notions of honor as practical issues of survival. Twenty-six years after his conviction, in "very precarious health," Mirams was never going to practice again. To be reinstated as a barrister would, however, be a final affirmation of his good character and, as he put it, bring comfort to his wife and children.

Faced with the arbitrary authority of the benchers, Gill threatened to sue, Mirams begged and pleaded, and other barristers publicized their complaints. William Digby Seymour, MP, faced disciplinary action from the Middle Temple for his 1856 letter to a creditor's solicitor, offering to hold briefs on the solicitor's instructions as a means of paying off his debts.[42] For Seymour, the discretionary and erratic proceedings of the benchers during his disciplinary hearings were antithetical to English notions of justice. In February 1862, Seymour wrote to the *Times*:

I was upon 15 different occasions before the benchers of my Inn, and I stood practically before 15 different tribunals, because upon no two occasions were my Judges the same. The examinations were conducted within closed doors ... they were conducted by men sitting down after dinner, varying in their numbers and attendance, and sometimes postponing the inquiry upon the most trivial grounds.[43]

Seymour's contentions named many of the same injustices that Bowyer endeavored to curb in his parliamentary reform of the bar. Seymour's editorial attempted to rally support against the arbitrary

---

[41] IT BEN.

[42] See Pue, "Moral Panic;" Cocks, "Middle Temple in the Nineteenth Century;" Woolley, "The Inns as Disciplinary Bodies," 358–359.

[43] MT MPA February 21, 1862. See also Pue, "Moral Panic," 49–118.

power of the Inns at a moment in time in which parliamentary investigations and bills made it seem realistic that the bar might be reformed from without. His case roughly coincided with several other well-publicized cases in the mid-century that made the bar's elite seem untrustworthy and the Inns incapable of adequately regulating their members. (These cases included a lord chancellor accused of unlawful conspiracy against his own client, a would-be attorney general disbarred, a country barrister disbarred for practices he had engaged in for a decade, and a prominent crusading barrister exposed to public criticism and censure by the Inns.) As W. Wesley Pue argues, the Inns were aware that too much public concern could lead to reforms from the outside, and they justified their autonomy by demonstrating that they were capable of stamping out the unvirtuous among their ranks. Press attention thus caused the benchers to exert a stronger role and tighten their authority on the Inns.[44] Publicizing his grievances thus did little good for Seymour, who was excluded from the bar mess of the northern circuit (though he nevertheless went on to take silk two years later).[45]

Shifting Geopolitics and Discipline in the Early Twentieth Century

In the early decades of the twentieth century, the societies' attention was once again drawn to the national press, but this time the Inns were not concerned by members critiquing the societies in their pages. Instead, the societies confronted members who publicized dissident opinions in response to a shifting geopolitical context. The Inns still disciplined their members for infractions like fraud or impropriety.[46] New infractions such as sedition, however, forced the Inns to define the parameters of gentlemanliness in relation to a political spectrum, and to contend with issues of Britishness and national loyalty. In the first three decades of the twentieth century, the Inner and Middle Temple conducted at least six disciplinary cases resulting from members' personal political commitments. Conscientious objectors, nationalists, and communists opposed or actively worked against the state and the law. These men challenged the Inns to refine and retool legal etiquette to consider whether professional honor was compatible with radical politics. The societies'

---

[44] Pue, "Moral Panic," 116–118.

[45] G. C. Boase, revised by Eric Metcalfe, "Seymour, William Digby," *Oxford Dictionary of National Biography* (Oxford: Oxford University Press, 2004).

[46] David Woolley, "The Inn as a Disciplinary Body," in *A History of the Middle Temple*, 365–368. Particularly interesting is a 1914 disbarment of a barrister attempting to blackmail his former lover into marrying him.

responses to radical politics were inextricably bound up in their perceptions of members' foreignness. The Inns may not have been especially sympathetic to any radical bent, but they gave English-born members more latitude for defending their actions and were more likely to disbar individuals with confirmed foreign loyalties.

The societies drew discrete but distinct lines between alien and Anglicized others. In 1908, for example, the Inner Temple considered the disciplinary case of two King's Counsels (KCs) whose preexisting tensions had erupted into insults and fisticuffs, including anti-Semitic slurs. The disciplinary committee dismissed the blows as not "calculated to do actual damage," but they especially denounced the phrase "insolent Jew cur," which they considered particularly "improper, insulting and provoking." Anti-Semitic slurs ran contrary to the bar's image of itself as an institution upholding a British liberal notion of religious freedom, the same notion that had led to the removal of disabilities against Catholics in the 1830s and Jews in the 1850s.[47] In his apology the KC explained, "I am particularly sorry for having used the word 'Jew' in this way, for many Jewish members of the Bar might properly resent it, as I would resent the use of the word 'Irish' in a like connection."[48] In making an empathetic connection between the Irish and the Jews, the speaker evidenced a surface-level respect for the diversity of the bar. His statement also implicitly drew a distinction between an Anglo-Jewish KC, socialized with English values, and the unassimilable Eastern European Jews of the East End, a line not always held fast in broader articulations of British anti-Semitism.[49] The prejudices and growing xenophobia of the legal profession were reserved for elements the bar perceived as more dangerous than an Anglo-Jewish KC.

If the Victorian bar's accommodation of Catholics and Jews created a moment's reprieve from policing moral difference among barristers, Indian nationalists in the 1900s and 1910s represented a newly perceivable foreign threat in the midst of the Inns and raised ethical questions as to how the societies could – and if the societies should – accommodate

---

[47] Frederick Pollock, "Oath of Allegiance," in *Cyclopedia of Political Science, Political Economy, and of the Political History of the United States by the Best American and European Authors*, ed. John Lalor (Chicago: M. B. Carey, 1899).

[48] IT DIS/1/R1. It might also have insulted high-ranking members. The *Pall Mall Gazette* reported that Lord Morris, an Irish-born judge elected a member of the bench of Lincoln's Inn, made a joke at the elevation of Sir Charles Russell, an Irish Catholic, to Lord Chief Justice in 1894. "You English ... are a tolerant people: your highest Court of Appeal consists of a Scotch-man, two Irishmen, and a Jew." *A Chance Medley Extracts from "Silk and Stuff" (Pall Mall Gazette)* (London: Constable, 1911), 280.

[49] See David Feldman, *Englishmen and Jews* (New Haven, CT: Yale University Press, 1994).

dissident personal politics. Nationalists did not have to commit illegal actions, or even directly violate legal etiquette, to find themselves under the scrutiny of the benchers. In 1909, for example, a representative of the Bar Council sent a letter to the Honorable Society of the Inner Temple, with a newspaper clipping attached. Based on the scrap of newsprint, the members of the council believed its author, Shyamji Krishnavarma, ought to be disbarred. The clipping contained Krishnavarma's response to a *Times* editorial that challenged his promotion of the Indian Martyrs' Memorial scholarship fund. The *Times* editorialist denounced the fund as "the glorification of murder," explaining that Krishnavarma's "martyrs" were in fact Indian nationalists who had been hanged for a May 1908 bombing that resulted in the death of two English women. In response, Krishnavarma dismissed the deaths of the two English women as "accidental and incidental," the attack having been intended for a magistrate.[50] Rather than upholding British power structures undergirded by law and thus intimately tied to the legal profession, Krishnavarma condoned their violent dismantling. Were such views, the Bar Council pressed, worthy of a barrister?

Krishnavarma's case confronted the Edwardian benchers with a question they had not before considered: could the expression of political views violate professional etiquette? Krishnavarma had not published anything illegal under British law, nor had he violated any of the societies' Consolidated Regulations.[51] Without a doubt, his inflammatory words would have found few sympathizers among the benchers. Yet in expressing his anti-British but perfectly legal political views, had Krishnavarma behaved in a manner unworthy of a barrister? To answer this question, the benchers demanded Krishnavarma "show cause why he should not be disbarred."[52] They did not outline their grievances with him, but Krishnavarma surmised that they "object[ed] to my attitude towards British rule in India." His response to the benchers, however, was mostly defiant. The British were in India, he contended, "for rapine and robbery," and Indians were "absolutely justified in getting rid of foreign despotism by all means in their power." Krishnavarma did highlight the uniqueness of his disciplinary case, the lack of precedent at the societies. "If ... you decide to disbar me for the expression of my political opinions ... you will ... be conferring a unique honour on me, for

---

[50] Shyamji Krishnavarma, "Indian Anarchism in England," *Times*, February 20, 1909.
[51] It would have been different had he published the same editorial in India. Consider, for example, V. D. Savarkar's 1909 conviction of sedition for his poems under Indian Penal Code sections 121, 121-A, and 124-A. IOR/L/PJ/6/939, File 1849.
[52] IT BEN March 25, 1909.

I believe that in the history of the Inns of Court in England never has a similar case arisen." Krishnavarma's appeal to precedent did not persuade the society. In April 1909, the benchers disbarred Krishnavarma, noting in their records only that his conduct "in publishing the [letter to the *Times*] was unworthy of a barrister."[53]

Why, precisely, did the society disbar Krishnavarma? They likely condemned his justification of violence more than his desire for Indian independence. His dismissal of the murder of British women would have appalled the benchers and would have constituted ungentlemanly behavior in their eyes.[54] Certainly the Inns of Court perceived anti-imperial, potentially violent Indian nationalists as a very real and troubling threat. As Chapter 5 elaborates, their concerns were part of broader fears in official circles that well-educated but discontented Indian students in Britain would find their way to extremist politics and thus export seditious views from the metropole back to India.[55] Quite possibly the benchers interpreted Krishnavarma's editorial as seditious, regardless of whether it had been prosecuted as such. Krishnavarma compared Indian nationalists to British heroes like Milton, but the benchers most likely understood them as closer to Irish and other agitators who sought to throw off British rule.[56] Krishnavarma cast the issue as one of free speech, implying that he should have the right to express his views, no matter how abhorrent. Yet as A. V. Dicey explained in his classic work on the constitution, "Freedom of discussion," a feature of the common law rather than constitutional principle "is ... little else than the right to write or say anything which a jury ... think it expedient should be said or written."[57] In this case, the benchers clearly did not think it expedient that Krishnavarma's views should be published.

In the decade following Krishnavarma's case, the four Inns disbarred at least two other Indian nationalists for similar approbation of political violence; by the time the Inner Temple considered the case of Mohandas

---

[53] IT DIS/1/K2; IT BEN April 23, 1909.

[54] Mrinalini Sinha, *Colonial Masculinity* (New York: St. Martin's Press, 1995); Indira Chowdhury-Sengupta, "The Effeminate and the Masculine," in *The Concept of Race in South Asia*, ed. Peter Robb (Delhi: Oxford University Press, 1995); Kenneth Ballhatchet, *Race, Sex and Class under the Raj* (London: Weidenfeld and Nicolson, 1980); Ronald Hyam, *Empire and Sexuality* (New York: St. Martin's Press, 1990).

[55] Shompa Lahiri, *Indians in Britain* (London: Frank Cass, 2000), 125–126.

[56] Fiction and plays of the late nineteenth and early twentieth centuries, for example, often featured Indian nationalists as sedition-mongering villains. Lahiri, *Indians in Britain*; Benita Parry, *Delusions and Discoveries* (London: Verso, 1998).

[57] Dicey, as quoted in David Feldman, "Civil Liberties," in *The British Constitution in the Twentieth Century*, ed. Vernon Bogdanor (Oxford: Oxford University Press, 2003), 411–415.

Gandhi in 1922, the Inn's views on Indian nationalists had calcified such that an endorsement of violence was no longer necessary for disbarment. In November of that year, the Inner Temple treasurer received a certified copy of Gandhi's conviction of sedition by the Ahmedabad Court of Sessions. The benchers of the Inn did not open Gandhi's actions to interpretation or debate, nor did they write to Gandhi, as was their standard practice, to ask him why he should not be disbarred. Instead the benchers agreed that Gandhi had been "convicted by a competent tribunal" of an offense that "disqualifie[d] him from continuing a Member of the Inn."[58] After all, rather than propagate the attitudes and values appropriate to a British barrister, Gandhi encouraged his followers to foreswear British culture and boycott British institutions – including legal institutions. Furthermore, as Chapter 5 details, Gandhi's case coincided with a spate of investigation of Indian membership of the Inns of Court by the Inns and the India Office. The societies were increasingly convinced that the English bar was not a place for Indians at all, let alone those who led seditious, anti-imperial campaigns.

The Inns' scrutiny of Indian nationalists coincided with increasing xenophobia throughout the UK in the first three decades of the twentieth century. Outside the Inns of Court, suspicion fell on Eastern European immigrants, especially Jews, who British officials perceived as bringing foreign religion, disease, destitution, and eventually the specter of communism to London in particular. A spate of legislation imposed restrictions on individual liberties in order to assuage growing fears about dangerous aliens and foreigners, beginning with the Aliens Act of 1905 and continuing with the Official Secrets Act 1911 and the Defence of the Realm Acts 1914–15.[59] The Inns did not always sympathize with such legislation, particularly when it required increased state intervention. Nevertheless, the societies were also suspicious of individuals who might hold loyalties outside Britain, and they were willing to intervene to discipline and regulate these individuals.

The Great War served as a crucible for many of these concerns, forcing the Inns to consider issues of citizenship and national allegiance in relation to personal conscience and wartime legislation. On December 5, 1916, the Inner Temple called Joseph Alan Kaye, a law student and undergraduate at St. John's College, Oxford, before a committee of benchers to account for an offense committed while at university. Kaye had been the secretary of the Oxford "No Conscription Fellowship."

---

[58] IT BEN November 7, 1922.
[59] David Feldman, "Civil Liberties," in *The British Constitution in the Twentieth Century*, 411–415.

During the Christmas vacation of 1915, in anticipation of a January bill promoting compulsory conscription, Kaye distributed a number of pamphlets to members of the Independent Labour Party (ILP) and the Oxford University Socialist Association, as well as to a few of his friends. The pamphlets read, "We will accept no military duties," encouraging opposition to the "Conscription Bill," which by March 1916 was the Military Service Act. That same month (March of 1916), Kaye was charged with sedition and convicted by a Bench of Magistrates at the Oxford Police Court. The magistrates described the material as "likely to prejudice the recruiting of His Majesty's Forces," a violation of the Defence of the Realm (Consolidation) Regulations 1914. The court sentenced Kaye to two months' imprisonment, later reduced to two weeks.[60]

After Kaye's conviction, the Inner Temple benchers formed a committee to investigate whether his particular actions "disqualifie[d] him from continuing a Member of the Inn."[61] Before Kaye, no one at the Inns had violated the Defence of the Realm Acts. This emergency legislation that placed restrictions on freedom of association, assembly, and expression had been in force for little over two years. Prior to the 1914 enactment of this legislation, Kaye's actions would not have been cause for censure. In fact, before the 1916 Military Service Act, Britain maintained only a volunteer army. At the time of Kaye's offense, support for the war and the men fighting it generally ran high, but conscription was less universally popular. Conservatives pushing for the Act feared for the nation's military preparedness, but Liberals understood compulsory service as a betrayal of national ideals of liberty.[62] It fell to the Inner Temple committee, then, to determine whether or not violating temporary legislation by speaking out against a contested measure was an act unbefitting a member of the bar.

In conducting their inquiry, the committee gave first consideration to the offender's national origin rather than to questions of political conscience. A committee report noted that Kaye was the son of a Liverpool merchant of German origin. Though naturalized as a British subject in 1879, Kaye's father only changed the family name from the German Kaufmann to the Anglicized Kaye at the outbreak of the war, when Joseph Kaye was already twenty-one years old. The committee highlighted his ancestry at a time when a German background

---

[60] "King's Bench Division. An Oxford Undergraduate and Recruiting. Kaye V. Cole," *Times*, October 28, 1916.

[61] IT BEN January 12, 1917.

[62] See Nicoletta F. Gullace, *The Blood of Our Sons* (New York: Palgrave Macmillan, 2002); K. D. Ewing and C. A. Gearty, *The Struggle for Civil Liberties* (Oxford: Oxford University Press, 2000).

immediately aroused suspicion. The General Council of the Bar, for example, suggested in 1916 that the Inns take measures to suspend aliens from warring nations from practicing in the UK.[63] The members of the committee would also have been familiar with the case of *R. v. Halliday*. In 1915, having committed no offense, a German-born portable railway contractor naturalized as a British subject in 1905 was imprisoned without trial under Regulation 14B of the Defence of the Realm Acts. The latter permitted the internment of any person of "hostile origin or associations." The defendant's counsel maintained that 14B was *ultra vires*, but the lord chancellor dismissed the appeal.[64] The war years were a dangerous time to have German associations in the UK. Though the Inner Temple committee did not explicitly argue that Joseph Kaye's standing as a loyal British citizen was in question, in light of the hostile climate, mere mention of his German origin spoke against him.

After determining his background, the committee then expressed interest in Kaye's intentions. Kaye insisted that he had not known that distributing the pamphlets violated the Defence of the Realm Regulations, adding that the same pamphlets had been published in the *Labour Leader*. This may not have helped Kaye's case much, as during the war years, the paper was frequently censored under the Regulations.[65] Any barrister who read the *Times* – or happened to be walking down Fleet Street – would have been aware of the massive 1915 raid on the London *Labour Leader* office, in which city police seized "nearly a van-load of publications."[66] Kaye went on to say, however, that "although he did not wish to contravene the law he would to-day distribute the circular in question if it were essential in his opinion to do so in order to avert such a calamity as the passing of the Conscription Bill." The committee concluded that not only the offense itself but the offender's "present attitude of mind" merited disqualification from membership of the society.[67]

The case proved, however, to be an unusually divisive one for the full group of benchers considering the committee report, suggesting that the benchers held markedly different views on conscription and conscientious objection. One of the members of the committee, Lord Justice John E. Bankes, agreed with the facts stated in the report, but not with the recommendation of the other members. After the full group of benchers read the report, some agreed wholly with the report; others with Justice

---

[63] IT BEN May 23, 1916.

[64] "House of Lords. Internment of a Naturalized British Subject. The King (at the Prosecution of Arthur Zadig) V. Sir Frederick Lock Halliday," *Times*, March 2, 1917.

[65] Ewing and Gearty, *The Struggle for Civil Liberties*, 64–67.

[66] "Raid on Offices of 'Labour Leader,'" *Times*, August 19, 1915.

[67] IT BEN January 12, 1917.

Bankes; and still others with neither. One member proposed that the report's recommendation – Kaye's disqualification – be adopted. This lost. Another proposed that as "the offence of which Mr. Kaye has been convicted was a grave one" that Kaye be excluded from the hall, library, reading room, and garden for one year. This lost. A third even proposed that no action be taken, but this too lost. Finally, a proposal that "having regard to extenuating circumstances no punitive steps be taken but that the Treasurer address Mr. Kaye pointing out the seriousness of the offence and warning him … that if the offence be repeated, punishment will ensue" carried. The treasurer subsequently spoke to Kaye, and the case was over.

Ten years later, the Inner Temple faced a new iteration of troubling individual politics in relation to a member whose communist views stood opposed to military action. On May 4, 1926, a special committee of benchers of the Inner Temple called Thomas Henry Wintringham, a law student, before them. Wintringham was one of nine members of the Communist Party of Great Britain (CPGB) who in 1925 were arrested on charges of sedition for publications in the party organ the *Worker's Weekly*. After an eleven-day trial, it took the Old Bailey jury ten minutes of deliberation to convict the defendants of conspiracy to utter seditious libels, of conspiracy to incite mutiny, and of inciting mutiny.[68] When summoned before the Inner Temple disciplinary committee, Wintringham readily admitted that he was a member of the CPGB and an assistant editor of the *Worker's Weekly*. He agreed that in the latter publication he had stated that "under no circumstances should 'the military in the case of civil commotion act against the people,'" a violation of the Incitement to Mutiny Act 1797. Though the presiding judge of the Old Bailey placed Wintringham in the second division (rather than the first division denoting political prisoners), Wintringham insisted to the Inner Temple that his offenses were political and should not disqualify him from membership of the Inn.[69] The Temple interviewing committee, save for one member, disagreed with Wintringham's contention and recommended that he be disqualified.[70]

The dissenting voice came from Llewellyn Arthur Atherley-Jones, a libertarian and Old Bailey judge whose feelings that the law should not

---

[68] Ewing and Gearty, *The Struggle for Civil Liberties*, 136–144.

[69] The 1898 Prison Act reserved the first division for those who had committed clearly political offenses, the second division for those who declined to commit to keep the peace, and the third division for blatant criminal offenses. See Constance Lytton, *Prisons and Prisoners* (London: Virago, 1914).

[70] IT BEN July 16, 1926.

intervene in matters of private morality had earned him a reputation for lenient sentencing for homosexual offenses.[71] Atherley-Jones' minority report argued that though Wintringham's offense was "of the utmost gravity ... it involved neither acts of atrocity or immorality." In fact, Atherley-Jones referred back to the standards set by the visiting judges in the 1869 case of William Gill. Wintringham's "unlawful act [cast] no stigma upon his honour or good faith which was the test Lord Chief Justice Cockburn applied in the case of Mr. Gill." Furthermore, there was no precedent, he maintained, for a barrister being disbarred for a conviction of sedition. This statement either forgot or conveniently ignored Mohandas Gandhi's disbarment in November 1922.[72] Lastly, Atherly-Jones argued, disbarring Wintringham would be inconsistent with the lenient sentence – six months without hard labor – given by the judge of the Central Criminal Court.[73] On July 16, however, the benchers adopted the majority report and disqualified Wintringham.

Why, for similar offenses less than a decade apart, did Kaye escape with a verbal admonition, while the society disqualified Wintringham from membership? Kaye's actions violated a new and temporary piece of legislation that placed restrictions on civil liberties that sat uncomfortably with some barristers and judges. Though the courts decided almost all cases that challenged the Defence of the Realm Acts in favor of the government during the war, they were also responsible for introducing a 1915 amendment that preserved the right to trial by jury in civil courts and began ruling parts of the regulations *ultra vires* at the war's end.[74] Furthermore, before the war, the ILP had worked closely with the Liberals to achieve its goals.[75] The ILP's wartime pacifism short-circuited many of these sympathetic ties, but even so, party affiliation was considered more distasteful than dangerous.

To identify as a member of the Communist Party, especially in 1926, was an entirely different matter. Though small in number, the CPGB's stated goal was to overturn the ruling system. Anti-Bolshevism flooded British papers, and the party's ties to Moscow particularly provoked hostility. No matter how suspect Kaye's German origins may have seemed, in the minds of the benchers, Wintringham's political allegiances unquestionably cast him as the agent of an adversarial foreign

---

[71] Matt Houlbrook, *Queer London* (Chicago: The University of Chicago Press, 2005), 252.
[72] IT BEN November 7, 1922.   [73] IT BEN July 16, 1926.
[74] Ewing and Gearty, *The Struggle for Civil Liberties*, 87.
[75] James Eaden and David Renton, *The Communist Party of Great Britain since 1920* (London: Palgrave, 2002), 2–3.

power. Anxieties stemming from the postwar economic downturn augmented these fears. One "Barrister-at-Law," for example, asserted in the *Times* that "it is well known that the unemployed are being exploited by Communist agitators paid by funds supplied by the Third International in Moscow. These agitators ... are boldly inciting the unemployed to smash shop windows and loot."[76] Moreover, the events of the 1926 General Strike, which began on May 4, the same day that the Inner Temple called Wintringham before the benchers, intensified worries over general violence. The nine-day walkout, which at its height involved over 11.5 million workers, was perceived as a clear threat to institutions of British capital. Though leadership for the strike remained largely in the hands of Labour, both during the events and afterwards, British officials and the national press cast the strike as a radical attempt to overturn Parliament and the government. They placed the blame with the CPGB and arrested about one-quarter of the party's members.[77] As the Temple committee deliberated in July 1926, the events of the strike two months earlier would have been fresh in their minds. Wintringham, a foreign agent, convict, and inciter of social upheaval, could have no place at the Inner Temple or the bar.

The final case in this chapter returns to William Stafford Levinson, with whom the chapter opened, to highlight the degree to which, by the 1920s, the British legal profession had become a global undertaking and the challenges that came with managing such a far-flung endeavor. Not only did colonial subjects travel to London to study law, but like Levinson, London-trained barristers of various backgrounds practiced law in imperial courts around the world. As far as the Inns were concerned, these cosmopolitan individuals might bring the values and liberal influence of British law to foreign outposts, but they just as easily might absorb dangerous ideas and practices abroad. Levinson committed at least six offenses in two hemispheres, yet remarkably managed to elude the discipline of the Inner Temple for seven years. Even with wired communication connecting the globe in unprecedented ways, barristers on the other side of the world were difficult to monitor.

Unlike most disciplinary cases in the early twentieth century, Levinson's did not include a public or press dimension, in part because of his active mystification of his identity and location.[78] The case, which

---

[76] "Seditious Preaching. Inadequacy of Present Measures," *Times*, October 14, 1921.

[77] Eaden and Renton, *The Communist Party of Great Britain*, 25–27.

[78] For conmen who sought publicity, the market for inside stories from the underworld was booming. Matt Houlbrook, "Fashioning an Ex-crook Self: Citizenship and Criminality in the Work of Netley Lucas," *Twentieth Century British History* 24 (2013): 1–30.

finally concluded in 1928, began with a December 1920 letter from the acting judge of the Supreme Court of Shanghai, along with enclosed affidavits from the Shanghai Consul General, bringing Levinson to the Inner Temple's attention. Levinson, who Consul General Sir Everard Duncan Home Fraser described as "a short man with a pale face, ... obviously of Jewish extraction," had been admitted to practice in the Supreme Court of Shanghai in August 1919. According to the affidavit, in early 1920, Fraser received two anonymous letters casting doubt upon Levinson's bona fides. When asked to produce his passport as a means of following up these claims, Levinson explained that it had been accidentally destroyed. Neither H. M. Consul at Riga nor Cook's in London, whom Levinson claimed had, respectively, issued and renewed his passport, had any record of passports under that name. Both the consul general and the acting judge of the Supreme Court pointed out that Levinson had listed three different fathers with three different statuses, from knight to pawnbroker, in various official documents. Levinson claimed to have been baptized and also to be a practicing Jew. His account of his war service did not check out with the Army List. According to the consul general, his "methods at the bar" had not earned him "the respect or liking of his colleagues," and he had become "notorious from the class of cases" he chose. That Levinson might be a Jewish pawnbroker's son who had evaded war service and posed as a Christian, titled veteran in an outpost of His Majesty's empire was already alarming. To these the consul general added one last, loathsome possibility: "the combination in this case of such places as Riga, Shanghai and Egypt, all three centres of unrest and Bolshevist agitation, appears to me highly suspicious and to make it more than ever necessary that strict enquiries should be instituted into Mr. Levinson's position."[79]

Levinson's mysterious background proved that, despite requiring two character witnesses, the societies could never be certain what sort of dangerous elements they admitted into their midst: the Inner Temple had reason to doubt both Levinson's nationality and his honorability. By December 1920, when the consul general and acting judge sent their letter, Levinson had already defrauded a widowed client, closed his bank accounts, and fled Shanghai – on a Russian emergency passport. Was Levinson, wondered the benchers, a British subject or not? (Whatever he was, the acting judge assured the benchers, he was not dead, despite reports from Japan to the contrary.) As a result of further

---

[79] IT DIS/1/L1 Affidavit of Sir Everard Duncan Home Fraser, K.C.M.G., October 20, 1920.

inquiries, the benchers received a copy of a report from the Director of Military Intelligence, by way of the Foreign Office. Levinson, the report confirmed, was a Russian subject. His first run-in with British authorities came in 1916, when he was convicted of falsely representing himself as an inspector of munitions in order to gain information about several wire and munitions works in Penrhiwceiber, Wales. Although only fined ten pounds, the report noted that during that period Levinson received "numerous telegrams ..., and these were invariably destroyed immediately he had read them."[80] Levinson appeared to be a Russian Jew and potential Bolshevist who had falsely represented himself as a British subject in order to gain access to privileged information during the Great War, and the higher echelons of the British justice system thereafter. It was the stuff of nightmares to Britons in the 1920s.

The Inner Temple had much to call Levinson to account for, but first they had to find him. When the benchers began their search for Levinson in 1921, they were unable to locate him, despite the acting judge's suggestion that Levinson was in Putney with Lady Cornwall. In 1923 the society received information – it is unclear from whom – that Levinson had set himself up in Paris under the name R. Stark Livingston on the fashionable Rue de l'Arcade.[81] Levinson or Livingston's hotel informed the society's representatives, after two failed attempts at delivery, that Livingston or Levinson had lately returned to London. The society lost sight of him again until 1927, when a Manchester machinery merchant informed the Inn that he might have seen a man matching Levinson's description. The merchant had met "a man who calls himself W. T. Livingstone and who says he is a barrister of the Inner Temple & ... later a practicing barrister at Shanghai!"[82] The society contacted a firm of notaries to see if they could help identify the man the merchant had encountered. The notaries suggested the Inn contact the Foreign Office, the Foreign Office referred them to the Home Office, and the Home Office suggested they try Scotland Yard. Finally in 1928 the society learned – again it is unclear from whom – that Levinson was to appear at the London Police Court "for having failed to re-register himself as an alien on his return to England in 1920 and for having landed in England in contravention of an order made by the Home Secretary on 30th September 1920."[83] The Inns sent their

---

[80] IT DIS/1/L1 Report of William Adams, Chief Constable, Doncaster, June 27, 1916.
[81] IT DIS/1/L1 Letter from the Acting Judge of Supreme Court of Shanghai, December 6, 1920; Letter from the sub-treasurer of the Inner Temple, March 12, 1923.
[82] IT DIS/1/L1 Letter from Leonard Parker, January 23, 1927.
[83] IT DIS/1/L1 June 1928.

summons via a shorthand writer who followed Levinson into the court anteroom and, in March 1928, after seven years of pursuit, handed Levinson the letter calling him to account for his actions. Levinson did not appear to defend himself – perhaps because he had been deported – and in November 1928, the benchers finally voted to disbar him.[84]

Levinson, like Krishnavarma, Kaye, and Wintringham, represented the threat of foreign infiltration in the UK. He was not an integrated, Anglicized Jew, but a Russian and likely a Bolshevik. Unlike the KC reprimanded for and regretful of his anti-Semitic comments in 1908, the various interlocutors in this case made clear that Levinson's Jewishness only fed their suspicions of him. If aligning with the Third International made Oxford-educated Wintringham a source of foreign danger, how much worse was an actual Russian citizen connected to international sites of communist unrest?

Conclusion

This chapter has shown the connection between legal etiquette and ideas of gentlemanliness, ideas which in the nineteenth century became especially important for securing the status of the bar in the face of both commercial capitalism and an increasingly middle-class membership. Gentlemanly ideals at the bar persisted from the nineteenth into the twentieth century, but were reinterpreted by the benchers of the Inns when confronted with members' radical political expressions. The elasticity of legal etiquette allowed the societies quite a bit of flexibility in responding to geopolitical trends, and they used this flexibility to selectively excuse or disbar members according to a logic unconcerned with consistency.

Furthermore, the types of difference the Inns were willing to accommodate narrowed as the twentieth century progressed. The empire opened up possibilities for rank-and-file members of the bar to advance careers that would have been stalled at home, but the Inns were overwhelmed by its size and scope. The societies worried that the colonial bars were not sufficiently steeped in the practices of the metropole, nor sufficiently able to discipline and control their members. It was difficult, if not impossible, to keep track of barristers practicing on the other side of the globe. In fact, many of the etiquette infractions brought before the benchers throughout the nineteenth and twentieth centuries came from the officials of various colonial bureaucracies. These officials tried to

---

[84] IT BTO July 24, 1928.

maintain the standards of an English bar with which they might only be vaguely familiar, depending on their route to their position and how much time they had spent in London. As the connections between the profession at home and the profession abroad became increasingly difficult to maintain, the Inns of Court began to wonder if overseas subjects and the colonial bars should be tied to the English bar at all.

5   Overseas Students

Mohandas Gandhi devoted relatively little space in his *Autobiography* to his experiences at the Inner Temple, to which he was admitted in 1888; those he included highlighted the myriad ways in which he differed from his English peers. As he recalled, initially he wore clothes styled after the fashion of Bombay, not London. He had a wife and child back in India, unlike most young law students. Meals at the Inns centered on meats and fish; Gandhi, a vegetarian, could not partake. On this latter point, Gandhi remained firm, and eventually the society prepared special meals for him so that he might keep term with more satisfying fare than bread, boiled potatoes, and cabbage. In other respects, however, Gandhi adapted to the culture around him. He noted that, shortly after his arrival in London, he bought new clothes, including a £10 "evening suit made in Bond Street, the centre of fashionable life." He affected the role of a bachelor like other young Indian students in England, "ashamed to confess that they were married." He began to study Latin, a language already mastered by his public school peers.[1] In the *Autobiography*, Gandhi cast himself as an outsider, ill at ease with the culture of the legal profession. Yet at the time, Gandhi's admission to the Inner Temple and his call to the bar excited little notice or debate from the benchers of that society. In the late nineteenth century, overseas students like Gandhi did not challenge – nor did the societies perceive them as a threat to – the resolutely English culture of the Inns.

In the first three decades of the twentieth century, however, the societies disbarred Gandhi and several other Indian nationalists after they were convicted of sedition. By 1928, the four Inns debated the "rationing of Overseas students" admitted each year to dramatically reduce their numbers. This chapter asks why the Inns of Court's attitude toward students from the empire shifted from one of acceptance and limited accommodation in the late nineteenth century, to one infinitely more

---

[1] Mohandas Gandhi, *An Autobiography* (Boston, MA: Beacon Press, 1957), 93, 113, 138; Rozina Visram, *Asians in Britain* (London: Pluto Press, 2002), 110.

wary and begrudging in the early twentieth. In doing so, it pushes forward the growing body of scholarship on imperial subjects in the metropole by considering the largest subset of them – Indian law students – in the particular context of legal culture and the legal profession.[2] A focus on overseas students at the Inns of Court bridges the gap between scholarship that privileges the activities of the governing elite or imperial bureaucracies and work that takes interactions in the home, street, school, or club as loci of imperial power.[3] The Inns, conduits to positions of prestige and authority throughout the empire, fed imperial hierarchies and faced pressure and scrutiny from governing powers to make sure they adequately disciplined their imperial members. Yet the societies were also sites of work and learning – day-to-day interactions between English and imperial subjects at the Inns tested the elasticity of the societies' fraternal culture.

A focus on overseas students at the Inns further contributes to work that considers the role of metropolitan institutions in transforming colonial members into ideal liberal subjects or even liberal citizens, in ways as likely to undermine as to further the imperial project. Membership at the Inns gave overseas students important trappings of the ideal bourgeois subject, namely creditworthiness and professional expertise.[4] Rather than behaving as the well-ordered subjects officials might hope, however, some imperial members of the bar used their legal learning and status as barristers to make claims for independence from the empire. For their part, the Inns of Court maintained a delicate balancing act between supporting the imperial project as befit an ancient anchor of British law and Britishness itself, and the overwhelming demands an increasingly heterogeneous population placed on the societies. Historians such as Catherine Hall and Sonya Rose characterize the influence of empire in the metropole as uneven, at times an unconscious presence, at others highly visible and the subject of widespread concern.[5] In the nineteenth century, the Inns of Court took it as a matter of course

---

[2] Visram, *Asians in Britain*; Shompa Lahiri, *Indians in Britain* (London: Frank Cass, 2000); Michael H. Fisher, *The Inordinately Strange Life of Dyce Sombre* (New York: Oxford University Press, 2010); Antoinette Burton, *At the Heart of Empire* (Berkeley, CA: University of California Press, 1998).

[3] Tony Ballantyne and Antoinette Burton, "Introduction: Bodies, Empires, and World Histories," in *Bodies in Contact*, ed. Tony Ballantyne and Antoinette Burton (Durham, NC: Duke University Press, 2005), 6.

[4] Sukanya Banerjee, *Becoming Imperial Citizens* (Durham, NC: Duke University Press, 2010), 8.

[5] Catherine Hall and Sonya Rose, "Introduction: Being at Home with Empire," in *At Home with the Empire*, ed. Catherine Hall and Sonya O. Rose (Cambridge: Cambridge University Press, 2006), 2–3.

that the societies should be the central node in the vast web of the imperial legal profession. By the early twentieth century, as the demands of empire became increasingly unwieldy, the Inns' role at the center seemed both less desirable and less sustainable to the societies and the imperial authorities with which they cooperated.

Several key factors account for the benchers' changes in attitude toward overseas students and the Inns' role in the imperial legal profession. Whereas in the mid-Victorian period the vast majority of students from abroad coming to the Inns were white, British-born, or British-descended, by the 1880s the number of imperial subjects of color began to steadily increase. The societies recorded only students' countries of origin, not their race, making it difficult to estimate the exact number of students of color at the Inns at any given time. Admission data from Inner Temple is suggestive, however. Between 1860 and 1870, 72 percent of students admitted to that Inn came from England and another 6 percent came from Ireland, Scotland, and Wales. Only 1 percent came from Canada or Australia (none from New Zealand), whereas 2 percent came from India and Siam. By the period 1890–1900, 82 percent of students were from the UK and 2 percent came from Canada or Australia, but 5 percent came from India and Siam.[6] White settler colonies made few attempts to integrate native populations of color into structures of governance, so it seems likely that the majority of students hailing from North America or the antipodes were white. In India, particularly during the Raj, efforts to integrate elite Indians into colonial governance meant that at least some portion of Indian students at the Inns were likely Asian or Eurasian.

The number of students of color was still on the rise in the early twentieth century, when burgeoning colonial nationalist movements gained visibility for their causes, sometimes through violent actions taken against British citizens in the colonies or in London. Members of the Inns came to distrust the potentially radical politics of their overseas members, equating all imperial subjects of color with anti-British actions. Indian students particularly alarmed the societies. The number of students from India far outstripped those from any other colony. In the early twentieth century, the Indian nationalist movement, though relatively small in terms of membership, caught the attention of imperial officials due to the exalted status of India in the empire.[7] It is impossible to

---

[6] MT MPA; IT BEN. According to the National Indian Association census, there were 160 Indians in Britain in 1887 and 308 in 1894. By 1910, Indians in Britain numbered between 700 and 1200. Visram, *Asians in Britain*, 88.

[7] Jonathan Schneer, *London 1900* (New Haven, CT: Yale University Press, 1999), 184.

quantify the actual number of nationalists among Indian law students and barristers. The actions of a prevalent few, however, provoked the Inns to fear that, rather than upholding structures of power undergirded by the legal profession, Indian students in their midst would work to undermine imperial authority or even bring bodily harm to the Britons around them. These fears made the Inns – institutions that had fiercely guarded their autonomy for centuries – uncharacteristically willingly to cooperate with, or even cede authority to and rely on, state bureaucracies.

In the first two decades of the twentieth century, the Inns and members of the legal profession collaborated with governmental agencies to discuss the best means of inculcating British values and containing radicalism among imperial subjects. These interactions rarely resulted in concrete policy changes, but they reveal a variety of concerns and attitudes among British authorities toward Indian students. The benchers of the Inns, high-ranking members of the English and imperial bars, and bureaucrats from the India Office all discussed the best ways to mold students from the empire into rational liberal subjects. The debates often centered on geographic location and the spatial logic of discipline. Was a three-year stay in England a beneficial means of Anglicizing imperial students, or was it a waste of time and money? While in England, should students be kept together and closely monitored, or spread diffusely among English families to better absorb English culture? The Inns, though active interlocutors, made no attempts to instate residential policies one way or the other, nor did they adopt proposed quotas for overseas students. The societies were not, they declared, schools or universities responsible for monitoring the behavior of undergraduates, nor could they deny spots to otherwise qualified applicants on the basis of country of origin.[8] Instead, the societies hoped to mold imperial subjects by the same methods they molded English barristers, through the absorption of the culture and values of the profession via ritual. The societies thus held fast to tradition even as they discussed its inability to meet their needs.

Some members of the English and imperial bars, however, critiqued the Inns' unwillingness to take action. They believed that rituals designed to induct students into the culture of the bar would do little to counteract

---

[8] Paul Deslandes, *Oxbridge Men* (Bloomington, IN: Indiana University Press, 2005); Elleke Boehmer and Sumita Mukherjee, "Re-making Britishness: Indian Contributions to Oxford University, c. 1860–1930," in *Britishness, Identity and Citizenship*, ed. Catherine McGlynn, Andrew Mycock, and James W. McAuley (Oxford: Peter Lang, 2011), 95–112.

the political radicalization of overseas students in London. Failing to instate policies that would aggressively weed out undesirable imperial members, claimed some, jeopardized "the good name of the profession."[9] Such charges rehashed nineteenth-century suggestions by critics and parliamentarians that both the admission and qualification requirements of the Inns were not stringent enough. In interviews conducted by the India Office in the 1910s and 1920s, members of the profession and bureaucrats alike went so far as to question the standard of a call to the bar as the requirement for exclusive right to plead in courts. In considering the superior training of Indian pleaders, or vakils, some interlocutors suggested that the position of barrister was itself superfluous. Thus, for the Inns, the controversy over overseas students raised not only the threat of dissident politics, it also revitalized the specter of Victorian debates about the societies' prerogatives over the upper half of the bar.

Significantly, until the late 1920s, race remained conspicuously absent from these conversations, at least in overt form. Indeed, "overseas students," the term most often used by the Inns to refer to members from outside the UK, could seemingly include white students as well as students of color – except that the societies were not in conversation with the Dominion Division of the Colonial Office or hosting joint gatherings of the four Inns to discuss the dissident politics of their Canadian members. If something about race was implied by the term "overseas students," up until the early decades of the twentieth century, that something remained unsaid, and the Inns of Court framed their concerns about overseas students in relation to dissident politics or the material exigencies of study at the bar. While their discussions sometimes incorporated negative tropes and stereotypes, particularly of Indian students, these critiques usually manifested as contentions that overseas students had failed to live up to masculine ideals. Reports and memoranda never explicitly referenced skin color, nor did they include the deterministic rhetoric of scientific racism. It was only in 1926 that the Middle Temple employed the term "coloured students," and even then the Inn shied away from explaining why "coloured" – rather than "overseas," "colonial," or "Indian" – students were a particular problem. As scholars such as Laura Tabili have pointed out, though undoubtedly pervasive, racism was never a hegemonic discourse. Rather, racism was merely one of many ways of talking about difference – gender was another – that Britons could adopt, particularly in moments of crisis or duress, to define

---

[9] IT BEN November 13, 1925.

an ever-shifting group of internal others.[10] Racial language appeared in the Inns' memoranda at a moment when the Middle Temple felt especially worried about its numbers of overseas students in relation to its English membership. Racial language disappeared when the Inns replaced these concerns with fears about "alien" and "foreign" students fleeing Hitler's Europe in the early 1930s.

The Exigencies of Overseas Studentship

The Inns' relationship to imperial students shifted alongside Britain's relationship to its empire. In the first half of the nineteenth century, the majority of law students coming to the UK from the colonies were Anglo-British civil servants hoping to advance their careers. Indian legal offices, for example, were some of the most valuable in the empire, opening doors to wealth, influence, and political power. In the second half of the nineteenth century, civil servants continued to study at the Inns, but imperial expansion and a shift in overarching imperial directives increased the number of subjects of color training to be barristers. Particularly after the 1857 uprising in India, officials in London took a more direct hand in Indian governance and developed imperatives to integrate Indians into an expanding bureaucracy. Over time an increasing number of Indian students, now working as civil servants or within the newly developing British courts, traveled to the UK to study law. Indians represented the first major group of non-Europeans to enter the Inns of Court as students, and though always far smaller in number than students from the British Isles, they remained the largest group of non-Europeans at the bar.

The particular structure of the Indian bar also motivated Indian law students to train in England rather than India. Indian courts had two branches of advocates: the UK-trained barrister and the India-trained vakil. Barristers enjoyed superior prestige and income, and they held a monopoly over pleading before the Supreme Courts in presidency towns (Calcutta, Madras, and Bombay). Vakils, who were largely non-European, enjoyed less prestige and lower salaries, but even European members of the bar agreed that their training was more difficult and rigorous than that at the Inns. Unlike barristers, who faced optional courses and examinations that, when eventually required, were notoriously simple, vakils had to take mandatory courses and pass a "severe

---

[10] Laura Tabili, "A Homogenous Society? Britain's Internal 'Others,' 1800–Present," in *At Home with the Empire*, ed. Catherine Hall and Sonya O. Rose (Cambridge: Cambridge University Press, 2006), 53–76.

test."[11] These disparities made an English legal education quite appealing to Indians, who saw it as a less demanding path to greater distinction and remuneration. By 1885, 108 men from India, recruited almost exclusively from the nation's elite, had been called to the bar. Believing that an English-educated legal intelligentsia would support British rule, the Government of India encouraged young men to study in the UK.[12]

That colonial subjects would become members of the Inns of Court, however, was never a foregone conclusion. White settler colonies developed native bars to provide alternate routes to becoming a barrister. As of 1885, for example, Irish students could be called to the bar from King's Inn, Dublin. For Indian vakils, study at the Inns might be desirable, but it was certainly not necessary for a legal career. Furthermore, as some officials reminded the Inns, the privileges of barristers in India could be subject to change. As Henry J. S. Maine, a member of the Council of India, informed Sir Edward Ryan, assessor to the Judicial Committee of the Privy Council on appeal from the Indian Courts, the "admission, without conditions, of Members of the English ... Bar to the *status* of Advocate [in Indian courts] is only a matter of grace; the High Courts are entitled ... to impose what conditions they please."[13] In fact, in later debates in the early twentieth century, some interlocutors campaigned for admitting vakils as pleaders in the High Courts to obviate Indians' need to train in London.

Nevertheless, members of the profession encouraged both British inhabitants and natives of colonial outposts to study at the Inns, contending that the traditions of the bar acted as a positive influence in empire building. Time at the Inns, proponents argued, might provide civil servants with the foundations of English legal thought requisite for enlightened colonial governance. In 1860, for example, a member of the Bengal Civil Service and student at the Inner Temple declared, "Studying for the English Bar while on leave at home ... [tends] to give sounder and more enlarged legal ideas and a habit of judging complicated cases more carefully than is often the custom in Indian Courts."[14] Studying for the bar, he implied, allowed him to bring the complexities of English jurisprudence to an otherwise simplistic court system. Other interlocutors emphasized the importance of the extra-legal values that the Inns instilled in their members, suggesting these values might then filter back to the colonies. A justice of the Calcutta High Court praised

---

[11] IOR/L/PJ/6/1067 October 18, 1911.
[12] Daniel Duman, *English and Colonial Bars* (London: Croom Helm, 1983), 131–132.
[13] MT MPA November 20, 1867.   [14] MT MPA March 20, 1860.

the "traditional notions of honor and self-respect brought out from the English Bar," which raised the overall tone of the Calcutta bar.[15] He suggested that the societies' inculcation of gentlemanliness was as important as, if not more important than, knowledge of the workings of the law. Study at the bar, he contended, helped overseas students absorb something quintessentially and culturally English.

Whatever benefits study at the Inns might provide, colonial students faced numerous difficulties in pursuing a call to the bar in London. Many found the length of time required, three years, unfeasible for a variety of reasons. In 1867, Edward Henry Turner, a native of Madras, asked for a remission of terms because "his health ha[d] been seriously impaired by his residence in England during the last severe winter." Enclosing several doctors' notes, he stated that he "fear[ed] the consequences of a much longer stay in th[e] Country."[16] Furthermore, civil servants who came to London because a call to the bar could promote them up the bureaucratic ranks were seldom granted three years' leave at one time. As George Maxwell, a civil servant of the Federated Malay States, explained, enrolling at the Inner Temple during his leave in 1897–98, he could only keep four terms. With three more kept during leave in 1902–3, it would not be until 1908–9 that he could finish keeping terms and be called to the bar, despite having already passed the final examination. To avoid a prolonged period of studentship at the Inns, students in these straights could either petition their respective bureaucracies for delayed departure back to their posts, or petition the Inns for a dispensation of terms.[17] Petitioners in either case met equally with success and failure in a seemingly arbitrary fashion.

Under these circumstances, civil servants dismissed the historic rituals that some bureaucrats saw as propagating much-needed Englishness as a waste of everyone's time. As one member of the Colonial Office griped, "The eating of Dinners, as a preliminary to being called to the bar, is a perfectly useless infliction not only upon Indians or Colonials, but upon all British subjects."[18] Such detractors resented requirements that prolonged their stay in the capital without corresponding legal learning. They saw little value in the bar's affective ties: keeping term across a decade was unlikely to forge strong social networks, and connections in legal London were not the surest bet for colonial advancement

[15] MT MPA September 25, 1867; IT BEN October 29, 1899.
[16] MT MPA June 7, 1867.
[17] MT MPA June 8, 1855; IOR/L/PJ/6/287 June 10, 1890; IOR/L/PJ/6/363 November 24, 1893.
[18] IOR/L/PJ/6/604 June 23, 1902.

regardless. Unlike the aforementioned proponents of legal education at the Inns, who extolled the ideological value of legal culture, these civil servants renounced tradition without pragmatic purpose.

As with other professions, such as the civil service, the financial cost of spending three years in the metropole proved a burden to colonial subjects seeking to become barristers.[19] Most overseas students came from elite backgrounds – the sons of landowners, businessmen, and other professionals.[20] Like their English counterparts, many of the men who came from abroad depended on their families for financial support. Cost of travel and room and board in London were no small sums even for the prosperous, and families that fell on hard times might find they could no longer support a relative studying law. In 1886, for example, after explaining that, "by an unforeseen misfortune, his people at Home have become quite unable to help him in any way with pecuniary matters," L. Rahman asked the India Office to supply him with translation work to support his continued studies at the bar.[21] Parents abroad, as in England, could also use financial incentives to control their children's behavior. Foreign students who were cut off might have fewer close ties to fall back on than their English peers. In 1909, for example, the Charity Organization Society wrote to the India Office on behalf of a law student whose mother stopped his allowance after he married an English woman.[22] Unfortunately for both this student and for Rahman, and for the majority of students who asked the India Office for financial support, the Secretary of State deemed that there was nothing the office could do to help.

In other respects, however, overseas students benefited from the efforts of organizations willing to intervene on their behalf. A variety of voluntary societies, such as the National Indian Association (founded in 1870), existed to help imperial students in the metropole. Government bureaucracies not only oversaw imperial rule, they also advocated for colonial subjects. Perhaps the two most important in this respect were the Colonial Office, created in 1854, and the India Office, created in 1858. Both offices repeatedly appealed to the Inns to make concessions for Indian and colonial students.[23] Throughout the nineteenth century, for example, the Inns resisted remitting terms for colonial students, fearing that barristers who had not kept a full three years' worth of terms might

---

[19] Visram, *Asians in Britain*, 127.   [20] Duman, *The English and Colonial Bars*, 132–133.
[21] IOR/L/PJ/6/182 August 19, 1886.   [22] IOR/L/PJ/6/953 March 31, 1909.
[23] CO 323/863/43 1921; CO 323/878/72 1921; CO 323/926/6 1924; CO 67/220/7 1927;
CO 323/1044/4 1929; CO 323/1478/11 1937.

be underprepared for practice. By 1903, however, the India Office and Colonial Office joined together to successfully petition the Inns for a remission of four of the twelve terms for all civil servants coming from abroad.[24] The offices could also intervene in relation to cultural or religious matters. In 1909 the India Office thanked the Middle Temple for their "concession in regard to the wearing of Turbans" rather than wigs for Sikh students called to the bar.[25]

The societies only reluctantly altered fundamental practices – such as the keeping of a fixed number of terms – but they readily accommodated overseas students' requests regarding less entrenched practices, particularly in the second half of the nineteenth century. In 1860 the Middle Temple allowed members of the Indian Civil Service to be admitted without paying the usual deposit of £100, greatly reducing the expense of study. Like Cambridge University, the societies permitted foreign students to substitute other ancient languages for the Latin examination. In 1869, at the request of students who said it would be useful to have instruction in the laws of their home countries, the Middle Temple appointed a reader of "Hindoo, Mahamedan, & Indian Law [sic]."[26] None of these changes threatened the core values or practices at the Inns, and as such the benchers raised few objections to implementing them.

Even with these concessions, colonial students nevertheless faced difficulties at the resolutely English Inns. Gandhi recalled that he and other married students from the subcontinent passed themselves off as bachelors, not only to engage in "more or less innocent" flirtation with young women but also, as he described it, to hide the shame of "child marriages." While some law students, both English and colonial, claimed that all students intermingled, others maintained that colonial students kept apart. When asked by interviewers from the India Office if overseas students participated in the social life of the Inns via activities such as the Hardwicke Debating Society, B. S. Vaidya, an Indian law student at Lincoln's Inn, replied that they did not. Their primary means of contact with English students was, he claimed, through dining, when they sat together "quite freely." Even so, he admitted, though he went to court and dined in hall, he did not know any barristers "personally."[27] For their part, English memoirists rarely mentioned interactions – let alone friendships – with overseas students, except to note that a "Mohammedan or a

---

[24] Yet as Maxwell pointed out, even under these circumstances, it took "a man six to ten years before he can keep his terms, whereas the ordinary student who lives in England can be called at the end of three." IOR/L/PJ/6/604 June 4, 1902.

[25] MT MPA January 15, 1909.   [26] MT MPA April 30, 1869.

[27] IOR/Q/10/3/4 July 14, 1921.

prohibitionist was welcomed eagerly in any [dining] mess" because the other members could drink their allotted portion of wine.[28]

Overseas students also faced outright exclusion in other social activities designed to foster masculine camaraderie at the Inns. In 1897, for example, H. K. Mullick asked the four Inns to intervene regarding the Volunteer Rifle Corps' refusal to admit "Natives of India, & other dominions of the Queen outside the United Kingdom." Membership in the corps not only extended homosociability beyond the borders of Inns; it also allowed men to embody a more martial and robust form of masculinity than that typically associated with urban white-collar employment. Exclusion from the corps may have been particularly galling in the face of broader British criticisms of Indian "aloofness," complaints about the failure of Indian students to adequately integrate themselves into social and sporting culture, and stereotypes about the effeminate Bengali.[29] Corps membership was also a means of demonstrating loyalty to the crown by participation in the pageantry of empire. Refusing to allow colonial and dominion students to volunteer may have slighted those who considered themselves faithful British subjects.[30] While the societies agreed the corps' decision to exclude overseas students was "to be regretted," they determined that the "exercise of the authority rested in the Commanding Officer" and that they had "no jurisdiction in the matter."[31] In reality, the Inns provided essential material resources like training space to the corps and could have wielded this clout on behalf of the students. There is no evidence, however, that they attempted doing so.

Policing Indian Students

The question of whether or not Indian students could be thoroughly integrated into British associational life took on new meaning in the late nineteenth and early twentieth centuries, as the growing Indian nationalist movement challenged the status of Indians as faithful British subjects. In the mid-1860s and 1870s, several organizations dedicated to fostering

[28] C. P. Hawkes, *Chambers in the Temple* (London: Methuen, 1930), 146–147.
[29] Lahiri, *Indians in Britain*, 119; Mrinalini Sinha, *Colonial Masculinity* (New York: St. Martin's Press, 1995); Indira Chowdhury-Sengupta, "The Effeminate and the Masculine," in *The Concept of Race in South Asia*, ed. Peter Robb (Delhi: Oxford University Press, 1995), 282; Sikata Banerjee, *Make Me a Man! Masculinity, Hinduism, and Nationalism in India* (Albany, NY: State University of New York Press, 2005), 53–58.
[30] For an example of appealing to imperial values as a means of subverting the image of Indians as transgressors or disruptors, see Deslandes, *Oxbridge Men*, 222.
[31] IT BEN March 2, 1897; MT MPA January 22, 1897.

Indian nationalism and questioning the nature of British rule in India sprang up in London.[32] Bodies like the Indian National Congress first focused on goals achievable within the framework of the Raj, such as expanded economic rights or access to positions in the civil service. Beginning in the late nineteenth century, however, and picking up steam in the early twentieth, leadership in the nationalist movement radicalized and the Congress split into two fractions. The moderates, led by men like Dadabhai Naoroji, still wished to work within the Raj to reform the structure of British rule. The radicals, however, rejected all things British and advocated for direct action to achieve Indian independence. The latter group's efforts in India included strategies ranging from publication of radical poems to violence directed against British officials. Yet the Raj constrained speech and actions by limiting various freedoms. Indians found they had more latitude to question British rule in the metropole, where they enjoyed greater freedom of the press, for example.

Indian nationalists in London troubled the Inns of Court, especially because the largest number of overseas students at the Inns by far came from India. Irish and pan-African nationalists were active both at home and in the metropole at this time, but the numbers of Irish and African students at the Inns of Court were relatively low. Their actions were less likely to be connected back to or reflect upon the Inns. Regardless of the actual political leanings of most Indian law students and barristers, a prominent few played instrumental roles in Indian nationalist movements in London and the empire. A number of the early organizers of the Indian National Congress in 1885 were members of the Inns of Court, including Womesh Chunder Bonnerjee, the first president.[33] In 1907, when the Congress split into two factions, members of the societies played key roles as leaders of the "hot faction," which advocated self-rule and did not reject violent means of achieving it. The societies feared both that they possessed inadequate means of determining which of their Indian members espoused radical beliefs, and that the dissident politics of actively nationalist members would be connected back to the Inns.

The societies' worries particularly intensified following Indian nationalist Madan Lal Dhingra's 1909 assassination of the India Office official Sir William Hutt Curzon Wyllie in South Kensington. Prior to this incident, nationalists had committed violent actions in India, including

---

[32] Visram, *Asians in Britain*, 124–125.

[33] Other later participants and members of the Inns included Badruddin Tyabji, Mohammed Ali Jinnah, and Chittaranjan Das. See Rakesh Batabyal (ed.), *The Penguin Book of Modern Indian Speeches* (Gurgaon: Penguin, 2007).

a botched 1908 assassination attempt on a magistrate that resulted in the death of the wife and daughter of a leading English barrister at the Muzaffarpur bar. The benchers may have been appalled by such actions, but prior to the 1909 assassination, nationalist violence still seemed far away from the Inns of Court. On the evening of his death, however, Wyllie, a political *aid de camp* to the Secretary of State for India, was attending an event organized by the National Indian Association. This organization promoted "social intercourse between the English people and the Indian people in London." As witnesses later testified, months earlier Dhingra had purchased a Colt automatic pistol in Holborn and began training at a shooting range in Tottenham Court Road. On the evening of July 1, 1909, Dhingra attended an evening of entertainment at the Imperial Institute, having been invited by the secretary of the National Indian Association. According to several guests, around 11:00 p.m. Dhingra appeared to be speaking to Curzon Wyllie when he "raised his arm and rapidly fired four shots in Sir Curzon's face – into his eyes." Dhingra also shot Cowas Lalcaca, an Indian doctor who attempted to restrain him. He then put his revolver to his own forehead, but found he was out of bullets.[34]

For the Inns of Court, as for other Londoners, Dhingra's assassination of Curzon Wyllie brought the threat of violence much closer to home in several unsettling ways. Firstly, Dhingra's actions violated both class and geographic boundaries: a high-ranking British official could be killed in gruesome fashion at an otherwise innocuous evening's entertainment in a respectable London neighborhood. Secondly, if a nonpartisan organization designed to promote good relations between English and Indians could become such a bloody staging ground for enmity, where else might death and violence strike? Perhaps most disquieting to the societies, Dhingra was a young university student like so many other Indians in Britain. He did not come to London a trained killer, but rather purchased his gun and learned to fire it in the midst of central London. If time in the capital radicalized him and drove him to violence, would not other Indian students – including law students – have similar experiences? Outside the Inns, politicians' and journalists' interpretations of the assassination varied from dismissing Dhingra as a lone and crazed figure to broader charges of a Hindu conspiracy for Brahmin domination. The standard response of the government, promoted by Prime Minister Asquith, was that there had been a conspiracy but that very few people were involved, and that the conspirators were dangerous

---

[34] "July 1909: Trial of Dhingra, Madan Lal," *Old Bailey Proceedings Online*, www .oldbaileyonline.org/browse.jsp?div=t19090719-55 (accessed March 3, 2015).

because of their violent methods, not because they represented a broader threat.[35] Yet even if metropolitan institutions did not believe all Indians had the potential to be violent, Curzon Wyllie's assassination propelled closer scrutiny of Indians in Britain.

The India Office, aware of tightening security measures in India via the establishment of the Criminal Intelligence Department, 1904 Official Secrets Act, and a clampdown on political activity, had begun an interventionist stance at home even before Curzon Wyllie's assassination. Their efforts included the monitoring of certain Indian law students and potential alerts to the Inns of Court if these individuals seemed suspicious. As early as 1906, the India Office profiled law student Basante Kumar Das, who gave a lecture in Edinburgh, "Is British Rule Beneficial to the Native Races of India?" Not only was Das' answer a resounding no, but he suggested that in order to throw off British rule, the people of India would have to reject capitalist government. In this case, the India Office saw only the need to monitor, rather than intervene or try and involve the Inns of Court in some form of policing. As one criminal intelligence officer declared to the Secretary of State, nothing Das said overstepped "the bounds of legitimate criticism." His anti-British, anti-capitalist speech was distasteful, but less cause for alarm than useful for giving "some idea of the status and antecedents of some of the Indians who proceed to England ... and of the associates with whom they ally themselves." Officials in the India Office even decided against communicating the contents of the criminal intelligence letters to the benchers of the Middle Temple, as Das had never been convicted by a court. They did, however, write to the Middle Temple to confirm Das was a student there, perhaps drawing suspicion to Das regardless.[36]

As with the cases in Chapter 4, concerns surrounding Indian nationalists were never just about political disagreements: they also raised questions about the gentlemanliness of the members in jeopardy. Both the India Office and the Inns of Court used negative tropes about Indians to connect radical politics to moral disorder and debased masculinity. The director of criminal intelligence, for example, included a letter to the Secretary of State for India linking Das's objectionable politics to other personal failings. According to the director, Das "took to bad habits, neglected his studies and kept a woman of the town," in addition to

---

[35] Simon Ball, "The Assassination Culture of Imperial Britain, 1909–1979," *Historical Journal* 56 (March 2013): 237.

[36] IOR/L/PJ/6/757 March 28, 1906. The following year the India Office wrote all four Inns asking if they had a Sunder Lal on their books. Lal's "views [were] of the most advanced type," and the Home Department suggested to the Judicial and Public Department that he be watched. IOR/L/PJ/6/831 September 26, 1907.

"misappropriat[ing] the property of his relatives and friends." For the director, radical politics were intimately bound up with profligacy and petty crime.[37] He drew on a wealth of negative stereotypes about Indians: that they were indolent; that they were less honest than other Asian students; that, corrupted by child marriage, they were sexual predators.[38] Thus, discussions of Indian students' political leanings were never exclusively about allegiance to Britain versus desire for self-determination, but also about upright gentlemanliness versus degenerate immorality. The benchers feared that the values of the Inns had not taken root in Indian students and adequately developed forms of masculinity appropriate to the English bar.

The dual association of radical politics and degraded masculinity jeopardized dissident Indian members' position at the bar, more so perhaps than their English peers. As Chapter 4 illuminates, it was not until 1926 that the Inns disbarred an Anglo-Saxon member for his political actions or opinions. The Inner Temple disbarred Shyamji Krishnavarma for similar reasons, however, as early as 1909 – three months before Dhingra's assassination of Curzon Wyllie. The benchers elected not to comment on their reasons for disbarring Krishnavarma, but significantly, his editorial to which the Bar Council objected justified the murder of two English women in the 1908 Muzaffarpur bombing. As Krishnavarma put it, even if the women had not been killed accidentally, "it would only prove that those who ... associate with wrongdoers or robbers (and Indian Nationalists regard all Englishmen in India as robbers) do so at their own peril."[39] Though perfectly legal to express such sentiments in England, condoning the murder of women violated British sanctification of the rule of law and contravened the notion of women as innocent, nonpolitical actors.

Indian nationalists' connections to particular organizations or places in London could also raise suspicion and jeopardize members' standing at the bar. Krishnavarma, for example, was one of several members of the Inns tangled in London's network of radical nationalists, an association which was cause for scrutiny from both the India Office and the Inns of Court. Although no evidence existed to connect Krishnavarma to Wyllie's assassination, Madan Lal Dhingra had in fact been Krishnavarma's political pupil. The two men knew each other through India House, a hotbed of Indian radicalism in Highgate. Launched to promote nationalist views among Indian students in Britain, the organization also raised funds, published the radical paper

---

[37] IOR/L/PJ/6/757 March 28, 1906.   [38] Lahiri, *Indians in Britain*, 120–122.
[39] Shyamji Krishnavarma, "Indian Anarchism in England," *Times*, February 20, 1909.

the *Indian Sociologist*, and maintained contact with revolutionary move-ments in India.[40] Aware of their connection to Dhingra, the India Office alerted the Inns of Court to three members of the bar who were also members of India House: Shyamji Krishnavarma, Vinayak Damodar Savarkar, and Virendranath Chattopadhyaya. By the time of the assassination, Krishnavarma had already been disbarred by the Inner Temple. Savarkar, already under investigation by Gray's Inn for poems encouraging guerrilla tactics and other evidence of seditious activities, had his call to the bar postponed and withdrew his membership the following year.[41] Virendranath Chattopadhyaya, previously free from disciplinary investigation, came under the scrutiny of the Middle Temple before the end of July 1909.

Like Krishnavarma, the benchers called Chattopadhyaya to account not for his actions but for his words, in this case letters to the editor following Curzon Wyllie's assassination, two in the *Times* and one in the *Daily Dispatch*. Citing his references to rumors of "methods ... practiced ... in Bengal ... to be imitated in London," the benchers accused Chattopadhyaya of knowing about Curzon Wyllie's assassination and doing nothing to prevent it. The benchers also objected to Chattopadhyaya's statement in the *Times*, "The catalogue of coming assassinations will prob-ably be a long one," claiming that he expressed "no reprobation" for those who would commit these crimes. They were most disturbed, however, by his statement in the *Dispatch*, "There is every hope that the women of New India will fight the battle too." By using the word hope, the benchers claimed, it "looks as if ... you recommended and approved of the action of those Indians ... that ... are executed for killing people with bombs." Apologizing that the article was written in haste in his second language, Chatto responded, "I did not mean 'hope.' I really should have put 'fear.'" The benchers, unconvinced, suggested that if he confused words like "hope" and "fear," he should perhaps not write in English at all.[42]

---

[40] Richard Popplewell, *Intelligence and Imperial Defence* (London: Frank Cass, 1995); Nicholas Owen, *The British Left and India* (Oxford: Oxford University Press, 2007).

[41] IOR/L/PJ/6/939 June 10, 1909; Edward Dicey, "Hindu Students in England," *Nineteenth Century and After* (August 1909): 349–360. In 1909 the Viceroy of India telegraphed the India Office to say that they were sending an Indian plainclothes policeman to London in an attempt to gather evidence against V. D. Savarkar to convict him on conspiracy charges. As the viceroy explained, the "best evidence against Savarkar will be obtained from Sikhs and therefore [we] have selected [a] Sikh deputy-superintendant." The India Office noted several risks with this plan, including the possibility of discovery by Savarkar or the deputy-superintendent working as a counteragent to spy on Scotland Yard. Ultimately, however, they agreed that if the viceroy could find "the right sort of man," the proposal was "well worth considering." IOR/L/PJ/6/939 July 9, 1909.

[42] MT MPA July 23, 1909.

The societies expected Indian members to demonstrate regret and condemnation of violent nationalist actions. Instead, Chattopadhyaya characterized the assassination as an inevitability, and one that not only would be repeated but also justifiably so. Such sentiments did not, the Middle Temple declared, accord with those proper to a barrister. "If a member of an English corporation and a student of the English Bar writes to a public paper advocating a violent revolution," the benchers asserted, "the question arises whether he is fit for that sort of magistracy which to be called to the Bar implies." After all, barristers were meant to interpret and uphold the laws of England, not support the extralegal execution of members of the government in hopes of eventually overturning British rule. On July 28, less than a month after Curzon Wyllie's assassination, the benchers voted to expel Chattopadhyaya.[43] The following year he moved to the continent and continued his organizing efforts from Paris and Berlin.

The benchers were disturbed not only by Chattopadhyaya's sentiments but also by the fact that he addressed his letters to the editor from the Middle Temple. Doing so, they explained, "seems to involve the Middle Temple in your views on the matter. Whatever they may be we do not wish that."[44] As an institution foundational to British law, the Inn recoiled from association with seditious, anti-imperial speech. The Middle Temple, in particular, was also becoming increasingly concerned about its reputation as the "most cosmopolitan" of the Inns. In the nineteenth century, this reputation attracted the wealth of colonial members to an Inn that, in the mid-century, had been in tough financial straits. By the early twentieth century, the benchers began to fear they had too many colonial members in relation to native Britons. At this point, however, the Inn was still willing to accommodate foreign students; their concession in regard to Sikhs wearing turbans came only a week before they expelled Chattopadhyaya.

In the face of nationalist violence, it became increasingly important for the societies to screen applicants before they joined, but the Inns of Court feared they could not appropriately evaluate potential Indian law students. A November 1909 report by the Council of Legal Education suggested that the requirement of a certificate signed by two barristers of five years standing to vouch for Indian applicants was not enough "to secure that only persons of good character... become member of an Inn." Other than the certificate of character, the Inns had to rely on outside bodies like the India Office to alert them to any impropriety on the part of

---

[43] MT MPA July 28, 1909.   [44] MT MPA July 23, 1909.

Indian students, or to vouch for students when possible.[45] The Council
of Legal Education's report expressed further concerns about cases of
"personation," as there were "no means of identifying Students, who can
adopt what names they please." The Council recommended that native
Indian applicants should have to have their certificates of good character
signed by an officer representing the Indian government in their district
or state.[46] Such an official, the Inns presumed, would be better informed
of an applicant's objectionable actions or affiliations than would the
barristers at the Indian bar. The four Inns adopted the council's recommendation and required Indian students to produce certificates signed
by the collector, deputy commissioner, or higher-ranking officers of their
native states. In so doing, the Inns placed judgment of character in the
hands of the state rather than members of the profession. That the
societies, fiercely territorial over their governance of the bar, willingly
handed power over to an outside authority indicated the depth of their
concerns over Indian members.

Indian students resented the Inns' requirement of a certificate of
character from the collector or deputy commissioner of their native
states, interpreting the requirement as a deliberate means of preventing
politically radical candidates from joining the legal profession. Leaders
at the Inns denied political motivations behind the new regulation.
W. G. Wrangham, sub-treasurer of the Inner Temple, claimed that he
was "not aware that there was any resentment ... at having to produce a
certificate from a Government Officer," and that he "had no idea that the
High Commissioner took political views into consideration at all." Sir
Thomas Arnold, educational adviser to Indian students to the Secretary
of State 1917–20, firmly maintained that political consideration had
nothing to do with the regulation. But as R. Ramachandra Rao, a district
collector of Madras, forthrightly explained, "It is a political question.
The political opinions of a candidate are always enquired into by the
Collector, and there is a certain amount of dissatisfaction in India on the
matter."[47] Nevertheless the Inns maintained the requirement.

Students objected to other measures designed to police Indian
students, especially rules that overtly privileged European over Indian

---

[45] IOR/L/PJ/6/1123 November 6, 1911. In 1911 W. Blake Odgers, representative of the
Council of Legal Education, wrote the India Office asking if they could vouch for a
student, Vanga Jagannadha Row, to be called to the bar. The India Office responded that
they knew nothing against him, but neither could they recommend him knowing nothing
about him either.

[46] IT BEN November 12, 1909.

[47] IOR/Q/10/4/14 July 27, 1921; IOR/Q/10/4/32 July 21, 1921; IOR/Q/10/4/
19 August 18, 1921.

barristers. For example, they opposed a 1913 rule that required advocates of the Bombay High Court to "read for at least one year in the chambers of a practicing *European* barrister of more than 10 years' standing." This rule prevented Indian barristers from taking on pupils who wished to read with them. According to officials, the Bombay High Court enacted the rule "to preserve as far as possible the best traditions and practice of the English bar."[48] Drawing overt distinctions between Indian and European barristers, the rule suggested that the former – despite their training in London – were somehow less than English barristers and had not actually absorbed the culture of the bar. On a material level, such a prohibition could make it difficult for Indian students to find a pupilage, jeopardizing their success at the bar.

Indian students also expressed grievances with the institutions governing their time in the capital, revealing deep mistrust of the British government and agencies they suspected were actively but secretly monitoring Indians in London. In 1914, for example, the Secretary of State and the National Indian Association bought a house at 21, Cromwell Road, ostensibly for meetings, lectures, and other forms of associational life. The house's ties to the government, and perhaps its South Kensington location, however, raised suspicions among Indian students. Even Indian student representatives of 21, Cromwell Road readily admitted to a 1921 India Office investigative committee that "there is a feeling amongst the students that they are being spied upon." As V. N. Sahai put it, "As long as the Government has anything to do with the institution it must be in disfavor with the public." Students had no proof of espionage, but Sahai pointed out that the lack of political lectures made it seem as if "there is something official behind it." It seemed clear that nationalists were being kept out. Sir Murray Hammick, a committee member, protested that the National Indian Association was nonpolitical, a sort of social club. "I do not suppose they allow politics there," he protested, "any more than they would allow them in a club in St. James' Square."[49] For Hammick the absence of politics in club life was a given, familiar from years of socialization in the West End's gentlemen's clubs. Yet for Indian students the absence of nationalist talk was conspicuous, fueling a deep and general mistrust of the government and the conviction that Indian students' actions and words would be used against them.

Well-meaning English volunteers at 21, Cromwell Road expressed sympathy and distress that the house would be so mistrusted.

---

[48] IOR/L/PJ/6/1067 December 4, 1913.   [49] IOR/Q/10/3/19 August 8, 1921.

Miss E. J. Beck, honorary secretary of the House Managing Committee, treasurer of the Distressed Indian Students Aid Committee, and secretary of the National Indian Association, regretted that "the House undoubtedly suffered on account of the suspicion ... that those in charge of it were agents of the Government for the purpose of spying" on the students. Sir Charles E. Mallet, secretary for Indian students at the India Office (1912–16), went even further, suggesting that perhaps Indian students' suspicions were not unfounded. He explained to the 1921 India Office committee that he "always told the students freely that he cared nothing about their opinions," but suspected there were others "at the India Office who did not altogether share this view."[50] Though he did not elaborate, Mallet implied that some of the India Office affiliates at 21, Cromwell Road did indeed report what they saw and heard to their superiors. Suspicion of spying also fell on those Indians who seemed too eager to cooperate or collude with the house.

Other India Office officials dismissed these concerns, asserting that regardless of their ties to the state, organizations like those at 21, Cromwell Road remained nonpartisan. Sir Thomas Arnold maintained that there had been no case of a student discriminated against "on account of his political opinions." Neither 21, Cromwell Road nor the Indian Students' Department was involved, he insisted, in the policing of Indians. In fact, while popular opinion claimed that the latter was formed after the death of Sir Curzon Wyllie, its existence actually dated to April 1909, several months before the assassination.[51] Nevertheless, N. C. Sen, OBE, joint secretary to the High Commissioner for India for Indian Students' Work, suggested that removing the offices of the local adviser from 21, Cromwell Road would "tend to diminish the feeling that the house was an official one." The house's South Kensington location, combined with the presence of India Office bureaucrats, further reinforced contentions that the house was connected to government oversight.

Should Indians Study in Britain?

As both the Inns and the India Office worried over what to do about Indian students, a clear question arose: did Indian law students really need to come to London at all? In order to assess Indian bar students' needs and training, in 1911 the India Office began surveying members of

[50] IOR/Q/10/4/40 August 24, 1921; IOR/Q/10/4/27 July 30, 1921.
[51] 21, Cromwell Road was, in fact, the result of the 1907 Lee Warner Commission. "Indian Students in England," *Times*, June 2, 1910; IOR/Q/10/4/32 July 21, 1921.

the Indian High Courts.[52] They drew responses, in the form of letters and testimonials, from over two dozen high-ranking members of the Indian bar and Indian bureaucracies, from Calcutta, Madras, Bombay, Bengal, United Provinces, Punjab, Burma, Central Provinces, and the North West Frontier Province. They also interviewed benchers and other key functionaries at the Inns of Court. The office's inquiry raised a number of questions: was it really necessary for Indian students to come to England? If it were necessary, or at least if it were to be an option for Indian students, how could British institutions and bureaucracies judge the suitability of students that came? Furthermore, how could those students who came be properly inculcated with British values?

Respondents to the India Office's survey – barristers and judges of both English and Indian descent – recapitulated arguments about empire building or degraded masculinity to express conflicting opinions as to whether or not Indian students should study law in London. A minority of those interviewed by the India Office rehashed earlier justifications for study at the bar, maintaining that the Inns of Court performed important work inculcating overseas students with key aspects of Britishness. C. C. Scott, the treasurer of the Middle Temple, contended that "the knowledge of our laws and customs" benefited not only the individual student but also "indirectly ... the Indian community." According to Scott, the best way to impart this legal knowledge was through pupilage in chambers, which allowed students to learn the letter as well as "the usages and the practice of the law." Scott admitted that requiring overseas candidates to pass an examination prior to departure for England would be a "useful check on students ... who were unfitted or had no intention of working," but insisted that among those students already at the Inns, "many of them are men of ability and well qualified to succeed." He concluded that it would be "undesirable to wholly discourage natives from being called to the English Bar." Notably, the Middle Temple had the largest population of overseas students. That Inn admitted ninety-two new Indian students in 1920–21 alone, compared, for example, with the Inner Temple's fifty-six total Indian students on the books in the same period.[53] Should Indian students stop coming to Britain, the Middle Temple's enrollment numbers would sharply decline.

Respondents without a vested monetary interest in overseas students at the Inns maintained that Indians had no reason to come to London as

---

[52] This work was an even more comprehensive inquiry than the 1907 Lee-Warner Committee.

[53] IT BEN November 12, 1926. Fifty-six out of a total of 1,158 students were from India and Ceylon at the Inner Temple.

they could train as vakils in India. Unlike Scott, they claimed that those who joined the Inns were "young men of mediocre educational qualifications," unwilling to face the rigor of vakil training. They were men eager to take advantage of "the numerous novel temptations of a strange city like London." A former principal of the Muhammadan Anglo-Oriental College at Aligarh and member of the Council of India suggested that Indian law students in London, "under less supervision and less compulsion to work," at best wasted time and money. At worst they spread or acquired "vicious habits" and "undesirable politics." A High Court justice claimed that these "failures" lowered the tone of the whole profession. Such commentators refigured mid-Victorian characterizations of barristers and law students as profligate wasters to critique only one ethnic subsection of the bar. Indian law students, these men suggested, were best kept in India to prevent indolence and immorality, but also – unlike their mid-Victorian counterparts – the spread of dangerous ideas.

Some India Office interviewees saw the problem in sending Indian students to London as the failure of the Inns to provide students with an adequate legal education. Viscount Haldane, Liberal imperialist and lord chancellor, put it bluntly: "Candidates for admission to the Indian Bar should be trained in India" because training in Britain was "out of date." Aware that critics might accuse him of cutting off "the light and influence of the English Bar" from the Indian bar, Haldane assured his readers that he saw the value in Indian advocates "imbibing something of [the English bar's] spirit and methods." He maintained, however, that Indians should come to London to observe the English bar after their training in India was complete. The best way to strengthen the Indian bar was "not by sending hordes of half-educated boys to hang about the Inns" but to utilize "Indian resources to build up ... an autonomous organization for training and selecting members of a profession ... open only to men of high attainments."[54] In Haldane's view, vetting Indian law students via training in India would ensure that only the subcontinent's best would pursue further study in London.

Perhaps the chancellor worried about exposing Indian students to English ideas that might, from an English perspective, be misinterpreted. According to an advocate of the Chief Court of Punjab, England and English ideas radicalized Indian students. "It is the British Rule of Law that they come in contact with," he stated, and "they feel inclined to apply these principles to their own country, and without studying all the conditions and ill-circumstances." Indian nationalists certainly drew on

[54] IOR/L/PJ/6/1067 January 30, 1914.

British figures and ideas to justify their freedom. Krishnavarma, for example, likened the nationalist cause to Milton's writing.[55] Indians also drew on nineteenth-century British liberal thought, especially John Stuart Mill, to advocate for political freedoms. Yet as historian Sukanya Bannerjee notes, for thinkers like Mill "universal capacities" rendered everyone *potentially* equal for political rights, but even Mill argued that there are "conditions of society in which a vigorous despotism is in itself the best mode of government for training the people in what is specifically wanting to render them capable of higher civilization."[56] As the advocate of the Chief Court of Punjab implied, Indians came to Britain and demanded political rights for which they were not yet ready.

Yet just as this advocate's individual political ideology led him to stress the dangers of thinkers like Mill, other interlocutors sympathetic to Indian reforms emphasized the benefits of liberal thought. The chairman of the India Office committee, the Earl of Lytton, then Undersecretary of State for India, suggested that the value of coming to England might be to learn about free enterprise and private undertakings. One of the most impressive English qualities, he maintained, was "the amount which is done by private individuals apart from State assistance," from which Indians who "look to the Government for everything" might take a cue. In so saying, Lytton suggested that it was not legal learning alone from which Indian students would benefit, but exposure to capitalist philanthropy and the workings of the laissez-faire liberal state. Lytton, a Conservative, nevertheless supported a variety of Liberal policies, including Edwin Montagu's Indian constitutional reforms. He believed in preparing India for eventual self-governance and was thus unworried about how Indian students would reconcile their appreciation for the successes of the noninterventionist English state with the paternalist oversight of the British Raj.[57] Lytton's intervention is an important reminder that members of the bar spanned the political spectrum; by the early twentieth century, barristers skewed Conservative, but their individual convictions might vary widely from party orthodoxy.[58]

If some respondents overtly tied their views to political ideology, others framed their convictions in terms of pragmatism, suggesting there were better reasons for Indian students to train in India than there were for

[55] IT BEN March 10, 1909.

[56] John Stuart Mill, as quoted in Banerjee, *Becoming Imperial Citizens*, 13.

[57] Tomes, "Lytton, Victor Alexander George Robert Bulwer-, Second Earl of Lytton (1876–1947)," in *Oxford Dictionary of National Biography* (Oxford: Oxford University Press, 2004).

[58] Duman, *The English and Colonial Bar*, 171–172.

them to study in the UK. Sir Lewis Coward, chairman of the Board of Legal Studies, pointed out the differences between legal practice in England and India, as the latter fused English law with preexisting Indian laws. It might make sense, he contended, to make allowances for students in other colonies where law more closely resembled that of Britain – not so for India, especially given the high quality of Indian legal training. Furthermore, Coward explained, the Inns of Court did not have the same disciplinary powers as the universities. As Coward put it, "They say, 'These men come here. It is not part of the contract with them that they have to pass their examinations or depart.'"[59] To his mind, the Inns' policy of letting students sink or swim without interference was a deplorable remnant of their early-modern function as a finishing school for gentlemen. Such an approach was not well suited, Coward implied, to a population of overseas students. For Coward, Indian students lacked the self-discipline, instilled in British students by the public schools and universities, to apply themselves to their studies without institutional oversight or consequences.

The problem for Coward was not just that the Inns did not take an active role in disciplining their students. Instead, Coward doubted the Inns' abilities to create true cohesion between English and Indian students. Although Indian and English students "read together in chambers, go into the Courts and mingle together, ... mix at the table and in the common rooms ... somehow or other they do not seem to cement." For centuries the Inns of Court had touted their customs and rituals as creating a sense of brotherhood and coherence among barristers. The societies relied on these practices to inculcate students with the values of the Inns. Yet the social life of the Inns did not seem, to Coward, to be able to surmount existing barriers. W. G. Wrangham agreed that in hall and in the common rooms, Indian and English students "did not mix."[60] If Indian students did not interact with English, then regardless of how often they dined in hall or lounged in the common room, they were not absorbing English values. For Coward and Wrangham, sociability at the Inns failed to properly induct overseas students into the societies' culture.

If the social life of the Inns could not provide reason for Indian students to study in London, could another frequently cited rationale, reading in chambers, justify their time in the UK? W. G. Wrangham felt that Indian students could probably learn Indian law better in the chambers of an Indian barrister, but he did not think that "the student could learn the etiquette of the profession unless he read in the chambers of an

[59] IOR/Q/10/3/1 July 11, 1921.   [60] IOR/Q/10/4/14 July 27, 1921.

English barrister." After all, unwritten professional etiquette was intimately bound up with English notions of gentlemanliness. At the same time, Wrangham acknowledged that Indian students often found it difficult to find a place in English barristers' chambers, as "English barristers usually preferred to take English students." Dr. William Blake Odgers, director of legal studies for the Council of the Bar, explained that this reluctance stemmed from barristers' fears that Indian pupils would not do well in front of a jury should they ever have to take a case to court. The treasurer of the Middle Temple was somewhat more defensive, claiming that Indians did not have any more trouble finding practice in chambers than "other people say from Jamaica or anywhere else." He admitted, however, that he could not think of a case of difficulties for someone hailing from white settler colonies like Canada or Australia. By contrast, Haldane, the former lord chancellor, dismissed the value of reading in chambers at all – for any student – as "very much exaggerated," claiming that a pupil was lucky if "his barrister will perhaps condescend to spend a few minutes with him looking over the drafts which he has done."[61]

In so saying, these men harkened back to Victorian debates about the standards for the legal profession imposed by the Inns of Court. Nineteenth-century members of the bar, reluctant to disrupt the traditions of the profession, challenged proposals for tightening the requirements for a call to the bar. Competent barristers, they contended, would always attract briefs while the unsuccessful eventually disappeared from the profession. Leaders of the bar in the early twentieth century now recognized that self-regulation did nothing to weed out deeply undesirable radical politics. Even the meticulous screening of candidates' affiliations would not be enough, the logic implied, to prevent violent Indian nationalists from infiltrating the bar. Only rigorous requirements for a call to the bar would make it unpalatable to any but those motivated to succeed in the profession – and success, of course, necessitated embracing existing British structures and hierarchies. In 1915 the lord chancellor, Secretary of State for India, and the judges of the Madras High Court considered taking measures a step farther and obviating the need for Indian law students to train at the Inns of Court altogether. The elite coterie planned to meet to discuss the training of Indian advocates outside the Inns, but hostile conditions made travel impossible. In the face of wartime emergency, the participants postponed the meeting indefinitely.

---

[61] IOR/Q/10/4/19 August 18, 1921; IOR/Q/10/4/16 July 29, 1921; IOR/Q/10/3/1 July 11, 1921.

The Spatial Logic of Discipline

At the same time that members of the bar and India Office officials debated the virtue of study in colony versus metropole, they also engaged in contestations over the geography of legal training at the local level, debating the spatial logics of the discipline of Indian students in London. At stake in these debates were questions as to how best to mold Indian students into both British and rational subjects. Should Indian students be spread across the city in the homes of good families that would encourage them to absorb proper English values, interlocutors asked, or should they be grouped together in dormitory-style housing that would allow for their close monitoring and observation? Aware of the glacial pace of change in the legal profession, the India Office foresaw that Indian students were likely to continue studying for the bar in London for some time. Thus, in the first three decades of the twentieth century, the India Office surveyed members of both the English and Indian bars to explore how to best manage overseas students in the capital.

Members of the bar who opposed grouping Indian students together invoked epidemiological language to voice their concerns about radical politics. In a 1915 India Office study, one barrister from Lahore worried about "contagion," while another worried about Indian students "herding together." Pandit Moti Lal Nehru, advocate of the High Court of Judicature, North Western Province, explained that in "the common rooms of certain Inns of Court" and "the lodgings of Indian students who lived in groups," ideas spread in a way "that it would have been best for those students to have stayed … in India." Nehru's comment on group housing may have been an oblique reference to India House, that hotbed of Indian radicalism in Highgate led by Shyamji Krishnavarma. Emissaries from India House met freshly arrived students at Victoria and Charing Cross stations and tried to persuade them to join the nationalist movement. The hostel only had twenty-four beds and a reportedly high turnover, but as one pleader in the North West Frontier Province stated, ideas in a hostel would spread in merely "a few weeks," whereas "the same work will require months and years if students are living apart." Instead of being allowed to live and socialize in groups, Justice Sir D. D. Davar proposed that "Indian students should be … assisted in securing residence in good English families."[62] Davar's proposal harkened back to Victorian philanthropists who advocated cottage

---

[62] Lahiri, *Indians in Britain*, 123; IOR/L/PJ/6/1067 February 25, 1911–March 12, 1915.

homes rather than barrack-style dormitories for orphaned paupers.[63] Exposure to wholesome British family life, Davar believed, would inculcate Indian students with desirable values and a healthy respect for established authority.

Other officials suggested the creation of some kind of hostel system, which would concentrate Indian students in London in a few readily policed buildings. Proponents like Mr. Justice Spencer of Madras imagined that such a system would replicate "the discipline of a public school and a University, where more attention is given to moral training and discipline than in Indian educational institutions." Like Coward, Spencer implied that the Indian education system failed to inculcate Indian students with the ability to self-regulate. A hostel would, he implied, provide this much-needed training and its resultant character development. To those who protested that living together in a hostel would not expose Indian students to English society, depriving them of valuable cultural exchange, Spencer countered, "What they learn of English ways in ... boarding houses is very often better unlearnt." Mr. E. B. Raikes suggested that, if not a hostel system, "it would be possible to form a club ... for young Englishmen and the Indians to live in... getting the Englishmen to join out of public spirit just as they do ... in Toynbee Hall." By likening his imagined club to the East End settlements, Raikes equated upper-class and well-educated Indian students with working-class denizens of London's slums. Sensitive to such slights, the Honorable Mr. R. N. Mudholkar pointed out that a hostel system "would be keenly felt as a slur and an indignity." As Mudholkar was no doubt aware, cultural norms held that elite men could control themselves; only the working-class rabble and women needed external restraints. Suggesting that Indian students required the supervision of a hostel implied that they had not acquired the self-discipline requisite for respectable manhood. The India Office agreed with Mudholkar that hostels would "rouse the bitterest resentment." Instead, they proposed "raising ... the educational standard," which would "eliminat[e] shirkers by making the profession of advocate one only to be attained by real work."[64]

Indian students themselves disagreed about whether a hostel would be a desirable living arrangement. In the India Office's 1921 investigative committee, two representatives of the students at 21, Cromwell Road

[63] Lydia Murdoch, *Imagined Orphans* (New Brunswick: Rutgers University Press, 2006); Seth Koven, *Slumming* (Princeton: Princeton University Press, 2004).
[64] IOR/L/PJ/6/1067 February 25, 1911–March 12, 1915; IOR/Q/10/3/24 August 15, 1921.

repeated the language used by members of the Indian bar in the 1915 study, explaining their objection to a hostel on the grounds that "Indian students would *herd together* and lose the benefit of their stay in [England]." They envisioned 21, Cromwell Road as a clearinghouse, a place for newly arrived Indian students to land before they took lodgings elsewhere, or a place for regional university students coming to London for short stays. Mr. Kuriyan, the YMCA representative, agreed. He appreciated the YMCA's meetings and lectures, but if all Indian students lived there instead of in lodgings, it would become "a bit of India." By contrast, Ariam Williams, secretary of the YMCA Indian Students' Union, envisioned a future in which the YMCA hostel would function as a "residential Club" where individuals "intellectually, culturally and spiritually" qualified would act as "interpreter[s] of India to the West." Others maintained that it was only through the organized efforts of hostels that Indians saw anything of English life at all. D. Runganadhan, general secretary for the YMCA Indian Students Union, for example, praised a recent outing to Epping Forest in which students had tea, tennis, and conversation at the country home of one Mr. and Mrs. Lister.[65]

In addition to the living arrangements of overseas students, the Inns of Court also worried over students' use of various spaces at the Inns. Officially, overseas students enjoyed access to the same areas as home students, and despite discussions with the India Office, the societies never enacted formal policies to keep overseas students from socializing with one another. Battles over Lincoln's Inn common room, however, suggest that the Inn did engage in discreet practices to prevent overseas students from congregating together. The common room at Lincoln's Inn came into existence in 1879, when the society reluctantly agreed to dedicate the ground floor of No. 7, Stone Buildings to its students and barristers, provided members would cover maintenance costs via a nominal fee. Yet in 1912, without explanation, the benchers passed an order excluding students from the common room. The common room had been losing money, and this seemingly counterintuitive decision reduced rather than expanded the financial support of the space.[66]

A report by a 1920 special committee, however, revealed that the earlier decision to exclude students was a calculated risk; the benchers hoped that by removing overseas students from the space, the common

---

[65] Italics mine. IOR/Q/10/3/19 August 8, 1921; IOR/Q/10/2/16 August 12, 1921.
[66] Black Books of Lincoln's Inn, 1879, 1880, 1912.

room would become more appealing to home members of the Inn. As the report explained, overseas students in the common room presented a twofold problem. The first issue, as other members of the profession had stated elsewhere, was that home and overseas students did not "intermix socially." The authors claimed that students' "mutual distaste" for one another meant that overseas students "monopolized" one end of the common room. It was not merely the inconvenience of this practice to which the committee objected. Instead, the report explained that overseas students, generally housed in "humble lodgings," were likely to "make the Common Room their home for the day – thus getting a sitting room with heating, lighting and attendance free." Home students seeking "legitimate" use of the space found overseas students' "excessive user [sic]" of the common room "distasteful." As a result, claimed the committee, home students "either cease[d] using the Common Room or ... resort [ed] to some room where the Overseas Students [were] not 'living.'"[67]

The authors' report raised several issues, including the tensions that arose when white and colonial students were expected to share social space as equals. When asked to comment on overseas students in other spaces at the Inns, such as the hall, most home students responded with indifference or off-handed jokes. But when they quipped that adding a Muslim student to their mess augmented the others' portion of wine, the joke was always framed as one Muslim to three British students. Overseas students could be tolerated so long as they were the minority. In the instance of the common room, the authors of the report protested not that a handful of overseas students spent their days in the room, but that a group large enough to "monopolize" it was "living" there. Both of the latter terms have proprietary implications and suggested that the common room was being used in ways that made it increasingly seem as if it belonged to overseas students. In documenting colonial student domination of British space, the committee described an uncomfortable reversal of the colonizing process.

Furthermore, in emphasizing overseas students' desire to take advantage of cheap comforts, the committee suggested that these students lacked not only financial resources but also the manners and insider knowledge of what was or was not "done." As Ben Griffin and others have argued, beyond wealth and pedigree, on a day-to-day basis, gentlemanliness was marked by factors like dress, manners, and deportment.[68]

---

[67] Black Books of Lincoln's Inn, 1920.
[68] Ben Griffin, *The Politics of Gender in Victorian Britain Masculinity, Political Culture and the Struggle for Women's Rights* (Cambridge: Cambridge University Press, 2012), 189.

Some home students at the Inns may have been wealthier than some overseas students; we know from the enormous range of incomes at the bar that plenty of home students also faced tight budgets and unglamorous living conditions.[69] The distinction the committee drew between the two groups was not truly financial but one that rested on years of accumulated cultural knowledge that clued home students into unspoken social rules. Lincoln's Inn's preoccupation with overseas students in the common room *may* have had to do with the spread of unsavory radical politics, though the Inns were rarely oblique when discussing such concerns. Instead, the society wanted to maintain the use of its common room according to implicit social rules and was willing to ban all students entirely in order to do so. Such a ban implied that no amount of legal learning at the Inns could provide overseas students with the requisite cultural knowledge for insider status in the society.

In fact, Lincoln's Inn did not wish overseas students to become insiders. The 1920 report revealed that the Inn's decision to exclude students from the common room was not only designed to make the room more appealing to home members, it was expressly designed to make the entire society less appealing to overseas students. The committee explained that when the common room had been open to overseas students, these students felt that they had "a home" at Lincoln's Inn, causing more overseas students to join the Inn. This feeling attracted "an undue proportion of the Overseas Students, in consequence of which Home Students became shy of joining the Society." The committee suggested that while the common room was open to students, the ratio of overseas to home students had reached the "startling figure" of five to one. They claimed that the 1912 policy prohibiting students from use of the rooms "has had a beneficial result in reducing the number of Overseas Students coming to this Inn."[70] According to this logic, the society was obliged to admit some proportion of overseas students, but there was no reason it should make itself more appealing to foreign students than any of the other Inns.

Despite the committee's recommendation to continue prohibiting students from the common room, the benchers decided to once again allow students' use of the room. Perhaps they were persuaded by the great number of students who had petitioned for its use: 400 students total, 275 home, 125 overseas. They may also have found the ratio of petitioners reassuring, for if overseas students made up slightly more

[69] Duman, *The English and Colonial Bars*, 144.   [70] Black Books of Lincoln's Inn, 1920.

than a fourth of those likely to use the common room, surely they could not monopolize it. The benchers decided to enact rules that would increase the chances of this being the case. They restricted the hours of the room's use and, following the example of the Inner Temple, insisted that no letters were to be addressed from the common room. This latter policy served two functions. According to the benchers, it prohibited overseas students from "obtaining credit on the strength of their address" and saved the societies the embarrassment of having police and collecting agents serving writs in the common room.[71] The implication was that overseas students – and overseas students alone – were not only impecunious but also lacked the self-discipline to responsibly borrow. Such a policy would also prevent overseas students from associating their views with those of the Inns, as Chattopadhyaya had done when he addressed his letters to the editor of the *Times* from the Middle Temple common room. In the society's view, students could be admitted into the common room, but only with rules in place to make up for the self-restraint and cultural knowledge that overseas students lacked.

The Inns Discuss among Themselves

Despite the India Office's repeated investigations (1907, 1911, 1921), only two alternatives existed to obviate the need for Indian law students to spend time in London. Either the Indian bar could change the requirements for pleading in Indian courts, or the Inns of Court could alter their regulations for a call to the bar for Indian or colonial students. In the mid-1920s the Indian legislature debated policy changes that would remove barristers' privileged standing in courts, but they did not go so far as to create a separate Indian bar. At the same time, the Inns speculated whether these limited legislative changes would actually reduce the numbers of Indian students coming to the UK, and they considered whether they should alter their own regulations. The Middle Temple began to push for changes and met resistance from the other Inns as underlying divisions between the four societies surfaced. The Middle Temple felt it was carrying an unfair share of the burden of colonial students. According to a confidential memorandum circulated among the benchers of the Middle Temple in 1926, more than half (56 percent) of "coloured students" called to the bar had been

---

[71] Ibid.

called by the Middle Temple.[72] The memo proposed that the Middle Temple reduce the average sixty incoming "coloured" students each year by half and recoup the loss of £2,700 per year this would create by taking steps to "induce an additional number of white students to join the Inn."

The memorandum did not outline the Middle Temple's objections to the uneven number of colonial students, but discussions at meetings of the benchers over the following three years suggest potential underlying logics. These sometimes-incompatible explanations likely reflected divergent political preoccupations among the benchers. By the second half of the 1920s, Britons' attitudes toward Indian self-governance sharply diverged: Liberals and Labour were committed to Home Rule, while Conservatives maintained that India should be content with the dyarchy established by the Government of India Act 1919.[73] Master Reading – former viceroy of India, current Liberal Party leader and believer in eventual Indian self-governance – did not doubt the merits of Indian students at the Inns. Instead, he stated that it was imperative for the "good government" of the societies "that there should be an adequate supply of Barristers ... who practice, or have practiced in England." Reading further expressed concern that given the large number of foreign students who "do not intend to reside in this country," the Middle Temple would eventually be hard-pressed to find "a sufficient number of members ... to provide suitable candidates for election to the Bench."[74] By this logic, overseas students created a problem because they returned to their countries of origin rather than remaining in London after being called to the bar. A motion by another bencher, Master Powell, contradicted this premise. Powell proposed that "students from abroad who shall declare in writing that it is their intention to leave this country for good as soon as ... they are Called to the Bar" might eat fewer dinners and keep fewer terms to speed along their call. For Powell, then, the problem with overseas students seemed not to be that they returned to their countries of origin but rather that they spent too much time in London to begin with. Asking for increased standards to guarantee that students had received "liberal education[s]" and "adequate knowledge of the English Language and Literature, and of Latin," Powell challenged colonial students' cultural credentials for membership in the Inns.[75] Overseas students did not come

---

[72] MT MPA March 4, 1926. Lincoln's Inn was responsible for 24.1 percent, Gray's Inn for 10.4 percent, and the Inner Temple for 8.8 percent. The memo does not account for the missing 0.7 percent of students called to the bar. Perhaps it took into account calls from the Irish or Scottish bars.
[73] Bernard Porter, *The Lion's Share* (New York: Longman, 1996), 302–303.
[74] MT MPA May 26, 1927.   [75] MT MPA January 24, 1929.

equipped, he implied, with the intellectual accoutrements necessary for gentleman barristers.

These disputes, however, do not explain why the Middle Temple's 1926 memorandum on "coloured students" framed the Inns' concerns in racial terms. In the past, the societies frequently used the term "overseas" to denote students from throughout the empire, or referred to particular groups by their country of origin, such as "Indian students." The 1926 memorandum, however, explicitly used the adjective "coloured," indicating that the issue was more than students returning to their countries of origin, or students not sharing a common academic pedigree. The students in question, the memorandum pointed out, were not white. As historians such as G. R. Searle argue, by the 1920s, the difference between whites and people of color – and the superiority of the former over the latter – would have been so ingrained in the minds of Britons as to be "self-evident."[76] The Middle Temple could thus adopt racial language to emphasize its duress and demarcate overseas from other students, without any explanation needed.[77]

In 1926, shortly after circulating its confidential memorandum to benchers of the Inn, the Middle Temple sent the other three Inns of Court a report to determine what changes, if any, were necessary regarding "the admission and treatment of members of the Society ... not of European origin." The report explained that it was "clearly undesirable that one Inn should become the ... favoured home for non-English students," as that would "affect its popularity in the eyes of English students." The report acknowledged that certain changes afoot in Indian courts, such as a move to abolish barristers' privileged standing over vakils, might somewhat reduce the number of Indian students at the Inns, but that "the prestige which attached to membership of the English Bar" would still mean fairly high numbers of Indian students at the Inns. The universities, the report pointed out, had taken steps to make sure that overseas students were equally spread throughout their colleges. While the Inns could not "deal with the question on a merely racial basis," surely there was something they could do to even out the distribution of students among all four societies. The Middle Temple suggested all four Inns meet to discuss.

After some resistance on the part of the Inner Temple, the societies finally convened in 1928, but could not reach a consensus. Lincoln's Inn,

---

[76] G. R. Searle, *A New England? Peace and War, 1886–1918* (New York: Clarendon Press, 2004), 32.
[77] Laura Tabili, "A Homogenous Society?" in *At Home with the Empire*, 53–76.

housing the second greatest number of international students, was sympathetic to reforms that would redistribute the number of overseas students. The other two Inns, however, especially the Inner Temple, remained opposed to such measures. The benchers of the Inner Temple circulated among themselves their own private report containing research on overseas student demographics. According to the Inner Temple report, most overseas students were of European origin and merely domiciled in the colonies. That being the case, the benchers could not support apportioning students between the Inns. It would be "impossible," they argued, "to treat students of [European descent] on a different footing from natives of Great Britain and Ireland."[78] Furthermore, the report maintained, sorting through and apportioning students would be an enormous drain on each Inn's time. The report's ultimate concern was not that the Inns should not discriminate against students of color but that it was highly impractical to do so.

After much cajoling by the Middle Temple, the other Inns finally agreed to alter the Consolidated Regulations in order to create a hierarchy of circumstances by which to privilege applicants for admission. The hierarchy descended as follows:

FIRST: Applicants intending to practice (when qualified) at the bar in England or Ireland or in some part of the British Empire where membership of the English, Scotch or Irish Bars is a necessary qualification for practice.

NEXT: Applicants already qualified to practice (under whatever title) as Advocates in a superior Court of the portion of the British Empire in which they are domiciled.

NEXT: Applicants educated between the ages of 13 and 18 mainly within Great Britain or Ireland.

NEXT: Applicants who are members of an University in Great Britain or Ireland.

NEXT: Other applicants.

On paper, at least, this list of priorities addressed the Middle Temple's concerns about replenishing its bench by allowing them to privilege students who intended to remain in the UK after their call. It also supported the notion that overseas students coming to Britain should have already studied law in some capacity in their countries of origin. It accounted for cultural differences by giving priority to individuals educated in the British Isles. A separate addendum to the regulations, added later that year, allowed overseas students to be called to the bar after keeping eight rather than twelve terms. All of these regulations,

---

[78] IT BEN November 13, 1928.

however, were prefaced by the caveat that the benchers of any Inn could "relax" any of the rules under "special circumstances," in effect allowing each Inn free reign to comply or not as it saw fit.[79] Such a provision would mean that the Middle Temple and Lincoln's Inn would comply with the new regulations, while the Inner Temple and Gray's Inn went about their admission processes as usual. The Middle Temple refused to adopt the changes, feeling that their "difficulties" would not be resolved by the proposed amendments. Further, they worried that the changes would "create a distinction between the subjects of the Crown which is not desirable in the interests of the Empire," and that the regulations would discriminate against "Indians who desire to study ... in this country" in particular.[80]

Conclusion

The Inns of Court faced yet another challenge to their heterogeneity as the makeup of overseas students shifted from white civil servants to native students of color. The societies proved capable of accommodating minor differences in members' dress or diet, but failed to cultivate meaningful relationships between British and colonial students. This failure raised questions for the benchers about how best to take on the (unasked for and, to some degree, unwanted) role of being a central node in the unwieldly network of imperial legal systems. The Inns collaborated with other institutional authorities, most notably the India Office, about how to regulate a group of students increasingly understood to be unassimilable.

The Inns never agreed upon a satisfactory resolution to the overseas student problem. Concerns about overseas students gradually disappeared from the Middle Temple's minutes in the early 1930s, supplanted by worries over "aliens" and refugees from Hitler's Europe, and then by the exigencies of air raids. Indian independence shortly after war's end dramatically reduced the number of Indian students coming to Britain. The numbers of students from other parts of the empire briefly spiked in the immediate postwar period, then similarly declined in the wake of newly formed independent nations throughout the 1960s.[81] Those overseas students who did come to the Inns, particularly students of color, faced unique disadvantages throughout the remainder of the century,

---

[79] IT BEN June 14, 1929.   [80] MT MPA July 16, 1929.
[81] Richard L. Abel, *The Legal Profession in England and Wales* (New York: Blackwell, 1988), 76–79.

particularly in terms of finding pupilage in chambers. Such exclusions represented the spatial logic of discrimination, informally shutting overseas members of the Inns out of spaces critical to professional advancement. A continuation of discriminatory practices beginning earlier in the century, these exclusions did not extend to foreign students alone. As Chapter 6 explores, in the 1920s and 1930s, the Inns denied women law students and barristers professional advantages through official and unofficial spatial regulations designed to marginalize women at the Inns.

6   Women and the Bar

On April 9, 1919, Lincoln's Inn hosted the Union Society of London's Ladies Night debate on whether or not the bar should be opened to women. Those who spoke against the proposition – led by I. A. Symmons, a metropolitan magistrate – claimed that women lacked the requisite masculine capacities to be lawyers, most especially the qualities of judgment and honor.[1] Such an argument rearticulated the logic of inadequate masculinity that underscored other instances of professional exclusion, from Victorian disciplinary cases to contemporaneous inter-war debates about overseas students. But the two participants who spoke in favor of opening the bar refused to argue over women's judgment and honor. Instead, Helena Normanton and Cornelia Sorabji insisted that women needed women lawyers. In fact, both Sorabji and Normanton had attempted to insert themselves into the legal profession to satisfy this need. Sorabji had studied law at Oxford in the 1890s, trained with a firm of London solicitors, then returned to India where she carved out a position for herself as a legal adviser to women in *purdah*. Normanton, a member of the suffragist Women's Freedom League (WFL), had refocused her efforts since getting the vote on entering the legal profession. She published editorials, gave lectures, engaged in debates. She also applied to be a student at the Middle Temple in February 1918, was rejected, then applied a second time in March 1919.[2]

Sorabji and Normanton were not the first women to try for careers in law. Prior to the twentieth century, a handful of women who succeeded as legal professionals had adopted strategies similar to Sorabji, circumventing the need for a call to the bar by finding niche work. In the 1870s, for example, Eliza Orme and Mary Eliza Richardson made careers out of conveyancing, setting up an office on Chancery Lane and taking in work

---

[1] Judith Bourne, *Helena Normanton and the Opening of the Bar to Women* (Sussex: Waterside Press, 2016), 74.
[2] Women's Library 7HLN/A/05.

from sympathetic barristers.[3] Women who espoused Normanton's strategy of confronting the Inns head on met with flat refusal. In 1873, for example, while Orme and Richardson were quietly establishing themselves, Lincoln's Inn denied the petition of ninety-two women who asked permission to attend lectures at the society.[4] When women applied for admission to the Inns, as Christabel Pankhurst did in 1904, the societies cited long-standing custom as prohibiting women from practicing as barristers.[5] In 1903, for example, Gray's Inn denied admission to a female applicant on the grounds that "there was no precedent for ladies being called to the English Bar."[6] Similarly, Normanton explained the Middle Temple's refusal to admit her in 1918, "As [long as] the customary tradition of the four Inns of Court persists no woman may be called to become a barrister."[7] Yet in the wake of the Great War, public opinion increasingly supported expanding women's educational and professional opportunities. Normanton and other women's rights activists continued to campaign for entry, and though the Inns refused to change their policy, Parliament ultimately intervened. The Sex Disqualification (Removal) Act forced the societies to open the bar to women in December 1919. Normanton was admitted to the Middle Temple in 1920, Cornelia Sorabji to Lincoln's Inn in 1922.

The Sex Disqualification (Removal) Act 1919 represented the most direct and significant parliamentary intervention the Inns of Court had ever experienced. As the preceding chapters detail, throughout the nineteenth century, the Inns faced potential parliamentary interference in everything from legal education to municipal governance. Developments like the Victoria Embankment encroached on the Inns' geographic bounds, but they ultimately did not threaten the independent governance of the Inns, nor did they change the fundamental makeup of the societies. In all other matters that came under parliamentary investigation, from ensuring the quality of admitted students and those called to the bar, to providing for the fair governance of the Inns, the societies undertook small, self-directed reforms. When it came to opening the bar to women, however, the benchers firmly refused to act even though

---

[3] Mary Jane Mossman, *The First Women Lawyers*, (Portland, OR: Hart, 2006), 120; Leslie Howsam, "Legal Paperwork and Public Policy: Eliza Orme's Professional Expertise in Late Victorian Britain," in *Precarious Professionals*, ed. Heidi Egginton and Zoë Thomas (London: University of London Press, 2020).

[4] Black Books of Lincoln's Inn, 1873.   [5] Black Books of Lincoln's Inn, 1904.

[6] "Why Women Need Women Lawyers!" *Vote*, November 21, 1919; "Women and the Bar," *Times*, December 3, 1903. Significantly women practiced as barristers in parts of Canada, New Zealand, and Australia as early as 1900. Mossman, *The First Women Lawyers* (Portland, OR: Hart, 2006), 14.

[7] "Women and the Law," *Vote*, March 15, 1918.

failure to do so would mean legislative intervention. The Inns found admitting women to their masculine domain so distasteful that they knowingly waited for outside intervention to force their hand rather than willingly spoil their homosocial preserve.

Once Parliament required the Inns to admit women, the societies took pains to preserve their masculine character by manipulating the built environment and its ties to tradition to marginalize female members. As Timothy Jones argues in his work on the Anglican Church, institutions that could not justify excluding women in terms of their physical or mental abilities appealed to long-standing and ritualistic gendered divisions of space.[8] The Inns and the law courts both relied on the scarcity of spaces like ladies' lavatories or cloakrooms to discourage women from joining. Moreover, the societies debated and enacted policies restricting women's presence in or use of key spaces of social interaction and professional development, such as the hall. In this regard, the societies went one step further than in their approach to overseas students: the Inns never officially segregated students on the basis of race or ethnicity, but at least one of the Inns established a formal policy to keep women separate from men.

Another major difference between the experiences of women and overseas students at the Inns lay in the ratios of these groups to the rest of the membership. Overseas members numbered in the hundreds; they may have been unwelcome, but they were impossible to ignore. The number of women at the Inns, by contrast, was miniscule. In 1920, for example, the Middle Temple admitted 33 women and 330 men, and the other three Inns combined took only thirteen women. Throughout the interwar period, these numbers fluctuated only slightly: between 1919 and 1939, women represented no more than 4 percent of the Inns' total admissions.[9] The deeply uneven ratio of men to women at the Inns not only ensured the societies' enduring masculine character, it also allowed agnostic male members to play ostrich in regard to women's presence at the Inns. Almost none of the histories of legal London discussed in Chapter 2, for example, acknowledged women's admission to the bar, even in sections devoted to the present rather than the past.

If some members of the bar were keen to minimize women's presence, the popular press had other ideas. Indeed, the attention the media

---

[8] Timothy Jones, "Unduly Conscious of Her Sex," *Women's History Review* (2012); see also Lucy Delap, "Conservative Values," in *Brave New World* (London: University of London, 2011); Alison Light, *Forever England* (London: Routledge, 1991).

[9] Richard L. Abel, *The Legal Profession in England and Wales* (Oxford: Basil Blackwell, 1988), 79–85; Patrick Polden, "Portia's Progress," *International Journal of the Legal Profession* 12 (2005): 295, 302, 314.

devoted to women's studentship and early careers magnified their presence at the Inns. The press acted as a representational subsidiary for debating women's place in the legal profession and forming popular attitudes about lady barristers. Newspapers were vociferous, if ultimately ambivalent, interlocutors in women's introduction to the bar. In his study of the interwar press, Adrian Bingham argues that editors, trying to please male and female audiences and raise advertising revenue from booming industries such as fashion, printed stories with conflicting messages and appeal.[10] After World War I, as before, suffragist papers such as the *Vote* and the *Common Cause* agitated for women's entry to the closed professions as well as for the franchise. At the same time, legal journals and the popular press, eager to garner copy from the women's movement, began to weigh in on women's place at the bar. Papers, whether Liberal or Conservative, often caricatured the lady barrister and mocked the retrograde Inns in the same column. Such satirical depictions appealed to a broad readership and sold more copies than columns that supported or condemned women's ambitions outright.

In addition to representations of women at the bar, this chapter traces various strategies women enacted to navigate the resolutely masculine legal profession. As previous chapters demonstrate, at the Inns a nexus of characteristics conferred insider and outsider status. For women, members of the Inns considered not only gender but also race, social connections, and political affiliation. The importance of any one of these characteristics fluctuated with context and could be highlighted or minimized by women themselves or other members of the societies in order to foster inclusion or further marginalize female members. The chapter departs from others in this book in that it relies heavily on two extended case studies. Cornelia Sorabji and Helena Normanton both preserved extensive archives; their letters, diaries, newspaper clippings, and other personal papers provide some of the richest accounts of women's experiences at the Inns. Furthermore, the two represented starkly different iterations of the female barrister, in terms of background, ethnicity, class, social connections, politics, age, and disposition. Sorabji spent her career working around barriers, Normanton spent hers charging directly at them. Sorabji, politically Conservative, invested in social hierarchies, and willing to accord herself with the status quo, described her time at Lincoln's Inn as marked by kindness and support. Meanwhile Normanton – active in public life, outspoken, flouting convention – came into her studentship with an adversarial attitude and an unwillingness to

---

[10] Adrian Bingham, *Gender, Modernity, and the Popular Press in Inter-war Britain* (New York: Clarendon Press, 2004).

demur. Her difficulties with the Inns appear in her own personal papers, in the Middle Temple's records, and in the press. No other woman law student left a similar trail of petitions, debates, and disciplinary hearings.

Significantly, while this chapter considers Sorabji and Normanton as opposite poles on a strategic spectrum, it does not hold either as representative of most women at the bar. The two were both exceptional, not least because they went on to practice law – most women law students did not. Of all the women admitted to the Inns in the interwar period, just under two-thirds were called to the bar. Even fewer pursued legal careers; it is possible that during the interwar period fewer than twenty women made a living exclusively from professional practice.[11] Why? The Inns did not enforce a marriage bar, as did professions like teaching, but nevertheless interwar women who married faced pressure to end their careers.[12] (Sorabji, for example, remained single; Normanton bucked the trend, but her nuptials drew considerable negative attention.) Women who tried to establish legal practices could find it difficult to get briefs from solicitors, to find a place in chambers, and to win over law clerks who distributed work. They had to navigate not only the homosocial world of the Inns but also that of the circuit messes connected to the assize courts. These later associations – more fiercely fraternal than even the Inns of Court – were under no obligations to admit women, and those which did still maintained cultures of carousing and casual misogyny in which women might feel particularly unwelcome.[13]

For women who did try to practice, a multitude of factors undergirded their success. The letters and diaries of Cornelia Sorabji, for example, highlight the importance of social networks. Sorabji took advantage of elite patronage to fund her Oxford education and carve out a legal career in the 1890s. These same connections supported her when she finally joined Lincoln's Inn in the 1920s. Male law students routinely exploited Oxbridge connections, but few women were in positions to do the same. Sorabji also highlights the complexity of the relationship between women and colonial subjects at the Inns, as well as the complexity of being a

---

[11] Abel, *The Legal Profession in England and Wales*, 79–85; Polden, "Portia's Progress," 295, 302, 314.

[12] Gerry Holloway, *Women and Work in Britain since 1840* (London: Routledge, 2007); Alison Oram, *Women Teachers and Feminist Politics, 1900–39* (Manchester: Manchester University Press, 1996); Dina Copelman, *London's Women Teachers: Gender, Class and Feminism 1870–1930* (London: Routledge, 1996); Mary Jane Mossman, "'The Law as a Profession for Women': A Century of Progress?" *Australian Feminist Law Journal* 30: 1 (2009): 134; Polden, "Portia's Progress," 328.

[13] Polden, "Portia's Progress," 325; Anne Logan, *Feminism and Criminal Justice* (New York: Palgrave, 2008), 84–85.

person at the intersection of these two categories.[14] Previous chapters of this book examined colonial subjects, particularly Indian students, whose nationalism clashed with the ideological priorities of the societies. Sorabji's conservative politics, however, made her extremely palatable to the Inns of Court – far more so, in fact, than did Normanton's liberal feminism. Moreover, Sorabji's race marked her as distinct from those around her, but in ways that only sometimes made her an outsider. For example, Sorabji was not likely to sit with English students at dinners in hall during term, but on Grand Night, because of the work she was doing for *purdah* women, she was introduced to the queen. Where other women law students faced derision because of their intention to compete with men for work, Sorabji's intention to practice in India nullified this threat.

For her part, Normanton represents a generation of women whose advocacy for suffrage and expansion of rights before and during World War I met with success in the interwar period. Normanton and other women's early efforts to be admitted to the Inns of Court grew in tandem with feminist agitation for the vote, as women's groups demanded not only suffrage but also professional and economic parity. Feminists campaigned to open some of the last remaining "gentlemanly" professions to women: Parliament, the church, and law.[15] Once the bar was open, many of the women who joined the Inns of Court in the 1920s and 1930s – like Cornelia Sorabji – did not share the feminist commitments of Normanton and her colleagues. This chapter nevertheless relies on Normanton's archive to complicate declension narratives of interwar feminism, contending that while some women law students tacitly accepted the Inns' existing culture, this did not preclude others, like Normanton, from pursing active feminist agendas.[16]

---

[14] Antoinette Burton, *At the Heart of the Empire*, (Berkeley: University of California Press, 1998), 114.

[15] Jenny Daggers, "The Victorian Female Civilising Mission and Women's Aspirations towards Priesthood in the Church of England," *Women's History Review* 10: 4 (2001): 651–670; Carol Dyhouse, "Women Students and the London Medical Schools, 1914–39: The Anatomy of a Masculine Culture," *Gender and History* 10: 1 (1998): 110–132; Anne Logan, "Professionalism and the Impact of England's First Women Justices, 1920–1950," *Historical Journal* 49: 3 (2006): 833–850; Lucy Delap, "Conservative Values Anglicans and the Gender Order in Inter-war Britain," in *Brave New World* (London: University of London, 2011), 149–168; Timothy Jones, "'Unduly Conscious of Her Sex': Priesthood, Female Bodies, and Sacred Space in the Church of England," *Women's History Review* 21: 4 (2012): 639–655.

[16] Brian Harrison, *Prudent Revolutionaries* (New York: Clarendon Press, 1987); Johanna Alberti, "Keeping the Candle Burning: Some British Feminists between Two Wars," in *Suffrage and beyond International Feminist Perspectives*, ed. Caroline Daley and Melanie Nolan (New York: New York University Press, 1994), 295–312; Susan Kingsley Kent,

Normanton's fight to enter and practice at the bar also highlights the issue of self-representation in the interwar period. Women's achievements, bodies, and fashion attracted national attention, but how much room did this leave women to cultivate their own public persona? Whereas Sorabji eschewed press attention, Normanton maintained a long but ambivalent relationship with the press. Media attention could result in unwanted notoriety; nonetheless, Normanton relied on publicity to establish her reputation and maintain her status as a public figure. Furthermore, to sidestep Inn-imposed injunctions against self-advertising, she had to court the press without seeming to, leaving little recourse against objectionable copy. Together, personal papers, institutional records, and newspaper articles offer a multifaceted view of the meanings of and possibilities for women professionals in the interwar period, and more broadly reveal the spatial underpinnings of gendered institutions.

Women and the Legal Profession before World War I

By the early twentieth century, women in other parts of the Anglophone world, as well as on the continent, had made inroads into their respective legal professions. Indeed, feminist publications like the *Vote* pointed to women's successes around the globe, featuring stories on women lawyers in Russia, France, the United States, Canada, and New Zealand.[17] Yet women in the UK, though they could take university law degrees, remained excluded from professional practice as barristers and solicitors by the Inns of Court and the Law Society. Instead, women operated at what feminist legal historian Mary Jane Mossman has termed "'the boundaries' of law."[18] Mossman deploys this metaphorical phrase to describe women who found legal work for which they did not need to qualify as barristers or solicitors, such as conveyancing, patent work, and estates. Mossman's phrase is particularly apt, because these women also

---

Making Peace (Princeton: Princeton University Press, 1993); Harold L. Smith, Pat Thane, and Esther Breitenbach have made convincing challenges to these assertions. Harold L. Smith, *The British Women's Suffrage Campaign 1866–1928* (Harlow: Pearson, 2007); Pat Thane and Esther Breitenbach, *Women and Citizenship in Britain and Ireland in the Twentieth Century* (London: Continuum, 2010).

[17] "Russian Woman Lawyer," *Vote*, November 25, 1909; "The Woman Lawyer," *Vote*, August 12, 1911; "Woman's Powers. The Idea of a French Woman Barrister," *Vote*, December 16, 1911; "Women Barristers in New Zealand," *Vote*, March 7, 1913; "The Success of a Woman Judge," *Vote*, March 28, 1913; "Madame – as Lawyer," *Vote*, March 6, 1914; "Maitre Marie Vérone," *Vote*, February 12, 1915.

[18] Mossman, "'The Law as a Profession for Women': A Century of Progress?" 138.

operated at the material boundaries of legal London. In 1875, Eliza Orme and Mary Richardson, for example, moved their conveyancing offices from Lincoln's Inn to Chancery Lane in order to "excite less attention" than they had in chambers at the all-male society.[19]

Cornelia Sorabji's professional practice, prior to the 1920s, stands as an example, as Mossman notes, of another woman at the "boundaries" of law. What's more, her experiences preparing for a career in law highlight the spatial constraints on women in the legal profession. Sorabji also indicates the relatively small scale of women's interventions into the profession prior to the turn of the century. Sorabji exploited individual connections and asked for personal exceptions to further her career, but did not attempt to clear barriers for subsequent women. Wary of press attention, she published journal articles on the condition of India and Indian women, but never advocated for women's admission to the Inns of Court or Law Society. When she gave speeches on the plight of women in *purdah* to women's philanthropic organizations like the YWCA, she did not frame the need for women lawyers as an end unto itself, but as a Christian and imperial imperative.[20] Such Christian philanthropy fell well within the bounds of elite respectability, unlike equal rights feminism – indeed, Sorabji took pains to distinguish herself from "what is called 'a shrieking sister.'"[21] Sorabji was also no doubt aware that the women who had managed successful incursions into the profession before her were ones who had placed themselves in positions of amity rather than enmity.

Sorabji's journey into the legal profession was launched by her particular familial circumstances and intellectual promise and the social connections she forged as a result. Sorabji grew up in Poona, a large city in western India, in a Christian family. Both of her parents were predisposed to British values and a British way of life.[22] Sorabji was instilled with a sense of pride for her Parsi heritage, but she and her siblings were, as she put it, "brought up English." Her father, a missionary, and her mother, the head of a girls' high school, both valued education, and they supported Sorabji in unconventional steps toward furthering her own. Sorabji was the first woman student matriculated at Deccan College (part of the University of Bombay), where she placed first in a degree examination that entitled her to a government scholarship at a British

---

[19] London School of Economics Eliza Orme to Helen Taylor, August 3, 1875, Mill-Taylor item 81, as quoted in Leslie Howsam, "Legal Paperwork and Public Policy," 3.

[20] For example, see "Our Correspondence," *Glasgow Herald*, April 24, 1890.

[21] MSS Eur 165/194 – Sorabji's reminiscences of Benjamin Jowett 1893, 1903; MSS Eur F 165/17 – Letters to Lady Hobhouse 1900–1905.

[22] Cornelia Sorabji, *Opening Doors*, (London: IB Taurus, 2010), 8.

university. The college refused to give the scholarship to a woman, but Sorabji received a "substituted scholarship" via the philanthropic influences of Lord and Lady Hobhouse – he a former law member of the Governor General's Council in India and both patrons of Indian women's education – and Madeleine Shaw-Lefevre, the principle of Somerville Hall, Oxford. A hefty donation from the Hobhouses and generous contributions from a list of other subscribers made possible the "English adventure" that would be Sorabji's Oxford education.[23]

For women to be successful even at the boundaries of the law required the help of sympathetic allies inside and outside the profession. The Hobhouses, who remained in touch with Sorabji for the rest of their lives, became the first critical node in a social network of British elite that would partly chart the course of her future. It was Madeleine Shaw-Lefevre – the outgoing principal of Somerville College, who convinced Sorabji that she should not study medicine, as she had originally intended – and Miss Maitland, incoming principal, who pointed her toward law.[24] Attracted to the possibility of working as a "lady legal [commissioner] ... taking evidence from zenana residents," Sorabji shifted her course of study.[25] When she proposed reading for a Bachelor of Civil Law (BCL), a degree usually reserved for barristers with years of practice under their belts, and which no woman at Oxford had read for, her mentor, Benjamin Jowett, master of Balliol, did not say no. Instead, he had her sit for the Indian Civil Service Law Course, an examination that no less than Courtney Ilbert (former counsel to the Viceroy, then parliamentary counsel to treasury) marked "very high." Having thus proved her potential, Sorabji was granted permission to read for the BCL.[26] She received tutelage from several Oxford professors, including legal luminary A. V. Dicey, whom Sorabji described as "very nice" and "very kind."[27] When the time came to take the examination, however, the London examiner refused to evaluate a woman. It ultimately required the intervention of the vice-chancellor of Oxford and an official university decree to allow Sorabji to sit for the exam. Sorabji passed with a third in 1892, though Oxford did not allow women

[23] Sorabji, *India Calling*, 24–25; Burton, *At the Heart of the Empire*, 110–111.

[24] As Antoinette Burton notes, Shaw-Lefevre's reasons were pragmatic: the course could not be completed in Oxford, nor was there adequate funding for her to pursue it in London. *At the Heart of the Empire*, 123.

[25] Burton, *At the Heart of the Empire*, 133, 124–125.   [26] Sorabji, *India Calling*, 28–29.

[27] MSS Eur 165/194 – Sorabji's reminiscences of Benjamin Jowett 1893, 190. Indeed, Sorabji seems to have had an almost filial relationship with the "shy" Dicey. She gave him slippers, which he praised, and stuck around for tea after her lessons, getting to know both Dicey and his wife.

to take degrees until after World War I. Sorabji formally took hers in 1922.[28]

In trying to launch her career, Sorabji's intentions to help women in *purdah* won her some degree of sympathy and assistance, but did not obliterate prejudice against her. Indeed, Sorabji lost various positions, including a Hyderabad commissionership and a Madras inspectorship, to English women, despite the fact that "none of these Ladies … [knew] Anything about India."[29] Hoping it might give her a leg up, the Hobhouses suggested Sorabji "try and get some training in the practice of Law."[30] The parents of a friend from Somerville had a solicitor son-in-law, and their daughter Lily contacted him to ask if his firm would take on Sorabji as a clerk. Lily Bruce acknowledged that her brother-in-law, Henry Whatley, might have to "overcome [his] partners' prejudices," though she did not specify prejudices against women, Indians, or both. Notably, Bruce's letter highlighted rather than minimized Sorabji's race and gender, insisting that if a firm did not take Sorabji on, "her career would be more or less spoilt – & the poor Zenana women [will] have to continue in the old way." In underscoring Sorabji's intention to work with zenana women, Bruce emphasized that Sorabji would be working in India – neutralizing any threat of the Indian student who overstayed their welcome in the UK – and that she would work with a population whose seclusion from men would not draw clients away from male solicitors. Bruce also vouched for Sorabji's character, alleviating fears stemming from stereotypes of ill-mannered or intractable Indians. She assured her brother-in-law that Sorabji was "very amiable & good-tempered – nothing oriental about her except her appearance."[31] The numbers of Indian students in Britain in the 1890s were growing, but few of them remained in the country after completing their training, and firms and chambers were reluctant to take on the ones who did. If the firm took on Sorabji, she would likely be one of the only people of color its employees would interact with on a daily basis.

Perhaps the partners found Bruce's logic persuasive; perhaps Whatley wished to ingratiate himself to his in-laws. Either way, the firm, Lee & Pemberton, agreed to take on Sorabji for six months at the adjusted fee of fifty guineas, which Lord Hobhouse paid.[32] Sorabji did not seem put out that this expensive training would not result in qualification. Instead,

---

[28] Sorabji, *India Calling*, 30.
[29] MSS EUR F.165/6 – Letters to Family January–July 1892.
[30] Sorabji, *India Calling*, 34.
[31] MSS Eur 165/19 – Letters to Henry A. Whatley of Lee & Pemberton.
[32] Ibid. The usual fee was 300 guineas.

Sorabji expressed gratitude and "joy" about her position with the firm. On her first day she wrote home, "It feels so swell being an articled clerk – and working in Lincoln's Inn Fields with that excellent Lee & Pemberton's."[33] "Excellent" was indeed an appropriate description: Lee & Pemberton's long-standing practice counted among their clients Lincoln's Inn itself. Sorabji's school chum had brokered her a position with one of the most prestigious firms in the city.

Sorabji's clerkship brought her into the all-male world of Lincoln's Inn, an environment she navigated by cultivating affective, almost filial relationships with her superiors. She referred to the firm's partners as her "Chiefs," which became a playful term of endearment. When Sorabji had to remain home with a cold, a few of the partners sent her a get-well card, saying "All your 'Chiefs' … miss you very much. Come back to us soon. We cannot get the work done at all."[34] The warmth of these paternal or avuncular sentiments was in keeping with the principal–clerk relationship, which had "a strong kin character."[35] The card's heightened playfulness in tone, however – the use of the nickname "Chiefs" in scare quotes, the hyperbole about not getting work done – signaled an affect of cuteness that, as Sianne Ngai argues, was "deeply associated with the infantile, the feminine, and the unthreatening." Affective cuteness "exaggerate[d] social difference."[36] Such a tone was rare in letters between male superiors and subordinates, but prevalent in communications between male bosses and female employees like stenographers and secretaries.[37] Yet in letters to Whatley, Sorabji embraced this language of cuteness, frequently describing herself in the diminutive, "very little & small & ignorant." Sorabji's self-deprecation – she often referred to herself as a "nuisance," and once as "so abjectly stupid" – undermined her extraordinary achievements and placed her in a position of perpetual deference and dependence.[38] Such a rhetorical strategy would have been anathema to champions of women's equality, but likely helped Sorabji minimize resistance to her incursion into male domain.

At Lee & Pemberton, paternal concern for Sorabji took a particularly spatial dimension, foreshadowing later spatial separations that the Inns of Court would undertake when forced to admit women to the bar. In their

---

[33] MSS Eur F 165/7 – Letters to Family August–December 1892.   [34] Ibid.

[35] Michael Burrage, "From a Gentlemen's to a Public Profession: Status and Politics in the History of English Solicitors," *International Journal of the Legal Profession* (1996): 53.

[36] Sianne Ngai, *Our Aesthetic Categories*, (Cambridge, MA: Harvard University Press, 2012), 59.

[37] Leah Price, "Stenographic Masculinity," in *Literary Secretaries/Secretarial Culture*, ed. Leah Price and Pamela Thurschwell (London: Routledge, 2005), 32–47.

[38] MSS Eur 165/19 – Letters to Henry A. Whatley of Lee & Pemberton.

letter agreeing to take Sorabji on, the partners specified, "We think it will be a sine qua non that you should have a separate room, to [work] in at our office."[39] Formalizing this arrangement in writing prior to Sorabji's start at the office suggests a deep concern with the presence of women's bodies in male spaces. Part of this concern appeared rooted in anxieties about proximity. As Sorabji described it, all the other male clerks worked in "one small room hoisted on stools eight feet high." To have Sorabji in such close quarters with a group of men would not have been proprietous, nor would be asking her to mount a stool. Instead, the firm outfitted "such a pretty room" for her, with "oak paneling & pretty yellow paper." Beyond the desire for decorum, the firm's partners seemed especially concerned with Sorabji's comfort, suggesting underlying assumptions about female frailty. Sorabji arrived at work one day to find a note from Whatley reading, "Please come & sit in my room" – he had discovered something wrong with the chimney in her room and "was afraid the room wd [*sic*] not be warm enough for [her]." One suspects a malfunctioning chimney in the room of the male clerks would not have caused similar preoccupation.

Much like the infantilizing rhetoric in communications with the partners, concern for Sorabji's comfort cut two ways. By her own account, Sorabji learned the same skills as the male clerks: she practiced draftsmanship and conveyancing, attended court, learnt estate administration and how to interview clients.[40] Yet at the firm, as at the Inns, legal learning was only one component of legal culture. As Michael Burrage argues, forcing clerks to undergo a period of hardship and drudgery built among them an *esprit de corps*.[41] Physically separating Sorabji meant that even if she undertook the same tasks as the male clerks, she was not undergoing the fundamental experiences – in this case, the physical discomfort of being cold – that built relationships among members of the profession. On the other hand, Sorabji's goal was not to secure for herself equal standing in the eyes of her future colleagues. Indeed, Sorabji considered it fortunate to receive gendered special treatment. She described the other clerks as "looking shy & miserable & dull" in their tiny room, declaring, "I did not envy them their sex. If I'd been a man clerk I'd have fared likewise."[42] Later women at the bar would regard spatial separation as a barrier to legal learning or form of inequality, but for Sorabji, these divisions were welcome – perhaps even expected – acknowledgments of the dictates of her gender.

---

[39] Ibid.   [40] Sorabji, *India Calling*, 35.
[41] Burrage, "From a Gentlemen's to a Public Profession," 54.
[42] MSS Eur F 165/7 – Letters to Family August–December 1892.

Sorabji may also have appreciated being separated from the other clerks because, however kindly she was treated by the partners, she may not have received such a warm reception from her supposed peers. The partners had nothing to lose by admitting a woman to train with them for six months, but for the junior clerks, sharing the same status as a woman may have reduced the overall prestige of their position. To be sure, this damage would have been mitigated by the fact that they could eventually become solicitors while Sorabji could not. Nevertheless, Sorabji wrote home of very few interactions with the other clerks, and those she detailed involved some degree of wariness on her part. For example, she described an encounter with a clerk who, "with many apologies" and requests to "forgive his curiosity," asked Sorabji for a copy of the magazine *Nineteenth Century* containing an article she had authored. Sorabji claimed that it would have been "affectation to refuse" his request, but she was haunted by "visions of the Clerks upstairs perhaps jeering over it."[43] It is impossible to know whether the clerks actually mocked Sorabji behind her back, but that Sorabji feared this possibility speaks to the degree to which she felt herself an outsider from them.

When Sorabji finally returned to India after finishing her time in chambers with Lee & Pemberton, she faced a certain degree of disappointment: after living (relatively) independently and being treated as exceptional, she now was once again in her parents' household. She faced a series of professional closed doors, followed by a series of hoops to jump through. In addition to her Bombay BA, Oxford BCL, and the solicitor's certificate from her training with Lee & Pemberton, Sorabji had to pass yet another examination, the Bombay Bachelor of Laws, which should have qualified her to practice as a vakil. Even then her admission to practice in the courts was contingent and not universal. She spent several years in a stressful limbo, patching together work, relying on the advice and encouragement of well-placed friends to find a more secure trajectory. Ultimately it took a campaign on the part of Sorabji and her allies to create a special position – legal adviser at the Court of Wards, under the purview of the Board of Revenue – for Sorabji to find steady work providing legal counsel to *purdahnashins*. This was an effort some ten years in the making, and with no lesser a personage than Princess Louise, granddaughter of Victoria, backing Sorabji.[44]

After finally securing the ICS position, Sorabji considered her story a success. She had not been allowed to practice as a solicitor; she had not been allowed to practice as a barrister; sometimes she had even been

---

[43] Ibid.   [44] Sorabji, *Opening Doors*, 130.

prohibited from practicing as a vakil. But her stated aim was never to explode the barriers barring women from these professions. She had intended to use her law degree to provide legal assistance to *purdahnashins*, and she was now employed by the government to do just that. True, it would be virtually impossible for any other women to follow in her footsteps, but Antoinette Burton has postulated that Sorabji preferred to maintain her exceptionality.[45]

Helena Normanton took a much different view.

Women and the Legal Profession after World War I

Broadly speaking, Normanton and Sorabji both understood female legal professionals as critical to righting economic and other injustices in women's personal and professional lives. Unlike Sorabji, however, Normanton was an outspoken suffragist and active member of the WFL.[46] Her political activity focused on empowering women to "plunge ever more fully into the public and economic stream of affairs" and, by so doing, benefit all women.[47] Growing up in a Brighton boarding house, Normanton watched her widowed mother support a family without male help. A promising student, Normanton won a scholarship to a Brighton grammar school and then a place at a Liverpool teachers' training college. She read for a history degree at London University and studied French language, literature, and history at Dijon University. Thereafter she supported herself by working as a tutor and lecturing at Glasgow and London Universities.[48] As a single professional woman, Normanton placed great weight on women's economic and legal independence. She frequently contributed to the *Vote*, press organ of the WFL as well as many of London's daily presses. She supported and corresponded with a number of women's unions and associations, particularly those composed of women teachers.[49] Her 1914 pamphlet "Sex Differentiation in Salary" advocated equal pay for equal work, emphasizing the plight of female breadwinners whose numbers increased due to wartime conditions.

---

[45] Burton, *At the Heart of the Empire*, 145.

[46] MSS Eur F 165/17 – Letters to Lady Hobhouse 1900–1905; Burton, *At the Heart of Empire*, 141.

[47] Helena Normanton, *Everyday Law for Women* (London: Ivor Nicholson and Watson, 1932), ix.

[48] Joanne Workman, "Normanton, Helena Florence (1882–1957)," in *Oxford Dictionary of National Biography* (Oxford: Oxford University Press, 2011), https://doi.org/10.1093/ref:odnb/39091 (accessed December 15, 2023).

[49] Women's Library 7HLN/A/05, 7HLN/A/06.

Normanton's frequent lectures and articles in the *Vote* and other papers focused on the necessity of opening both sides of the legal profession, barrister and solicitor, to women. Her arguments were similar to those of other pre- and postwar equal-rights feminists. Prohibiting women from practice, she asserted, did not serve the public interest. It discouraged wronged women from seeking out legal rather than extralegal redress. It prevented individuals with a talent for law from contributing to their nation.[50] Female teachers and civil servants, who had already made inroads for women's rights, could never fully press for equal opportunities as long as they could not hire female legal advisers. Similarly, Normanton spoke of the negative consequences of impeding laboring women's ability to consult with female counsel "in intimate and utter confidence."[51] Women would not realize their full legal rights or redresses as long as they had to endure the embarrassment of confiding intimate harms to male legal professionals.

Whereas Sorabji accepted the Inns of Court as an all-male preserve – "I'm not going to practice as a Barrister … I am not 'Called' and cannot be" – Normanton made herself a metaphorical battering ram at the Inns' gates, first petitioning the Middle Temple for admission in 1918.[52] The women's differing strategies for entering the legal profession stemmed from a variety of factors. Conservative Sorabji had greater respect for tradition and hierarchy, and she often let the authority figures in her life open the doors to the opportunities she would pioneer. The more-than-twenty-five-year difference between their forays into the profession is also significant. In the early 1890s when Sorabji was beginning her career, women were just beginning to make inroads into the professions and to agitate for better legal protections and political rights. To be sure, they had some successes – for instance, the existence of Oxbridge women's colleges, like Somerville. Legally, the 1870 and 1882 Married Women's Property Acts released wives from the laws of coverture, declaring all wages and property acquired by women a separate estate from that of their husbands. But women still could not take degrees from any institutions of higher learning; they could not vote, sit on juries or serve as justices of the peace. In 1918, when Helena Normanton petitioned the Middle Temple, British women still faced many legal inequalities, but were no longer – at least not entirely – legally incapacitated. After World

---

[50] Helena Normanton, "Women and the Law," *Vote*, March 15, 1918.
[51] Helena Normanton, "Oppose Lawyers Who Oppose Women as Lawyers," *Vote*, December 6, 1918; "Women and the Law," *Vote*, May 30, 1919; "Why Women Need Women Lawyers!" *Vote*, November 21, 1919.
[52] MSS EUR F.165/6 – Letters to Family January–July 1892.

War I, and less than three weeks before Normanton submitted her petition, the 1918 Representation of the People Act enfranchised English women over the age of thirty meeting minimum property requirements. By the terms of this Act, a significant number of women, though deliberately less than half the voting population, could make their opinions felt at the ballot box.[53] Normanton encouraged women to vote strategically for women's benefit. In an editorial in the *Vote* from December 1918, she enjoined readers to "Oppose Lawyers Who Oppose Women as Lawyers."[54]

Women in early twentieth-century Britain also enjoyed more cultural support for their professional advances than had their Victorian counterparts. Newspapers dedicated to the legal profession, such as the *Law Times*, frequently reported on women's issues and expressed support for moderate suffragist campaigners in the years preceding the Great War.[55] Contributors did not explicitly extend this approbation to women entering the legal profession, but neither did they raise opposition to the idea until war altered professional demographics. With the obituaries of young lawyers overflowing the pages of the *Law Times* and a population of nonmembers filling newly vacant chambers at the Inns, one anonymous 1917 contributor stated that "with regard to the admission of women to practice as barristers, ... the present time is hardly opportune – to use a no stronger expression." Another unsigned article accused women who sought entry to the bar of trying to "take advantage of the absence of those who have sacrificed their existing positions or future careers to uphold the cause of this country."[56] After the war, however, with demobilization under way and surviving members trickling back into the Inns, the legal press became more receptive to opening the bar to women. Women had not only assumed many new occupations during the war, but they were widely viewed as having sustained the

---

[53] Cheryl Law, *Suffrage and Power* (New York: St. Martin's Press, 1997), 34.

[54] Normanton, "Oppose Lawyers Who Oppose Women as Lawyers."

[55] Using 1910 as an example: "Is Forcible Feeding Justifiable," *Law Times*, February 5, 1910; "Occasional Notes," *Law Times*, March 12, May 7, June 25, July 9, August 6, August 27, September 3, September 24, October 8, November 5, December 10, 1910; "Women Suffrage Measures in America," *Law Times*, June 4, 1910.

[56] "Bar Meeting," *Law Times*, January 6, 1917; "Admission of Women," *Law Times*, July 20, 1918. See also, "Women and the Bar Meeting," *Law Times*, January 20, 1917; "Admission of Women to the Bar," January 27, 1917; "Women as Solicitors," *Law Times*, February 3, 1917; "Women as Solicitors," *Law Times*, February 24, 1917; "Women as Solicitors," *Law Times*, March 10, 1917; "Women as Solicitors," *Law Times*, March 17, 1917; "The Profession during the War," *Law Times*, July 14, 1917; "1917," *Law Times*, December 29, 1917; "Women and the Law," *Law Times*, March 23, 1918; "Admission of Women," *Law Times*, July 20, 1918.

efforts of the home front. In keeping with a popular argument regarding female suffrage, some articles in the legal press claimed that women had proved their worth and deserved a just reward. Given "the facts of the last four years," one correspondent to the *Law Times* wrote in 1919, "The time is arriving when the doors of the Profession should be opened to all persons irrespective of sex."[57]

The Inns of Court, institutions which had defined themselves as exclusive and masculine from the beginning of their 600-year existence, were not easily swayed by the dictates of popular opinion, however. At a meeting of benchers in 1918, the Middle Temple treasurer reiterated the importance of precedent for continuing to exclude women from the society. "The question of the admission of women to [the Inns] was settled," he explained, "on the principle that their legal incapacity appeared from the uninterrupted usage of many centuries ... and this principle ... is the basis upon which numberless rights rest[;] indeed the whole body of the Common Law has no other foundation."[58] Women could not be called to the bar, he argued, because historically women had not been called to the bar. To question this precedent would be akin to questioning the foundation of the English legal system. The treasurer further referred to the 1913 case of *Bebb v. Law Society*, in which four women applied to sit for the solicitors' examination and were refused. The women appealed the case, but the presiding judge upheld the Law Society's decision, maintaining that women were not "persons" according to the meaning of the 1843 Solicitors Act.[59] Common Law, affirmed by the decision of an appellate court justice, clearly excluded women from the legal profession. The society rejected Normanton's application.

In February 1918, after receiving the society's rejection, Normanton sent a petition against the benchers' decision to the lord chancellor and the judges of the High Court. Together these bodies constituted a tribunal of appeals. Lord Chancellor Finlay ignored Normanton's appeal, as did his successor the following year, Lord Birkenhead. By the time Normanton wrote to the lord chancellor reminding him of her petition, he had already begun to push through parliament a short but significant bill that would prohibit the disqualification of a person "by sex or

---

[57] "Women and the Law," *Law Times*, February 1, 1919; "Women and the Law," *Law Times*, March 15, 1919; "Women and the Law," *Law Times*, March 29, 1919; "Women and the Profession," *Law Times*, April 5, 1919; "Admission of Women as Solicitors," *Law Times*, April 5, 1919; "Barristers and Solicitors (Qualification of Women) Bill," *Law Times*, July 5, 1919.

[58] MT MPA February 21, 1918.

[59] "Women as Solicitors," *Law Times*, March 10, 1917.

marriage" from "carrying on any civil or professional vocation." Not especially sympathetic to women's rights, Lord Birkenhead acted to preempt the passage of a similar bill put forward by the Labour Party. The latter legislation would have allowed women to hold civil and professional offices, but also to vote at the age of twenty-one and to sit as peeresses in the House of Lords. The lord chancellor's bill relieved the pressure to open the professions without altering the ratio of male-to-female voters or opening the Lords to women.[60] For her part, Normanton said curiously little for or against either party's bill. A letter to the director general of the BBC thirty years later revealed that the bills may have run contrary to Normanton's sense of her own importance. She cast herself as poised to open the legal profession to women single-handedly, until legislation made her appeal to the lord chancellor disappointingly unnecessary.[61]

Aware that Lord Birkenhead's bill was very likely to pass, in January 1919 a joint committee of the four Inns of Court met to discuss the "desirability and the legality of women being admitted as Students and called to the Bar."[62] The benchers' worries were threefold. Allowing women to become members of the Inns would disrupt six centuries of tradition, highly distressing for institutions founded almost exclusively on precedent. Further, having their hands forced by parliamentary legislation was anathema to the benchers, who preferred to view their authority over their societies as extra-governmental. If the legislation passed, the societies also needed to prepare for the material reality of women joining the Inns. Just as Lee & Pemberton had concerned themselves with the spatial dynamics of Sorabji's tenure in their office, so the Inns of Court had to confront this problem on a grander scale. Would women take chambers? Dine together or separately from men in hall? Where would the societies fit a ladies' lavatory? Throughout the nineteenth century, the benchers had forestalled state intervention through self-initiated reform.[63] Yet at their February meeting, the benchers refused to act.

---

[60] Sex Disqualification (Removal) Act 1919, 9 & 10 Geo 5, c. 71. F. A. R.; Bennion, "The Sex Disqualification (Removal) Act – 60 Inglorious Years," *New Law Journal*, December 13, 1979, 1240–1241; Sandra Fredman, *Women and the Law* (Oxford: Oxford University Press, 2002), 65; Charles R. Epp, *The Rights Revolution: Lawyers, Activists, and Supreme Courts in Comparative Perspective* (Chicago: The University of Chicago Press, 1998), 123.

[61] Helena Normanton, "Oppose Lawyers Who Oppose Women as Lawyers," *Vote*, December 6, 1918; Women's Library 7/HLN/A/17 October 28, 1952.

[62] MT MPA January 16, 1919.

[63] Daniel Duman, *The English and Colonial Bars* (London: Croom Helm, 1983), 55–68; William Cornish, J. Stuart Anderson, Ray Cocks, Michael Lobban, Patrick Polden, and Keith Smith, *The Oxford History of the Laws of England, Vol. XII* (Oxford: Oxford

The societies decided to resist women's presence until coercive legislation mandated otherwise.[64]

To the disappointment of the benchers, Parliament passed the Sex Disqualification (Removal) Act on December 23, 1919. The following day, Normanton petitioned the Middle Temple for admission.[65] The Inns of Court may have disliked the legislation, but even self-regulating bodies could not defy an act of Parliament. The society granted her petition, and by the end of 1920, the Middle Temple had admitted thirty-three female students. The other Inns likewise followed suit, though they admitted only thirteen students between them that year.[66] Sorabji used her due leave from her ICS position to qualify for the bar and take her Oxford degree; she was admitted to Lincoln's Inn in 1922. The benchers set about reorganizing common spaces and formed a committee to take any necessary steps "in regard to lavatory accommodation, etc."[67]

The benchers and residents of the Inns regarded the use and divisions of space as more than a practical concern. As Chapter 2 contends, the elevated status of tradition at the Inns derived not just from the role of precedent in common law but also from a deep regard for past styles and values as manifested in embodied rituals. As they had since the Middle Ages, men donned black gowns, proceeded into hall two by two, broke into groups of four, and shared a meal of roast meats and wine. On special occasions members might drink a Loving Cup, a goblet full of a mysterious Elizabethan recipe. All sipped from the same cup, flanked on either side by brethren members to "guard" them, another medieval remnant. Calls to the bar were held in hall three times a year at ceremonies reserved for members only. Friends and family could watch from the minstrel's gallery above, but even after the Inns admitted women law students, they refused to allow female nonmembers to participate in occasions like Guest Night.[68]

Members of the Inns purported to be more perturbed by changes to the use of space than by female competition or the propriety of female pleaders. Exploiting their historic link to Fleet Street, indignant members of the societies expressed their misgivings in the daily press. In an editorial in the *Pall Mall Gazette*, one member of an Inn explained, "To the dining halls attaches a tradition which has been built up by many famous

University Press, 2010); Raymond Cocks, *Foundations of the Modern Bar* (London: Sweet & Maxwell, 1983).

[64] IT BEN February 19, 1919.   [65] "Another Barrier Down!" *Vote*, January 2, 1920.
[66] "Women Law Students," *Vote*, June 18, 1920; Polden, "Portia's Progress," 295.
[67] MT MPA December 19, 1919; see also Black Books of Lincoln's Inn, 1921.
[68] Black Books of Lincoln's Inn, 1921.

men, and some of us … cherish that tradition and the customs. The presence of women has not been one of those customs." He did not dispute that it was in the public interest to allow female barristers. But why, he asked, not institute a separate Inn, "a kind of London Girton?"[69] Similarly, a barrister correspondent to the *Evening Standard* proposed that, rather than "intrude into the semi-collegiate life of the Inns of Court," women from all four Inns should take their meals together in a separate location.[70] Neither author objected to female barristers professionally, they claimed, but to the disruption to their homosocial spaces. Yet beneath their assertions lay the reality that at the Inns sociability was intimately connected to professional success. The writers' references to colleges, especially Girton, are particularly revealing. Girton was located 2 miles outside of central Cambridge, meaning the women pupils were geographically removed from the rest of university life. Furthermore, as Cornelia Sorabji knew all too well, at Oxbridge women's colleges before the 1920s, women could sit exams but could not take degree titles and, even with titular degrees from their colleges, were excluded from the privileges of full university membership.[71] The model the newspaper correspondents proposed would not only preserve masculine homosociability at the Inns, it would also ensure female professional subordination.

Views on women at the Inns appeared not only in barristers' editorials but also in the feminist and legal presses. Immediately after the passing of the Sex Disqualification (Removal) Act, the *Vote* responded with the triumphant headline, "Another Barrier Down!"[72] Subsequent articles appeared monthly, if not more frequently, to update readers on female law students' progress and examination results. The *Law Times*, by contrast, though seemingly supportive, gave little coverage to women's entry. The paper had reported on debates over opening the profession to women throughout the Great War, but in 1920, only one January article covered women's recent admission to the bar. A brief paragraph in the "Occasional Notes" section mentioned that several women had applied to the Inns. The paper suggested their presence as an "opportunity for an appreciation of [women's] ability in law and administration." This ambiguous comment might have lauded women's introduction to the bar, but it might equally have implied that women were best suited for the work of legal clerks, rather than barristers. The article concluded,

---

[69] M. T., "Women and the Bar," *Pall Mall Gazette*, January 1, 1920.
[70] Untitled, *Evening Standard*, January 13, 1920.
[71] Carol Dyhouse, *Students: A Gendered History* (London: Routledge, 2006), 124–125; Christopher N. L. Brooke, *A History of the University of Cambridge, Volume IV* (Cambridge: Cambridge University Press, 1993), 326.
[72] "Another Barrier Down!" *Vote*, January 2, 1920.

however, by noting the recent first – and successful – brief of the first woman to enter the legal profession in Nova Scotia.[73]

Eager to capitalize on female accomplishments, the daily national and London press was a much more frequent participant in covering women's early experiences at the Inns. Liberal and Conservative papers alike, including the *Pall Mall Gazette, Daily Mirror, Morning Post, Evening Standard,* and *Daily News,* published a number of articles clustered around "firsts" relating to women at the bar. The initial cluster was printed in January 1920, just after women had been admitted. Some articles expressed great approbation for women's presence in the Inns, and others great cynicism, sometimes both within the same article or paper.[74] A feature in the *Daily Mirror,* for instance, mocked the Inns for being pretentious and retrograde – not a "preserve of the law" but rather "a fort." At the same time, the news article lampooned an imaginary woman barrister holding conferences in her Mayfair drawing room over tea, or, worse, scrubbing and curtaining the windows of a set of Temple chambers. The idea of a woman "clear[ing] up the dust and bring[ing] in the muslin curtains" was, the author suggested, as comical as the stodgy Inns themselves.[75]

The press paid particular attention to women's participation in rituals and events that marked rites of passage for law students. In January 1920, for example, the *Morning Post* announced that for the first time in history three women, "suitably enveloped in the Bar student's robe," would be dining in the Middle Temple Hall. The article cheerfully anticipated these women's acquaintance with Queen Elizabeth's Pudding, a concoction after the recipe of one supposedly made by the eponymous monarch herself. Women law students would, the article suggested, eagerly learn "this and other traditions."[76] The first tradition the benchers of the Middle Temple attempted to inculcate, however, was that of restrictive homosociability. The benchers resolved, "That all Lady Students ... in Hall must sit at the table reserved for their exclusive use."[77] The society had been forced to admit women, and these women would dine in hall. But there was no reason, the benchers concluded, for women to join men at table and further disrupt dining fraternity.

Both the Conservative and Liberal press reacted to the Middle Temple's decision to separate women with indignation and scorn.

---

[73] "Occasional Notes," *Law Times,* January 3, 1920.

[74] Bingham, *Gender, Modernity, and the Popular Press,* 10.

[75] "How Will Lady Lawyers 'Practice'?" *Daily Mirror,* January 6, 1920.

[76] "Women Bar Students. Dinner in Hall," *Morning Post,* January 10, 1920.

[77] MT MPA January 16, 1920.

"Are the Benchers of the Middle Temple after all a little frightened of the women law students they have admitted into their midst?" sneered the *Daily News*. "It seems rather like it."[78] Papers that similarly appealed to women readers described women students' experiences at the Inner Temple – which had not followed the Middle Temple's example – as evidence of the absurdity of separating female diners. An Inner Templar wrote the *Daily Mail*, "Personally I have dined in Hall when two women students were present. So far as I could see … they fitted into the routine of student dining ways in the most normal manner."[79] Even the Conservative *Morning Post* reported, "The change in students' corporate life has hardly been perceptible, and as most of the women students have come down from the Universities they have assimilated themselves on the whole satisfactorily to their new surroundings."[80]

Contributors to the daily press opposed the benchers' decision to separate women because they connected dining in hall to important tutorial and networking functions. Students could learn the tenets of the law from books and treatises, but the tenets of legal etiquette did not exist in printed form. Members of the bar argued that when they dined in hall, established barristers imparted the culture and etiquette of the bar to new members. Students, as many commentators observed, learned the practices and attitudes appropriate to the profession at table. "Nothing serves to fashion the outlook of a newcomer … more effectively than rubbing shoulders with those who are even a little more senior to himself," wrote one memoirist.[81] Relegating them to their own table denied the women students at the Middle Temple the opportunity of interacting with senior members of the bar. "How are the women to acquire the tradition of which the legal profession prides itself," asked a contributor to the *Daily News*, "if they are not to mix in social intercourse with the men?"[82]

In an unpublished letter to the editor of an unidentified newspaper, Normanton suggested a more covert reason for segregating male and female diners. The "current speculation," she informed the editor, "ascribes the separation … to a desire to prevent contact between the women and the numerous Oriental students [at the Middle Temple]."[83]

---

[78] "Women at the Inns. Must Dine at Separate Tables in the Middle Temple," *Daily News*, January 21, 1920.
[79] "Women Bar Students. Dining Routine," *Daily Mail*, January 31, 1920.
[80] "Women Lawyers. Twenty Portias in the Middle Temple," *Morning Post*, August 14, 1920.
[81] Gilchrist Alexander, *After Court Hours* (London: Butterworth, 1950), 71.
[82] "Women's Tables," *Daily News*, January 27, 1920.
[83] Women's Library 7HLN/A/17 undated.

As authors repeatedly emphasized, the Middle Temple admitted the greatest number of overseas students of the four Inns. The entrance of women to the societies also coincided with the height of the Inns' concern about Indian nationalists. Nothing in the society's records corroborates Normanton's contention, however, or connects the society's separation of women to a desire to shield them from people of color. More likely this explanation circulated as a rumor among the bar's rank and file. Such a rumor suggested that, regardless of the motivations of the benchers, members of the bar worried about contact between women members and colonial subjects. Given the separation that overseas students described between themselves and English members of the bar in all other aspects of professional life, English women and colonial members were most likely to intermingle at dinner. Rather than the political concerns that sparked official surveillance of radical colonial students, members responsible for the rumor likely grounded their fears in racial stereotypes of hypersexual oriental men.

Of course, such concerns figured all colonial members of the Inn as male, whereas in reality at least half of the women admitted to the Middle Temple were themselves from overseas.[84] Furthermore, Sorabji's experiences dining at Lincoln's Inn suggest that while male and female students mixed freely in hall, English and colonial students were less likely to do so. In her life outside the Inns, Sorabji had no shortage of English friends, and given her frequent frustrations with other Indians in Britain, she may have preferred British dining companions. But Sorabji's diaries, which frequently noted the members of her mess, overwhelmingly indicated companions that hailed from locations such as Murshidabad, Allahabad, Ceylon, and Burma; that had worked as vakils or "soldiered in India" or were "Congress-Wallah[s]"; that had subcontinental surnames such as Tata, Sinha, and Desai. In May 1922 Sorabji recorded that she "sat by a young Eng man who is going into Parlt & doing the Bar on the way." Her dinner next to this Englishman was the exception that proved the rule: the fact that Sorabji noted his nationality indicates the rarity of having an Anglo-Saxon member of a mess.[85] In this respect, Sorabji, regardless of her proimperial politics, had a similar experience dining in hall to those Indian students in Chapter 5 who described a de facto segregation between British and colonial students.

---

[84] The figures vary by period, but Polden estimates between 44 and 69 percent of women called to the bar annually came from overseas, in greatest number from India. Polden, "Portia's Progress," 295.

[85] Personal Diary of Cornelia Sorabji 1922 IOR MSS Eur F 165/84.

Regardless of the logic behind the formal separation of male and female diners at the Middle Temple, Normanton intended to oppose the new rule. Almost immediately after the Middle Temple benchers announced their decision regarding the women's table, she contacted the other women students at the Inn to confer about taking action. She received in response a letter from Monica Geikie Cobb, a rector's daughter who would later achieve the distinction of being the first woman in England to hold a brief. Cobb's letter explained that while dining in hall together one evening, six of the ten women students had discussed the matter and unanimously felt "that no concerted action should be taken" regarding the segregation. The women did not "wish to do other than fall in with any arrangements" made for them, stating that they believed the benchers' decision to be "the outcome of kind thought for [their] comfort."[86] It remains unclear whether the other women students were really satisfied with the arrangement or just wished to draw as little extra attention to themselves as possible. In either case, Normanton could not count on their support if she decided to challenge the benchers. Though she remained opposed to women dining apart, Normanton agreed to "subordinate [her] views," foregoing published criticism in hopes that the women students' "own demeanour should give sufficient reason for the change whenever the benchers should see fit to reconsider the matter."[87]

Normanton would soon learn that she had good reason to hesitate in publishing anything that might recount her experience at the Inns. As we have seen, legal etiquette forbade any form of self-advertising; barristers received briefs by making connections with solicitors and pleading successful cases, not through newspaper ads.[88] In theory, proscriptions against advertising applied only to material that would promote Normanton's legal career. Other barristers active in civic life frequently appeared in print in their roles as MPs, public officials, and even authors. Indeed, Victorian fiction had popularized the trope of the struggling barrister-cum-journalist printing scraps of writing to make ends meet.[89] Even Sorabji, cash-poor despite her elite connections, published articles on a variety of topics in journals like the *Nineteenth Century* throughout her career. Yet in Normanton's case – and Normanton's case alone – the

---

[86] Women's Library 7HLN/A/17 January 19, 1920.
[87] Women's Library 7HLN/A/17 undated; MT MPA May 18, 1933.
[88] MT MPA January 13, 1899; MT MPA January 15, 1910.
[89] Duman, *The English and Colonial Bars*; Cornish et al., *The Oxford History of the Laws of England*; Raymond Cocks, *Foundations of the Modern Bar. A Chance Medley Extracts from "Silk and Stuff"* (London: Constable, 1911).

benchers chose to interpret self-publicizing more broadly than as advertisement for legal services.

The Middle Temple deliberately reinterpreted rules about advertising to handicap Normanton's public presence and threaten her standing at the Inn. When women barristers like Sorabji appeared in print, they did not face disciplinary action because they were not outspoken feminists. (If anything, Sorabji's articles disparaging Gandhi and "the emancipated woman" likely would have pleased even the most conservative benchers.)[90] Even articles about women law students' progress at the Inns did not seem to cause trouble for anyone but Normanton. In November 1920, for example, the *Law Journal* featured an article on women students' examination results, making special mention of Monica Geikie Cobb's first-class marks in criminal law and procedure.[91] Though it was unusual for papers to publish anything more than a list of the names of those who passed, the Middle Temple offered Geikie Cobb no reproach. The following January, however, when the *Evening Standard* ran an article, reprinted by several other papers, on Normanton's first-class marks in constitutional law and legal history, the benchers required her to explain how her name came to be in print.[92] Normanton sent them letters from the editors of over a dozen presses, including the *Pall Mall Gazette*, *Evening Standard*, *Daily Mail*, *Daily Telegraph*, and *Times*, all stating that she had not sought publicity or willingly given them interviews. The benchers accepted her explanation, but took the occasion to warn her to be cautious and avoid future appearances in print.[93] Yet before the year was out, Normanton faced another committee of benchers to account for newspaper articles on her marriage, particularly her printed correction in the *Times* stating that she had not assumed her husband's surname. Again in 1922 she came before the benchers to explain photographs of her in wig and gown published after her call to the bar generated fresh press attention.[94] On neither occasion did the benchers take disciplinary action, but repeatedly calling her to account for herself reiterated the benchers' absolute authority over the bar and their ability to prevent her from practicing should she step too far out of line.

---

[90] MSS Eur F 165/195 – Proofs and Cuttings and Offprints by Sorabji from the Nineteenth Century; MSS Eur F 165/196 – Proofs and Cuttings of Articles and Letters by Cornelia Sorabji in Other Periodicals and Newspapers.

[91] "Women and the Bar Examinations," *Law Journal*, November 6, 1920.

[92] Women's Library HLN/A/07 undated.

[93] MT 1 LBO December 25, 1920–November 1921, January 17, 25, 28 1921, February 7, 1921, May 31, 1921.

[94] Women's Library 7HLN/A/07 November 11, 1921, November 18, 1922.

Normanton's conflicts with the press and the benchers illustrate her difficulties in navigating the restrictions of legal culture and etiquette while continuing to function as a public figure. Becoming a member of the Middle Temple severely limited Normanton's ability to respond to printed criticism just as it thrust her more prominently into the scrutinizing eye of the press.[95] Caught between the press's willingness to capitalize on the details of her life and career, and the bar's censure for any newspaper appearances, even corrections, Normanton found little room to fashion her own public representation. Yet renown was crucial to her professional success: she understood her work to be for women's advancement and expected her success to come from pleading particular kinds of cases. It was crucial that solicitors with female clients seek her out in instances of property disputes, rape, and divorce. Normanton therefore endeavored to placate the benchers by appearing to adhere to legal etiquette and avoid press attention. At the same time, she rationalized deliberate violations of injunctions against publicity by appealing to her ignorance of the minutiae of legal etiquette, the fault of the benchers' restrictions on mixed-gender socialization in hall.[96]

The small crop of soon-to-be lady barristers presented the benchers with yet another challenge to legal tradition: proper female attire at the bar. By the 1920s, changes in fashion had relaxed the formal and conservative cuts of the late nineteenth century for men and women alike.[97] The benchers and older members of the bar found the new male professional uniform of bowler and lounge suit a startling contrast to the former fashion of top hat and tailcoat. As one memoirist recalled in the 1930s, "What a shock the old-time barrister would get if he saw the modern easy fashions."[98] The possibility of women's colorful or revealing attire disrupting the stark white wig and black gown of the barrister distressed the benchers even more than men's casual apparel. When in April of 1922 a joint committee of the Inns met to decide the parameters of acceptable female attire, they concluded that lady barristers would wear the ordinary wig and gown traditional to the profession. Women barristers must, they emphasized, take care that the wig should "completely cover and conceal the hair." Dresses were to be "plain, black or very dark, high to the neck, with long sleeves, and not shorter than the gown, with high, plain white collar and barristers' bands." Upon reporting of this decision,

---

[95] Women's Library HLN/A/07 undated.   [96] Women's Library 7HLN/A/07 undated.
[97] Christopher Breward, *The Hidden Consumer* (Manchester: Manchester University Press, 1999); Brent Shannon, *The Cut of His Coat* (Athens, OH: Ohio University Press).
[98] Gilchrist Alexander, *The Temple of the Nineties* (London: William Hodge, 1938), 3; Robert Blackham, *Wig and Gown: The Story of the Temple, Gray's and Lincoln's Inn* (London: Sampson Low, Marston, 1932), 187.

the *Law Times*, enjoying a laugh at the benchers' expense, quipped, "The committee is to be congratulated upon the successful termination of their difficult deliberations."[99]

In their decision regarding women's clothing, the benchers transferred the elements of the conservative male attire they preferred – "dark clothes, stiff white shirt with cuffs" – to female attire – "long sleeves, ... high, plain white collar."[100] Though they also disapproved of contemporary casual male fashion, it was only female attire and the female body that the benchers took pains to regulate. Hiding skin and hair beneath a high collar, wig, and long-sleeved robe removed interwar markers of femininity from the female barrister. The regulation created a conservative dress code, but also degendered the body of the female barrister.

For Sorabji, attire at the Inns carried with it not only expectations about femininity but also cultural valuations of color and style. When in the UK, Sorabji wore a sari in the Parsi style, draped "over the right ear, behind the left."[101] Despite her love of all things English, she maintained this costume from her time in Oxford in the 1890s through her years as a law student at Lincoln's Inn in the 1920s. The sari demonstrated pride in her Parsi heritage (she noted in her autobiography that the style was different from how Hindus wore their saris) and distinguished Sorabji from the women around her. When special occasions arose, Sorabji chose her sari with care, for example writing home to ask for material just the right shade of white to wear during an audience with the queen in the 1890s. During her time at Lincoln's Inn, Sorabji had the good fortune to win a raffled ticket to the society's much-anticipated quincentennial banquet. On the night of the occasion, Sorabji noted that only she and one Miss Ashworth had been successful in the ballot, making them the only two women members in a room of 350 men. As if that were not enough to make her self-conscious, Sorabji also noted that in her "Benares red and gold" sari, she was "the only person in colours in the crowd," as "Ashworth wore black."[102] In this sea of monochrome eveningwear, Sorabji's colorful sari must have caught the eye; the only other bright colors in the room were the "pale yellow to orange" chrysanthemums decorating the tables.

Unlike Sorabji, most female law students and barristers understood that their best chance of success at the bar was to deemphasize their gender and embrace the styles and culture of the Inns. Accounts of

[99] "Robes for Women," *Law Times*, April 8, 1922.
[100] Alexander, *Temple of the Nineties*, 3; "Robes for Women," *Law Times*, April 8, 1922.
[101] Sorabji, *India Calling*, 13.
[102] MSS EUR F 165/12 – Sorabji Letters to Her Family 1922.

women diners in hall recorded a "masculine solidity," down to the "shade and style of the costumes they wore beneath their students' gowns."[103] Women barristers and students socialized in the common room, joined the Hardwicke Debating Society, and played lawn tennis and stoolball with their male peers.[104] Such efforts did not mean that they were forced to abandon current women's fashions altogether. At least one woman lunching in Middle Temple Hall wore a "grass-green woolen waist-coat with a high collar and jaunty bow." This flash of color defied the Temple's preferred blacks and grays, but it also carried what might otherwise have been an unremarkable lunch into the evening news.[105]

Normanton and other women at the Inns were subject to renewed press interest in women barristers sparked by the call of Ivy Williams at the Inner Temple in May 1922. Holding an Oxford BA, MA, BCL, and London University LLD, Williams was the first woman to be called to the bar in England. Though she enjoyed a long career as an Oxford lecturer, she never intended to or attempted to practice.[106] This left her largely out of the eye of the press. After their call to the bar in 1922, Normanton and other women who sought briefs at the law courts had a far different experience. Reporters lingered outside the court, waiting for female "firsts" to generate copy. Shortly after her call, Normanton found herself the subject of the headline of an *Evening Standard* article, "Portia in Court. Mrs. Normanton Dons Wig and Gown. No Brief Yet, But—." Once more she was required to explain to the benchers that under no circumstances had she spoken to a reporter at the *Standard*. The next day she was forced to do the same regarding a report in the *Lady Chronicle*.[107]

Newspapers particularly seized on women in wig and gown as a source of sensation and humor. The *Evening Standard*, in keeping with its fashion obsession, proclaimed in 1922, "Women Barristers' Hidden Tresses. Wigs Make Them Look Like Men."[108] Just as they had when women entered other uniformed professions or the universities, papers treated women's appearance as deviant and representative of the

---

[103] "Women in the Inns," *Law Journal*, January 17, 1920.
[104] "Stoolball in London Match in Temple Gardens," *Sunday Times*, October 24, 1920.
[105] "Women Barristers' Clothes," *Daily Mirror*, February 14, 1924.
[106] Polden, "Portia's Progress," 316.
[107] "Portia in Court. Mrs. Normanton Dons Wig and Gown. No Brief Yet, But—,"*Evening Standard*, November 20, 1922; "Women's First Day in Wig and Gown. Two Portias Attend the Law Courts," *Lady Chronicle*, November 21, 1922; Women's Library 7HLN/A/07 undated.
[108] "Women Barristers' Hidden Tresses," *Evening Standard*, November 18, 1922.

inadequacies of the female professional or student.[109] Even papers more enthusiastic about female barristers took the opportunity to mock the women. A *Daily Mail* article detailed the "many handicaps" of the woman barrister. Women's bodies, by virtue of size, vocal pitch, and tresses, were rendered comical when decked with the trappings of the profession. In addition to women's lesser height and voices, the author asserted, women were handicapped by their hair. "How is a woman to wear her wig? If she waves her hair and puts her wig on top of it she looks as if she were varying a beehive. Alternatively, if she wears ... short, straight hair she looks like a female convict when she takes it off."[110]

Despite press caricatures, some male barristers welcomed their new female peers, even as they expressed uncertainty about how women would fit into established bar culture. Traditionally, all law students and barristers, regardless of rank, dropped honorifics and addressed each other by surname only. In 1924, A. J. Fox-Davies sent a short note to Normanton to congratulate her on winning her first case. He addressed the note, "Dear Normanton," but hastened to add, "(I presume you wish to adopt the ordinary rule of the Bar.)" When offering advice on a case the following year, Cartwright Sharp erred on the side of caution. "Dear (Mrs) Normanton," he wrote, "(I never quite know how to address a fellow barrister who is a woman.)" Sharp's parenthetical "Mrs." captured both men's dilemma: was the lady barrister primarily a lady, to be treated courteously, or a barrister, to be acknowledged as one of the fold by fraternal familiarity? Either way, the letters avoided the affective cuteness that had characterized the correspondence between Sorabji and Henry Whatley. Indeed, acknowledging uncertainty regarding honorifics made clear that both men wished to convey respect for a peer. The contents of the letters further supported this aim. Cartwright Sharp included legal turns of phrase, indicating confidence in Normanton's professional expertise, and Fox-Davies used slightly rough humor to signal collegiality. He closed his letter with the crude, "Isn't old Blacherley a priceless ass," a joke suggesting shared knowledge of other members of the bar.[111]

Not all men at the Inns welcomed women barristers, though the means by which they exhibited their resistance varied. In her diary, Sorabji noted a day in which she "stupidly [broke] down" when an instructor corrected her for referring to Lincoln's Inn's "Grand Night" as

---

[109] Paul Deslandes, *Oxbridge Men* (Bloomington, IN: Indiana University Press, 2005); Dyhouse, *Students*; Martha Vicinus, *Independent Women: Work and Community for Single Women, 1850–1920* (Chicago: University of Chicago Press, 1985).

[110] Hervey Middleton, "Do Not Envy the Woman Barrister," *Daily Mail*, June 29, 1938.

[111] Women's Library 7HLN/A/06 June 2, 1924; 7HLN/A/17 July 6, 1925.

"Guest Night." It wasn't so much the correction itself that upset her, she explained, as it was her "own sense of futility" as she prepared for upcoming exams. Her fear of failing the examination was compounded by pressure from her brother, Richard (Dick) Sorabji. Dick received his call to the bar from Lincoln's Inn in 1896, and it seems that he was less than supportive about his sister's efforts to follow in his footsteps.[112] According to Sorabji, Dick met her efforts to be called to the bar with bullying and denigration. Sorabji worried that if she failed the exam, Dick would gloat, "People shd not go in for Exams who...."[113] Sorabji's ellipsis suggests his smugness was all too familiar.

If Sorabji received some degree of derision from a jealous sibling, Normanton had to face far more underhanded forms of resistance to her presence at the Inns. In November of 1924, Normanton received an anonymous letter from the Middle Temple Common Room sent by members who described themselves as "consistently opposed" to women's entry to the bar. "Feminine jealousy," the writers warned, had placed Normanton at the center of much gossip, perhaps because her "partial successes" in scoring briefs and winning cases had "caused the other women envy." The writers wondered why Normanton ignored what was being said about her, especially by one Miss Ethel Bright Ashford. Called to the bar at the same time as Normanton, Ashford's interests lay in municipal law. The writers informed Normanton that Ashford "openly makes statements about your mode of life, literary work, marriage, and what is most important to us, your professional code." There is no way of knowing whether or not Ashford actually made the alleged comments about Normanton, though Ashford may have been jealous of the press attention Normanton attracted.[114]

The writers of the letter to Normanton used the long-standing trope of women as gossips to set sly, secretive female behavior against forthright, honorable male behavior. Though they assured Normanton that they did not believe the gossip, the writers warned her that her "own impassity [sic] [was] being remarked upon." She should not, the writers cautioned, continue to invite Ashford to her home and treat her like a friend. Such behavior was incongruent with the male codes of honor the writers conflated with professional etiquette. Not to challenge the rumors was, in terms of such codes of honor, to acknowledge them as true. Of course,

---

[112] Sorabji, *Opening Doors*, 68.   [113] MSS Eur 165/85 – Personal Diary of Sorabji 1923.
[114] The following articles, however, mention both Normanton and Ashford by name. "Women Barristers' Hidden Tresses," *Evening Standard*, November 18, 1922; "Portia in Court," *Evening Standard*, November 20, 1922; "Women's First Day in Wig and Gown," *Lady Chronicle*, November 21, 1922.

the men's own letter – critical and sent anonymously – was hardly an open and forthright action. Furthermore, by addressing the letter from the Middle Temple Common Room, the authors aligned their viewpoint with one of the physical spaces of the Inns, implying that all barristers in the common room agreed that the gossip surrounding Normanton had too long gone unchecked. The letter was signed simply, "Your Wellwishers."[115]

Women's ability to lay claim to common spaces – or male efforts to see that they could not – signaled deeper issues of belonging at the Inns. Sorabji's letters and diaries indicate ready comfort in and familiarity with Lincoln's Inn, in part because of her preexisting connections to the society through Lord Hobhouse and her work for Lee & Pemberton. Whereas some students spent little time at the Inns aside from required dinners, Sorabji regularly attended lectures and studied there. In addition, she frequently lunched in hall, sometimes with other law students, but just as often with female friends from outside the Inn. When her dear friend Elena Rathbone dined with her one afternoon in July 1922, Sorabji recorded in her diary, "Elena lunch chez moi at the Inn."[116] Sorabji's use of "chez moi" is doubly significant. The possessive "moi" indicated ownership, a space in which not only Sorabji belonged, but one that belonged to her. Furthermore, most often used to refer to one's house, the phrase characterized the Inn with the comfort and familiarity of home.

But there were limits to Sorabji's comfort. Her diaries almost never mention the common room, save for one day when she retreated there in between lecture and dinner in hall. On that occasion she described it as a "filthy place."[117] It is impossible to say for certain why Sorabji felt this way about the room. It seems unlikely that she was referring to the cleanliness of the space, as it no doubt would have been regularly attended to by one of the society's laundresses. Indeed, Lincoln's Inn's student common room only opened for use in October 1920, meaning it had little more than a year and a half to accumulate grime before Sorabji's derisive description in May 1922. Perhaps Sorabji meant the adjective, then, as more of a visceral reaction to her being in the room. With a dozen or fewer women students admitted to the Inn, the space would have been overwhelmingly male. In addition, as Chapter 5 discusses, Lincoln's Inn had long hesitated to even provide the students with a common room as it might "attract an undue proportion of the Overseas Students."[118] It seems entirely in keeping with Sorabji's

[115] Women's Library 7HLN/A/17 November 21, 1924.
[116] Personal Diary of Cornelia Sorabji 1922 IOR MSS Eur F 165/84.   [117] Ibid.
[118] Black Books of Lincoln's Inn, April 12, 1920.

frustration with Indians in Britain that she might dismiss any space dominated by colonial students as "filthy."

Sorabji's potential prejudice regarding the common room is not to diminish the fact that basic material resources for women's comfort might be limited or absent at the Inns or in other legal spaces. These limitations could create rivalries between women barristers. For example, in a 1933 letter to Helena Normanton, Chrystal Macmillan, a feminist activist and barrister, explained that the London Sessions Court had provided female barristers with a special changing room, but that it contained only six lockers for eleven women. Macmillan and three other women barristers decided among themselves that they would distribute the lockers according to seniority of membership in the Sessions, a method that awarded a locker to Macmillan and left Normanton without one. Normanton responded with a lengthy letter detailing her distaste for the "undemocratic" method of locker allocation. In an attempt to shame Macmillan for the decision she had reached, Normanton haughtily closed her letter, "I not only object to being left lockerless myself, but I should feel it very invidious and embarrassing if I had a locker at the expense of any other woman equally entitled."[119] On the one hand, Normanton's desire for a locker stemmed from practical concerns. She had injured her ankle and found it difficult to carry her barristers' robes with her from court to court. More importantly, having to carry robes to the London Sessions marked Normanton as an outsider; having a locker in which to store them at the court was a symbol of belonging to and at that court.

Belonging was a central issue for women barristers in relation not only to the courts but also to their associated circuit and sessions messes. Corollaries to the Inns of Courts, circuit and sessions messes were technically the "disciplinary bod[ies] controlling the members of the bar attending a particular circuit" or sessions court. In reality they functioned primarily as "social club[s]," spaces to provide food, lodging, and company for barristers away from home.[120] Unlike the Inns of Court, whose rituals were widely documented in print, it is difficult to recover the precise activities of messes, "since a member of one circuit mess [was] not permitted to divulge even to a member of another circuit mess anything of the doings and ceremonies of his mess, under penalty of expulsion from membership."[121] In their extreme secrecy, the messes were even more like fraternities than the Inns themselves.

---

[119] Women's Library 7HLN/A/17 June 29, 1933.
[120] "Women Barristers and Bar Messes," *Law Times*, February 24, 1923.
[121] Ernest Bowen Rowlands, "The Etiquette of the Bar," *Law Times*, November 30, 1895.

When the Inns admitted women to the bar, there arose the question of whether or not women would also be admitted to the messes. Traditionally, barristers who pleaded in a particular court or local sessions – for example, the London Sessions or the Northern Circuit – joined the associated mess. The Sex Disqualification (Removal) Act of 1919 ensured that no organization could deny women barristers the right to plead in court, but legally "the King's Courts [were] open to any barrister" whether or not he or she belonged to the mess.[122] Some circuit and sessions messes readily welcomed women. Normanton's supposed rival, Ethel Bright Ashford, for example, was one of the first two women elected to full membership by a circuit mess (of the South Eastern Circuit) in 1923.[123] Other messes chose to admit women exclusively on special occasions, for example, "on Grand Night only."[124] Still others proposed to allow women barristers to plead cases at their particular circuit or sessions court, but prohibited them from joining the mess altogether. As one *Law Times* correspondent asked, what "do women barristers lose? ... [T]he answer is: the doubtful pleasure of dining in inadequate numbers at what is a men's dinner."[125]

Normanton became a member the North London Sessions Mess in 1931, nine years after her initial application was rejected for reasons that would, she contended, not "have been raised if I had not been a woman."[126] Among her papers is an undated poem composed by a member of the sessions mess, likely read at a dinner in the late 1940s. Written in a lower-class dialect, each stanza poked fun at various members of the mess. The verse on Normanton read.

> The lady's 'Elena Normanton
> A Winner, a real blinkin' pearl,
> She's the queen of the mess and its sweetheart.
> She's the Old Bailey's own pin-up girl.

On the one hand, the quatrain pointed to the degree that even in the late 1940s, Normanton was still one of the few women at a "men's dinner." The lines began, "*the* lady," indicating she was the only one in the mess. The verse in fact drew all its humor from Normanton's gender and, perhaps, her appearance: in her sixties, bespectacled, and on the

---

[122] "General Intelligence. Women Barristers and Bar Messes," *Law Times*, February 24, 1923.
[123] "General Intelligence. Women Barristers and Bar Messes," *Law Times*, March 10, 1923.
[124] C. P. Hawkes, *Chambers in the Temple* (London: Methuen, 1930), 74–75.
[125] "General Intelligence. Women Barristers and Bar Messes," *Law Times*, March 10, 1923.
[126] Women's Library 7HLN/A/17 June 29, 1933.

stouter side, Normanton hardly resembled a "pin-up girl." Yet there is another way one could read the stanza. The fact that Normanton was included at all was a sign of affection and belonging to the group. It would have been far more effective to signal her outsider status by omitting her completely from the poem. The author's possessive language certainly suggests inclusion: "the Old Bailey's own." Though it drew attention to Normanton's greatest difference, her gender, perhaps the reason she saved a copy of the poem was because she was laughing along with the men.

Conclusion

Helena Normanton's integration into professional culture was exceptional rather than representative. Even when the circuit messes unreservedly admitted women, or the Middle Temple allowed women students to dine with men, as they did in 1933, other exclusions remained.[127] Late in her career, for example, Normanton noted women's difficulties in finding pupilage – an apprenticeship-like jump-start to success at the bar – in male-headed chambers. Some barristers had blatantly decided "not to take any … women students;" others made excuses on the grounds of inadequate lavatory accommodation.[128] Refusing to take female pupils was yet another of the many spatial logics that undergirded professional resistance to women members. From separating women diners in hall to subtly claiming common space as men's domain, from excluding women from circuit mess socialization to providing insufficient changing facilities at court, male members of the legal profession manipulated the built environment and its ties to tradition to maintain resolutely masculine institutions. These forms of resistance discouraged women from joining or succeeding in the profession. Normanton and a handful of others like Rose Heilbron reached prestigious heights, but of the 428 women admitted to the Inns between 1919 and 1939, less than one-eighth to one-quarter of them practiced as barristers.[129] Even Sorabji, who returned to India after her call to the bar, was confined to preparing opinions on cases rather than pleading in court, until she retired in 1929. The stark disparities between men and women at the bar remained through the end of the century, and embedded practices of preferment still persist in the organization of the contemporary legal profession.

---

[127] MT MPA May 18, 1933.
[128] Women's Library 7HLN/A/18 November 30, 1933; Polden, "Portia's Progress," 322.
[129] Polden, "Portia's Progress," 314–318.

Epilogue

After decades of preoccupation with questions of women's and foreigners' place at the Inns, in 1939 the societies' priorities rapidly shifted to the material exigencies of the nation's war with Germany. Even before the Blitz began, the Inns of Court felt the negative effects of the conflict on both their revenues and their long-standing traditions. By January 1940 the Middle Temple worried about maintaining the society's income from letting chambers, as many barristers and law students had joined the armed forces or were otherwise engaged in war work. The society tried its best to operate "so far as possible on Customary lines," but they were forced to suspend dinners in hall. The Inn had neither the funds nor the labor force to continue with this ancient ritual. Foregoing dinners saved the Middle Temple about £800 each term; moreover, at least thirty-one members of the serving staff had left to help with the war effort.[1] The following month the Inner Temple closed the gates to the garden as it could not afford to maintain the flowerbeds.[2] Throughout the summer the societies found other ways to cut costs and gain income, sharing one library between the two of them, renting vacant chambers to the Home Office. Meanwhile, fewer and fewer members populated the Inns, either joining up or evacuating the capital.

Come September, German bombs transformed the Inns, long characterized by literary fiction and topographic guidebooks as medieval relics, from figurative to literal London ruins. That month a high explosive bomb destroyed the roof and interior of the Inner Temple Hall. Another set a gas main on fire. Still others smashed windows, toppled masonry, blew off roofs.[3] In October a landmine attached to a parachute virtually demolished all of Elm Court, and the flying debris from its impact damaged other Middle Temple structures, most notably the hall. In addition to smashed glass and warped panels, flying masonry and stones destroyed a portion of the hall's much-valued double-hammer

[1] MT MPA January 10, 1940.   [2] IT BEN February 28, 1940.
[3] MT MPA October 3, 1940.

beam roof and collapsed its elaborately carved screen.[4] The societies undertook repairs as best they could and relocated their more portable treasures and documents to facilities outside London. The Luftwaffe continued to drop explosives on the Inns, and in May 1941, incendiary bombs destroyed significant portions of the Temple Church, including all but one of its famed medieval stone effigies.[5] The rump population of inhabitants at the Inns sustained no casualties, but by 1942, almost no building was left unscathed.

The war depopulated the mythic Inns of Victorian fiction and interwar histories and razed them to the ground; how different, then, were the societies that rebuilt themselves at the war's end? The contests over and issues surrounding the postwar Inns of Court may have come in the trappings of decolonization, revitalized feminism, and the welfare state, but at heart they echoed the concerns raised by reformers and members of the bar a century before: were the Inns enduring professional models or outmoded institutions in need of reform? Should that reform come from parliament or be driven by the societies? To what degree did – or should – the Inns accommodate or incorporate their female and overseas members? Of course, the postwar moment spurred certain noticeable changes at the Inns. Fewer members of the societies came from affluent backgrounds, bringing to the profession, as Gilchrist Alexander put it, "an air of practicality."[6] Immediately after the war, the numbers of overseas students spiked to an all-time high, outstripping British students for the first time in the societies' history. Gradually, however, the societies reestablished their resolutely English, masculine character, emphasizing custom, precedent, and self-directed education. English male barristers and law students slowly returned to the Inns; dining rituals resumed in newly rebuilt halls. Much of the Inns of the postwar era looked – in terms of governance, architecture, culture, and practice – like their Victorian predecessors.

Postwar parliamentary initiatives, like those a century before, resulted in very few changes to the bar. The nationwide commitment to social welfare that drove other sweeping transformations in Britain caused the Labour government to evaluate the failings of the legal system. Parliamentary committees concluded that litigation should be more affordable to a wider swathe of society but, rather than alter the courts or the legal system, instituted an immense system of legal aid. One or two individual reformers, such as eminent legal scholar Glanville Williams, highlighted the Inns of Court as sites likewise in need of revision.

---

[4] MT MPA November 28, 1940.   [5] MT MPA May 29, 1941.
[6] Gilchrist Alexander, "The Modern Outlook at the Bar," *Law Times*, October 20, 1950.

Williams and others contended that the societies did little, if anything, to prepare law students to practice law. They pointed, for example, to examinations that privileged antiquated subjects such as Roman law over knowledge of contemporary branches like taxation. Much like their Victorian counterparts, however, Parliament largely ignored these individuals. The Inns, in turn, responded with small conciliatory reforms, such as making pupilage in chambers compulsory.[7]

In rebuilding the bombed-out portions of the Inns of Court, the societies chose architectural styles in keeping with those they had emphasized over the past century and a half to evoke the Inns' storied past. In other areas of London, architects replaced buildings destroyed by the war with those of decidedly modern, postwar styles. Brutalism, for example, with its straight lines of poured concrete, gained popularity both for its relatively low cost and its architectural "honesty."[8] The Inns of Court, however, rebuilt and repaired their buildings with painstaking historicism. Papers like the *Illustrated London News* celebrated the completion of Temple repairs with headlines like: "Restored Again … The Historic Beauties of the Middle Temple Hall." Such articles detailed the meticulous reconstruction of the Elizabethan screen, joined so artfully that one could not detect any of the individual splinters.[9] Elsewhere the societies replaced Georgian brick facades with new brick facades, neogothic buildings with new (if somewhat less ornate) neogothic buildings. The Middle Temple relocated its library, but left the stone steps and arched entranceway of the demolished 1857 structure on its western border, a ruin of the past.

The societies' rule over their newly rebuilt domain remained autonomous, their status as local authorities unscathed by the war. In fact, postwar legislation reaffirmed the Inns' independence. To be sure, the Temples Order 1971 ceded certain responsibilities, ranging from flood protection to dog licenses, to the City's Common Council. Many of these functions would have been impractical for the societies to carry out themselves, however, or related to a residential population no longer occupying the Inns. Overall, the legislation confirmed the Inner and Middle Temples' functions as like those of any "inner London borough." The societies to this day remain in charge of their own paving and lighting, refuse collection, liquor licensing, and environmental

---

[7] Brian Abel-Smith and Robert Bocking Stevens, *Lawyers and the Courts* (London: Heinemann, 1967), 247, 315, 358.

[8] Alexander Clement, *Brutalism: Post-war British Architecture* (Wiltshire: Crowood Press, 2011); Owen Hatherley, *A Guide to the New Ruins of Great Britain* (London: Verso Books, 2010).

[9] "Restored Again after the Damage of War," *Illustrated London News*, July 9, 1949.

protection, among other things.[10] The 1971 legislation may have shifted the nonphysical boundaries between the Temple and the City, but in doing so it explicitly empowered local authorities and reinscribed the division between the two bodies.

Much like their predecessors, the postwar Inns met the dramatic increase in both numbers and percentage of overseas students with superficial conciliations while subtly bolstering engrained practices of discrimination. The prospect of independence motivated colonial students to join the Inns more than ever, because they viewed qualification as barrister a useful tool for carving out prestigious careers in newly-formed states. Given that the number of English law students had declined with the war, overseas students went from just 12 percent of the bar in 1885 to a full three-quarters of those called by 1963. The Inns responded by offering more studentships for overseas members, as well as special funds for holidays in the country and other recreational practices. At the same time, the postwar societies were mercenary in their approach to overseas students, eager to earn money on admissions, call fees, and interests on deposits, but not particularly generous in the academic resources they extended to students with diverse educational backgrounds. Overseas students' pass rate on the final examination with its Anglo-centric legal and historical topics was significantly lower than that of domestic students. In 1964 the societies decided to limit the number of re-sits for the exam, an action calculated to reap the benefit of forfeited deposits of those who did not pass.[11] The societies also instated a contested measure that required law students to declare whether they intended to practice in England or overseas, dividing them into two sections. Students who would practice overseas believed they "would have to settle for a second-class degree."[12]

Those students who protested in response found little solidarity among their peers, many of whom refused to recognize racial issues at the Inns. Overall, law students and barristers engaged in far fewer and less dramatic direct actions than students at other metropolitan institutions, such as the London School of Economics. The Inns had no tradition of politically active student unions on which to draw, and dissent fell along the lines of national origin. Newspapers reported wide

---

[10] NA HLG 120/2556 Temples Order 1971.

[11] Beginning in the mid-1960s, the numbers of overseas students began to rapidly decline as newly independent nations, especially those in Africa, established their own bars. Richard L. Abel, *The Legal Profession in England and Wales* (New York: Blackwell, 1988), 76–77.

[12] Hugh de Wet, "Bar Students in Protest to Race Relations Board," *Times*, November 11, 1969.

variations in levels of participation depending on their sources: anywhere between 5 and 15 percent of the total student body took part in demonstrations.[13] In 1968 a group of students formed the Bar Students' Reform Committee to protest overcrowding at lectures, the limited number of exam re-sits, and the division of law students based on their intent to practice in Britain or overseas. They held a one-day sit-in at a building in Gray's Inn, in which about a hundred students "organized discussions on law and held sing-songs." In response to this action and a similar one the following year, members of the Senate Students' Committee, the Student Link Committee, and the Federation of Conservative Students denounced the efforts of their peers as "irrelevant," "pathetically small," and a "rag-bag of demands."[14] *Times* editorials written by students of English origin, along with reports in the *Guardian*, empathized with protestors' grievances over class sizes, but dismissed direct action as an inappropriate channel for change. These student groups largely ignored the race-related elements of protestors' demands, as well as the fact that protest leadership, and perhaps participation, lay in the hands of people of color.[15]

If women slowly worked their way into associational life at the postwar Inns, it was because their marginal presence did not seem obtrusive, particularly when they took on typically feminine roles. In 1952, for example, when members formed a student union, the only female elected officer was Cynthia Allen, secretary.[16] The numbers of women at the bar remained low in the immediate aftermath of the war, and newspapers devoted significantly less ink to women barristers than they had in the 1920s. Women in the postwar Inns, after all, achieved fewer "firsts" than in early days. When papers did discuss women barristers, articles retained the interwar press's ambivalent focus on female dress and embodiment, describing women as "glamourous, dramatic personalities" or deriding the "woman barrister clutching a brief and wearing a

---

[13] In 1968, nearly 550 out of 3,000 LSE students attended a meeting to decide on occupation of the school. According to one report from a protest leader, about 600 out of 4,000 bar students attended a similar meeting at the Inns of Court that same year. Another article suggested that merely 180 out of 4,000 bar students attended a meeting in 1969. The *Times* reported a hundred students at a sit-in in November 1969, whereas the *Guardian* put the number at forty. "Students May Drop Plan for LSE Takeover," *Times*, October 22, 1968; Mohammed Arif, "Law Students' Sit-In," *Times*, November 22, 1968; "Bar Students Hold Sit-in," *Times*, November 25, 1969.

[14] Alex Cloudesley Seddon, Donald Hamilton, and Guy H. C. Frankham, "Law Students' Sit-In," *Times*, November 14, 1968; Hugh de Wet, "Bar Students Hold Sit-in," *Times*, November 25, 1969; "40 Law Students Sit In," *Guardian*, November 25, 1969.

[15] Christine Doyle, "We'll Sit in, Say Bar Students," *Guardian*, November 23, 1969; "40 Law Students Sit In," *Guardian*, November 25, 1969.

[16] "Inns of Court Students' Union," *Times*, August 14, 1952.

mini-skirt."[17] The resurgence of campaigns for women's rights, which steered women into higher education and professional life, meant that women's presence at the Inns began to increase significantly after 1965. By the early 1980s, women represented 10 percent of barristers.

Of course, from the moment they set foot at the Inns, women faced significant barriers to successful careers. Women law students in the 1970s reported difficulty in finding pupilage in chambers, a prerequisite for call to the bar. Legislation required the Inns to admit female applicants who met their standards, but nothing compelled individual barristers to take on able pupils. Women also reported difficulties and delays in finding tenancy in chambers after their call to the bar and further noted that they were disadvantaged in obtaining work once in practice. Such discrimination abounded in part because of the almost exclusive dominance of men as chamber heads. In 1984, out of 219 London chambers, only nine had women heads. Women who did find work were more likely to have careers that plateaued: in the 1980s women were only 2 percent of all QCs, and they represented merely three benchers out of the four Inns' combined 481.[18]

To practice as a barrister in England today still requires a call to the bar from one of the four Inns of Court, though this requirement is now combined with a stringent program of university training and examination, as well as mandatory pupilage in chambers. The entire training process is overseen by the Bar Standards Board (BSB), an independent entity created in 2006 to better regulate the bar according to public interest. This board is governed by a mixture of barristers and "lay" (that is, nonbarrister) members and has taken over many of the regulatory duties of the Inns, including setting standards of conduct for barristers and responding to complaints of barrister misconduct. If deemed necessary, the BSB can refer a disciplinary case to the Bar Tribunals and Adjudication Service, another independent entity made up of judicial, barrister, and lay members, all of whom were appointed to their positions by yet another independent entity, the Tribunal Appointments Body. The creation of these several independent bodies, and the power they hold to discipline and potentially disbar barristers, shifted control over the profession and practice away from the arbitrary authority and ad hoc proceedings of the benchers of the Inns, an

---

[17] "On the Side of the Law," *Times*, April 20, 1959; "Beating the Clock in High Court," *Times*, October 11, 1966; see also Phyllis Heathcote, "Parisienne at the Bar: Robed and Commanding – with Little Sky-Blue Shoes," *Guardian*, June 23, 1958.

[18] It is worth noting that one of these women benchers was Elizabeth II, an honorary member of the Middle Temple. Abel, *The Legal Profession in England and Wales*, 80–84.

acknowledgment that barristers serve a public function and should be regulated and held accountable in a transparent fashion. All disciplinary hearings, for example, are now open to the public.

The function of the present Inns is to offer resources and support to law students, including scholarships to cover the costs of the bar course all would-be barristers must take. (The course is not given by the Inns, but by university law schools authorized by the BSB.) Scholarships may also cover the cost of the twelve qualifying sessions students must attend, the present-day equivalent of keeping term. These sessions range from focused professional seminars and debates to traditional dinners in hall to leisure activities, including "a rather raucous boat party on the Thames."[19] In this regard, the Inns still emphasize socialization as a key component of professional success, and indeed some guides for law students suggest the networking opportunities the Inns provide are essential. There are far fewer chambers that offer pupilage than there are applicants – as of 2019, less than half of those who successfully completed the bar course in the previous five years had secured a pupilage in chambers.[20] Guides for prospective law students point to the connections made at an Inn, or the experiences the societies provide in exercises like mooting, to help competitive students secure a spot.

If ancient, change-resistant institutions are no longer the singular gatekeepers of the upper half of the legal profession, and if independent, transparent, and publicly accountable organizations have taken over many of their roles, has the bar become significantly more equitable and meritocratic? The short answer is no. The cost of training to become a barrister can prevent those who do not secure a scholarship from undertaking it. To this day, women and minorities at the bar are under-represented, particularly among senior counsel and the judiciary.[21] Women, for example, are admitted to the profession in almost equal numbers as men, but are not equally retained. Both women and minorities are more likely than their peers to be pushed toward the lowest paid work in criminal and family law. Both are more likely to be shut out of the most competitive chambers. Many ethnic minorities and immigrants have less access to elite public schools and universities – assets prized

---

[19] "The Inns of Court," Chambers Student, www.chambersstudent.co.uk/the-bar/the-inns-of-court (accessed April 6, 2022).

[20] "BPTC Key Statistics 2019: An Analysis of Students over Three Academic Years," Bar Standards Board, 2019.

[21] Abel, *The Legal Profession in England and Wales*, 79–85; "A Current Glance at Women in the Law," *American Bar Association*, February 2013; "Trends in the Solicitors' Profession: Annual Statistics Report 2012," *Law Society*, 2013; "Statistics," *Bar Council*, 2006–10.

by the top firms. Fierce competition and inadequate maternity leave policies often force women to choose between family and practice. In a 2016 survey by the BSB, two of every five women said they had suffered harassment and discrimination at the bar, though only one in five had reported it for fear of negative career impact. The survey concluded that rather than an issue with particular policies, it was "elements of *the culture* of the Bar and legal profession more generally" that created a "barrier to the retention of women."[22]

Examining the nineteenth- and twentieth-century Inns of Court does not account for the disparities in the contemporary bar, but the conclusion of the BSB report that those disparities are perpetuated by professional culture rather than policy is very much in keeping with the central contention of this book: change-resistant institutions like the Inns successfully maintained their status quo by adopting formal policy revisions that seemed to acquiesce to outside pushes for reform, but which did little to shift institutional culture. The Inns did not avoid parliamentary interference by staunchly refusing to bend; they did so by surface-level deference to public opinion. When Parliament did interfere, such as with the admission of women, the societies relied on professional culture to temper the effects of outside legislation. Examining this strategy explains how ancient institutions weathered Victorian rationalization with their authority largely intact and how the gender and racial makeup of the bar remained relatively consistent into the interwar period and beyond.

The Inns' strategy of small concessions also invites those of us invested in racial and gender equity in the twenty-first century to look critically at processes of reform across a variety of contemporary institutions. Policies that encourage museums to hire more black curators, or banks to place more women in mergers and acquisitions, do little to unpack the gendered and racialized logics of power and preferment that undergird these institutions. A strategy for meaningfully challenging institutional disparities is beyond the scope of this book, but an examination of the historical bar suggests that we need to think not only about the numbers of women and people of color within an institution but also about the norms of relationships within that institution, about the unspoken affective dictates that determine how members of a profession interact with and connect with one another, and about the expectations they hold regarding those relationships and the ways they might react when those expectations are not met.

---

[22] Bar Standards Board, "Women at the Bar," 4, 58. www.barstandardsboard.org.uk/media/ 1773934/women_at_the_bar_-_full_report_-_final_12_07_16.pdf (accessed September 27, 2018) (italics mine).

Bibliography

British Library
    India Office Records (IOR)
    MSS EUR Cornelia Sorabji Papers

Inner Temple Archives
    IT BEN Bench Table Orders
    IT DIS Disciplinary Records
    IT PLA Architectural Plans

Liddell Hart Military Archives
    Wintringham Papers

London Metropolitan Archives
    LMA 1907 Inner Temple Petition to the House of Lords
    LMA Inns of Court Rifle Volunteers Diaries and Scrapbooks
    LMA Photographs

Middle Temple Archives
    MT LBO Letter Books
    MT MPA Minutes of Parliament
    MT RBW Building Records
    MT Scrap Albums Volumes 1–3
    MT SRV Staff Records

National Archives
    CO Colonial Office Records

Select Newspapers and Periodicals
    Bell's Life in London and Sporting Chronicle
    Daily Mail
    Daily Mirror
    Daily News
    Evening Standard
    Graphic
    Guardian
    Illustrated London News
    Lady Chronicle
    Law Journal

Law Times
Lloyd's Weekly Newspaper
Morning Chronicle
Morning Post
Pall Mall Gazette
Punch, or the London Charivari
Times
Vote

Women's Library
HLN Helena Normanton Papers

Printed Sources

Abel, Richard L. *The Legal Profession in England and Wales*. New York: Blackwell, 1988.

Abel-Smith, Brian, and Robert Bocking Stevens. *Lawyers and the Courts*. London: Heineman, 1967.

Ahmed, Sara. *The Cultural Politics of Emotion*. Edinburgh: Edinburgh University Press, 2014.

    On Being Included: Racism and Diversity in Institutional Life. Durham, NC, and London: Duke University Press, 2012.

Alberti, Johanna. "Keeping the Candle Burning: Some British Feminists between Two Wars." In *Suffrage and Beyond International Feminist Perspectives*, ed. Caroline Daley and Melanie Nolan, 295–312. New York: New York University Press, 1994.

Alexander, Gilchrist. *After Court Hours*. London: Butterworth, 1950.

    Middle Temple to the South Seas. London: John Murray, 1927.

    The Temple of the Nineties. London: William Hodge, 1938.

Allbut, Robert. *Rambles in Dickens' Land*. London: S. T. Freemantle, 1899.

Archer, R. L. *Secondary Education in the XIX Century*. Cambridge: Cambridge University Press, 1921.

Baedeker, Karl. *London and Its Environs: Handbook for Travellers*. Leipzig: Karl Baedeker, 1911.

Bagehot, Walter. "The English Constitution." In *The Works and Life of Walter Bagehot*, ed. Mrs. Russell Barrington. London: Longmans, Green, 1915.

Bailey, Peter. *Leisure and Class in Victorian England: Rational Recreation and the Contest for Control, 1830–1885*. London: Routledge & Kegan Paul, 1978.

Baker, John H. *The Common Law Tradition: Lawyers, Books, and the Law*. London: Hambledon Press, 2000.

Baldick, Robert. *The Duel: A History of Dueling*. London: Spring Books, 1965.

Ball, Simon. "The Assassination Culture of Imperial Britain, 1909–1979." *Historical Journal* 56 (March 2013): 231–256.

Ballantyne, Tony, and Antoinette Burton. "Introduction: Bodies, Empires, and World Histories." In *Bodies in Contact Rethinking Colonial Encounters in World History*, ed. Tony Ballantyne and Antoinette Burton, 1–18. Durham, NC: Duke University Press, 2005.

Ballhatchet, Kenneth. *Race, Sex and Class under the Raj: Imperial Attitudes and Policies and Their Critics, 1793–1905.* London: Weidenfeld and Nicolson, 1980.

Banerjee, Sikata. *Make Me a Man! Masculinity, Hinduism, and Nationalism in India.* Albany: State University of New York Press, 2005.

Banerjee, Sukanya. *Becoming Imperial Citizens: Indians in the Late-Victorian Empire.* Durham, NC: Duke University Press, 2010.

Batabyal, Rakesh (ed.). *The Penguin Book of Modern Indian Speeches.* Gurgaon: Penguin, 2007.

Beckett, Ian F. W. *Riflemen Form: A Study of the Volunteer Rifle Movement, 1859–1908.* Barnsley: Pen & Sword, 1982.

Bellot, Hugh. *The Inner and Middle Temple, Legal, Literary and Historic Associations.* London: Methuen, 1902.

The Temple. London: Methuen, 1914.

Bennett, Tony. *The Birth of the Museum: History, Theory, Politics.* London: Routledge, 1995.

Bennion, F. A. R. "The Sex Disqualification (Removal) Act – 60 Inglorious Years." *New Law Journal* (December 13, 1979): 1240–1241.

Berlant, Lauren. *Cruel Optimism.* Durham, NC: Duke University Press, 2011.

Bingham, Adrian. *Gender, Modernity, and the Popular Press in Inter-war Britain.* New York: Clarendon Press, 2004.

Blaas, P. B. M. *Continuity and Anachronism: Parliamentary and Constitutional Development in Whig Historiography and in the Anti-Whig Reaction between 1890 and 1930.* Boston: M. Nijhoff, 1978.

Blackham, Colonel Robert J. *Wig and Gown: The Story of the Temple Gray's and Lincoln's Inn.* London: Low, Marston, 1932.

Boehmer, Elleke, and Sumita Mukherjee. "Re-making Britishness: Indian Contributions to Oxford University, c. 1860–1930." In *Britishness, Identity and Citizenship,* ed. Catherine McGlynn, Andrew Mycock, and James W. McAuley, 95–112. Oxford: Peter Lang, 2011.

Booth, Charles. *Life and Labour of the People in London. Volume IV Part I.* New York: AMS Press, 1970.

Boswell, David, and Jessica Evans (eds.). *Representing the Nation: A Reader. Histories, Heritage and Museums.* New York: Routledge, 1999.

Bourne, Judith. *Helena Normanton and the Opening of the Bar to Women.* East Sussex: Waterside Press, 2016.

Bowen, Marjorie. *The Story of the Temple and Its Associations.* London: Griffin Press, 1928.

Boyce, D. G. "Public Opinion and Historians." *History* 63 (1978): 214–228.

Braddon, Mary Elizabeth. *Lady Audley's Secret,* edited by Natalie M. Houston. Peterborough, ON: Broadview Press, 2003.

Breward, Christopher. *The Hidden Consumer: Masculinities, Fashion and City Life 1860–1914.* Manchester: Manchester University Press, 1999.

Brooke, Christopher N. L. *A History of the University of Cambridge, Volume IV.* Cambridge: Cambridge University Press, 1993.

Brooks, Christopher W. *Lawyers, Litigation, & English Society since 1450.* London: Hambledon Press, 1998.

Brown, Tim. "The Making of Urban 'Healtheries:' Transformation of Cemeteries and Burial Grounds in East London." *Journal of Historical Geography* 42 (October 2013): 12–23.

Burrage, Michael. "From a Gentlemen's to a Public Profession: Status and Politics in the History of English Solicitors." *International Journal of the Legal Profession* (1996): 45–80.

Revolution and the Making of the Contemporary Legal Professions: England, France, and the United States. Oxford: Oxford University Press, 2006.

Burton, Antoinette. *At the Heart of Empire: Indians and the Colonial Encounter in Late-Victorian Britain.* Berkeley: University of California Press, 1998.

Butler, Judith. *Bodies That Matter on the Discursive Limits of "Sex."* London and New York: Routledge, 1993.

Button, Anne. "Ariel." In *The Oxford Companion to Shakespeare*, ed. Michael Dobson and Stanley Wells, 21. Oxford: Oxford University Press, 2001.

Cannadine, David. "The Context, Performance and Meaning of Ritual: The British Monarchy and the 'Invention of Tradition,' c. 1820–1977." In *The Invention of Tradition*, ed. Eric Hobsbawm and Terrence Ranger, 101–164. New York: Cambridge University Press, 1983.

Ornamentalism: How the British Saw Their Empire. London: Allen Lane, 2001.

Carnes, Mark C. *Secret Ritual and Manhood in Victorian America.* New Haven, CT: Yale University Press, 1989.

Carpenter, Wilson, and Mary Wilson. *Health, Medicine and Society in Victorian England.* Santa Barbara, CA: Praeger, 2010.

Castronovo, David. *The English Gentleman: Images and Ideals in Literature and Society.* New York: Ungar, 1987.

A Chance Medley Extracts from "Silk and Stuff" (Pall Mall Gazette). London: Constable, 1911.

Chandos, John. *Boys Together: English Public Schools, 1800–1864.* London: Hutchinson, 1984.

Chapman, Raymond. *The Sense of the Past in Victorian Literature.* New York: St. Martin's Press, 1986.

Chowdhury-Sengupta, Indira. "The Effeminate and the Masculine." In *The Concept of Race in South Asia*, ed. Peter Robb, 289–300. Delhi: Oxford University Press, 1995.

Clement, Alexander. *Brutalism: Post-war British Architecture.* Wiltshire: The Crowood Press, 2011.

Clifton, Gloria. *Professionalism, Patronage, and Public Service in Victorian London: The Staff of the Metropolitan Board of Works.* London: Athalone Press, 1982.

Cocks, Raymond. *Foundations of the Modern Bar.* London: Sweet & Maxwell, 1983.

"The Middle Temple in the Nineteenth Century." In *History of the Middle Temple*, ed. Richard O. Havery, 288–333. Portland, OR: Hart, 2011.

Cohen, Deborah. *Family Secrets: Shame and Privacy in Modern Britain.* Oxford: Oxford University Press, 2013.

Household Gods: The British and Their Possessions. New Haven, CT: Yale University Press, 2006.

Cole, Sarah. *Modernism, Male Friendship, and the First World War*. Cambridge: Cambridge University Press, 2003.

Coleridge, Stephen. *Quiet Hours in the Temple*. London: Mills & Boon, 1924.

Collini, Stefan. *Public Moralists: Political Thought and Intellectual Life in Britain 1850–1930*. Oxford: Clarendon Press, 1991.

Conlon, Deidre. "Productive Bodies, Performative Spaces: Everyday Life in Christopher Park." *Sexualities* 7 (2004): 462–479.

Conway, Hazel. *People's Parks: The Design and Development of Victorian Parks in Britain*. Cambridge: Cambridge University Press, 1991.

Cook, Matt. *Queer Domesticities: Homosexuality and Home Life in Twentieth-Century London*. Basingstoke: Palgrave Macmillan, 2014.

Cooper, John. *Pride versus Prejudice: Jewish Doctors and Lawyers in England, 1890–1990*. Cambridge: Cambridge University Press, 2019.

Copelman, Dina. *London's Women Teachers: Gender, Class and Feminism 1870–1930*. London: Routledge, 1996.

Corfield, Penelope J. *Power and the Professions in Britain 1750–1850*. London: Routledge, 1995.

Cornish, William, J. Stuart Anderson, Ray Cocks, Michael Lobban, Patrick Polden, and Keith Smith. *The Oxford History of the Laws of England, Vol XII*. Oxford: Oxford University Press, 2010.

Cortazzo, Emma Cullum. *Emma Cullum Cortazzo, 1842–1918*. Meadville: Shartle, 1919.

Cruchley, G. F. *Cruchley's London in 1865*. London: G. F. Cruchley, 1865.

Cullwick, Hannah. *Diaries of Hannah Cullwick, Victorian Maidservant*, ed. Liz Stanley. London: Virago, 1984.

Cunningham, Hugh. *The Volunteer Force: A Social and Political History, 1859–1908*. Hamden: Archon, 1975.

Cunningham, Peter. *Hand-book of London*. London: John Murray, 1850.

Daggers, Jenny. "The Victorian Female Civilising Mission and Women's Aspirations towards Priesthood in the Church of England." *Women's History Review* 10: 4 (2001): 651–670.

Daniell, Timothy, and J. M. B. Crawford. *The Lawyers: The Inns of Court. The Home of the Common Law*. London: Wildy and Sons, 1976.

Davidoff, Leonore. "Class and Gender in Victorian England: The Diaries of Arthur J. Munby and Hannah Cullwick." *Feminist Studies* 5: 1 (1979): 87–141.

Davidoff, Leonore, and Catherine Hall. *Family Fortunes: Men and Women of the English Middle Class, 1780–1950*. London: Hutchinson, 1987.

Delap, Lucy. "Conservative Values: Anglicans and the Gender Order in Inter-war Britain." In *Brave New World: Imperial and Democratic National Building in Britain between the Wars*, ed. Laura Beers and Geraint Thomas, 149–168. London: University of London, 2011.

Deslandes, Paul. *Oxbridge Men: British Masculinity and the Undergraduate Experience, 1850–1920*. Bloomington, IN: Indiana University Press, 2005.

Deutsche, Rosalyn. "Boys Town." *Environment and Planning D: Space and Society* 9 (1991): 5–30.

"Men in Space." *Strategies* 3 (1990): 130–137.

Dicey, A. V. *Lectures on the Relation between Law and Public Opinion*. Indianapolis, IN: Liberty Fund, 2008.

Dickens, Charles. *Barnaby Rudge: A Tale of the Riots of Eighty*. New York: Start, 2013.

   Bleak House. London: Bradbury & Evans, 1853.

   Great Expectations, ed. Margaret Cardwell. Oxford: Clarendon Press, 1993.

   The Life and Adventures of Martin Chuzzlewit. London: Oxford University Press, 1966.

   Our Mutual Friend. Oxford: Oxford World Classics, 2008.

   Sketches by Boz Illustrative of Every-Day Life and Every-Day People. Philadelphia, PA: Getz, Buck, 1852.

Dowling, Linda. *Hellenism and Homosexuality in Victorian Oxford*. Ithaca, NY: Cornell University Press, 1994.

Duman, Daniel. *The English and Colonial Bars*. London: Croom Helm, 1983.

Dyhouse, Carol. *Students: A Gendered History*. London: Routledge, 2006.

   "Women Students and the London Medical Schools, 1914–39: The Anatomy of a Masculine Culture." *Gender and History* 10: 1 (1998): 110–132.

Eaden, James, and David Renton. *The Communist Party of Great Britain since 1920*. Houndmills: Palgrave, 2002.

Elliot, Brent. *Victorian Gardens*. London: Batsford, 1986.

Emerson, Ellen Tucker. *The Letters of Ellen Tucker Emerson, Vol. 1*, ed. Edith W. Gregg. Kent, OH: Ohio State University Press, 1982.

Epp, Charles R. *The Rights Revolution: Lawyers, Activists, and Supreme Courts in Comparative Perspective*. Chicago: University of Chicago Press, 1998.

Ewing, K. D., and C. A. Gearty. *The Struggle for Civil Liberties: Political Freedom and the Rule of Law in Britain 1914–1945*. Oxford: Oxford University Press, 2000.

Feldman, David. "Civil Liberties." In *The British Constitution in the Twentieth Century*, ed. Vernon Bogdanor, 411–415. Oxford: Oxford University Press, 2003.

   Englishmen and Jews: Social Relations and Political Culture, 1840–1914. New Haven, CT: Yale University Press, 1994.

Feltham, John. *The Picture of London, for 1803*. London: Lewis, 1802.

Fenton, Laurence. *Palmerston and the Times: Foreign Policy, the Press and Public Opinion in Mid-Victorian Britain*. London: IB Taurus, 2012.

Fisher, Michael H. *The Inordinately Strange Life of Dyce Sombre: Victorian Anglo-Indian MP and a "Chancery Lunatic."* New York: Oxford University Press, 2010.

Flanders, Judith. *Inside the Victorian Home: A Portrait of Domestic Life in Victorian England*. New York: Norton, 2003.

Foucault, Michel. "Governmentality." In *The Foucault Effect*, ed. Graham Burchell, Colin Gordon, and Peter Miller, 87–105. Chicago: University of Chicago Press, 1991.

   History of Sexuality: An Introduction, Vol. I. New York: Vintage, 1978.

Fredman, Sandra. *Women and the Law*. Oxford: Oxford University Press, 2002.

Freeman, W. Marshall. *A Pleasant Hour in the Temple.* London: M. Hughes & Clarke, 1932.

Friedberg, Anne. *Window Shopping: Cinema and the Postmodern.* Berkeley: University of California Press, 1993.

Furneaux, Holly. *Queer Dickens: Erotics, Families, Masculinities.* Oxford: Oxford University Press, 2009.

Gandhi, Mohandas. *An Autobiography: The Story of My Experiments with Truth.* Boston: Beacon Press, 1957.

Goldman, Lawrence. *Science, Reform, and Politics in Victorian Britain.* Cambridge: Cambridge University Press, 2002.

Goodman, Joyce, and Sylvia Harrop. "'The Peculiar Preserve of the Male Kind': Women and the Education Inspectorate, 1893 to the Second World War." In *Women, Education Policy-making and Administration in England: Authoritative Women since 1880,* ed. Joyce Goodman and Sylvia Harrop, 137–155. London: Routledge, 2000.

Graham, Clare. *Ordering Law: The Architectural and Social History of the English Law Court to 1914.* London: Routledge, 2003.

Greenberg, Kenneth. "The Nose, the Lie, and the Duel in the Antebellum South." *American Historical Review* (1990): 57–74.

Griffin, Ben. *The Politics of Gender in Victorian Britain: Masculinity, Political Culture and the Struggle for Women's Rights.* Cambridge: Cambridge University Press, 2012.

Gullace, Nicoletta F. *"The Blood of Our Sons:" Men, Women, and the Renegotiation of British Citizenship during the Great War.* New York: Palgrave Macmillan, 2002.

Hall, Catherine, and Sonya Rose. "Introduction: Being at Home with Empire." In *At Home with the Empire: Metropolitan Culture and the Imperial World,* ed. Catherine Hall and Sonya O. Rose, 1–31. Cambridge: Cambridge University Press, 2006.

Hamlett, Jane. *At Home in the Institution: Material Life in Asylums, Lodging Houses and Schools in Victorian and Edwardian England.* New York: Palgrave Macmillan, 2014.

Hamnett, Chris, and Bill Randolph. *Cities, Housing and Profits: Flat Break-up and the Decline of Private Renting.* London: Taylor & Francis, 1988.

Harris, José. *Private Lives, Public Spirit: A Social History of Britain, 1870–1914.* New York: Penguin, 1994.

Harrison, Brian. *Prudent Revolutionaries: Portraits of British Feminists between the Wars.* New York: Clarendon Press, 1987.

Hart, E. A. P. *The Hall of the Inner Temple.* London: Sweet & Maxwell, 1952.

Hatherley, Owen. *A Guide to the New Ruins of Great Britain.* London: Verso, 2010.

Hawkes, C. P. *Chambers in the Temple.* London: Methuen, 1930.

Haynes, Douglas Melvin. *Fit to Practice: Empire, Race, Gender, and the Making of British Medicine, 1850–1980.* Rochester, NY: University of Rochester Press, 2017.

Hide, Louise. *Gender and Class in English Asylums, 1890–1914.* New York: Palgrave Macmillan, 2014.

Hilliard, Christopher. *English as a Vocation: The Scrutiny Movement*. Oxford: Oxford University Press, 2012.

Hindson, Catherine. *London's West End Actresses and the Origins of Celebrity Charity, 1880–1920*. Iowa City: University of Iowa Press, 2016.

Hobsbawm, Eric. "Introduction: Inventing Traditions." In *The Invention of Tradition*, ed. Eric Hobsbawm and Terrence Ranger, 1–14. Cambridge: Cambridge University Press, 1983.

Hoeflich, M. H. "The Americanization of British Legal Education in the Nineteenth Century." *Journal of Legal History* 8: 3 (1987): 244–259.

Hoffman, Stefan-Ludwig. "Civility, Male Friendship, and Masonic Sociability in Nineteenth-Century Germany." *Gender & History* 13 (2001): 224–248.

Holloway, Gerry. *Women and Work in Britain since 1840*. London: Routledge, 2007.

Houlbrook, Matt. "Fashioning an Ex-crook Self: Citizenship and Criminality in the Work of Netley Lucas." *Twentieth Century British History* 24 (2013): 1–30.

   Queer London: Perils and Pleasures in the Sexual Metropolis, 1918–1957. Chicago: University of Chicago Press, 2005.

Howsam, Leslie. "Legal Paperwork and Public Policy: Eliza Orme's Professional Expertise in Late Victorian Britain." In *Precarious Professionals*, ed. Heidi Egginton and Zoë Thomas, 107–124. London: University of London Press, 2020.

Howse, Carrie. "From Lady Bountiful to Lady Administrator: Women and the Administration of Rural Nursing in England, 1880–1925." *Women's History Review* 3 (2006): 423–441.

Hughes, William Richard. *A Week's Tramp in Dickens-Land*. London: Chapman & Hall, 1891.

Hunt, Robert. *Guide A Londres et a L'Exposition de 1862*. London: W. Jeffs, 1862.

Hyam, Ronald. *Empire and Sexuality: The British Experience*. New York: St. Martin's Press, 1990.

Jones, Gareth Steadman. *Outcast London: A Study in the Relationship between Classes in Victorian Society*. London: Verso, 1971.

Jones, Timothy. "'Unduly Conscious of Her Sex:' Priesthood, Female Bodies, and Sacred Space in the Church of England." *Women's History Review* 21: 4 (2012): 639–655.

Joyce, Patrick. *The Rule of Freedom: Liberalism and the Modern City*. New York: Verso, 2003.

Kenny, Colum. *Tristram Kennedy and the Revival of Irish Legal Training, 1835–1885*. Dublin: Irish Academic Press, 1999.

Kent, Susan Kingsley. *Making Peace: The Reconstruction of Gender in Interwar Britain*. Princeton: Princeton University Press, 1993.

Koven, Seth. *Slumming: Sexual and Social Politics in Victorian London*. Princeton: Princeton University Press, 2004.

Kriegel, Lara. *Grand Designs: Labor, Empire, and the Museum in Victorian Culture*. Durham, NC: Duke University Press, 2007.

Lahiri, Shompa. *Indians in Britain: Anglo-Indian Encounters, Race and Identity, 1880–1930*. London: Frank Cass, 2000.

Lane, Christopher. *The Burdens of Intimacy: Psychoanalysis and Victorian Masculinity*. Chicago: University of Chicago Press, 1999.

Lane, Joan. *A Social History of Medicine Health, Healing and Disease in England, 1750–1950*. London: Routledge, 2001.

Law, Cheryl. *Suffrage and Power*. New York: St. Martin's Press, 1997.

Lefebvre, Henri. *The Production of Space*. Cambridge: Blackwell, 1991.

Lemmings, David. *Gentlemen and Barristers: The Inns of Court and the English Bar, 1680–1730*. Oxford: Clarendon, 1990.

Light, Alison. *Forever England: Femininity, Literature and Conservatism between the Wars*. London: Routledge, 1991.

Lippincott, Sarah Jane. *Haps and Mishaps of a Tour of Europe*. Boston: Ticknor, 1854.

Loftie, W. J. *The Inns of Court and Chancery*. Curdridge: Ashford Press, 1893.

Logan, Anne. "Professionalism and the Impact of England's First Women Justices, 1920–1950." *Historical Journal* 49: 3 (2006): 833–850.

Long, Vicky. *The Rise and Fall of the Healthy Factory: The Politics of Industrial Health in Britain, 1914–1960*. Basingstoke: Palgrave, 2011.

Longstaffe-Gowan, Todd. *The London Square: Gardens in the Midst of Town*. New Haven, CT: Yale University Press, 2012.

Lowenthal, David. *The Past Is a Foreign Country*. New York: Cambridge University Press, 1985.

Lynch, Eve M. "Out of Place: The Masquerade of Servitude in Victorian Literature." *Pacific Coast Philology* 31 (1996): 86–106.

Lytton, Constance. *Prisons and Prisoners: Some Personal Experiences*. London: Virago, 1914.

Mackay, Lynn. *Respectability and the London Poor 1780–1870: The Value of Virtue*. London: Pickering & Chatto, 2013.

Maltby, Josephine. "'To Bind the Humbler to the More Influential and Wealthy Classes.' Reporting by Savings Banks in Nineteenth Century Britain." *Accounting History Review* 22 (2012): 199–225.

Mandler, Peter. *The Fall and Rise of the Stately Home*. New Haven, CT: Yale University Press, 1997.

Marcus, Sharon. *Apartment Stories: City and Home in Nineteenth-Century Paris and London*. Berkeley: University of California Press, 1999.

Marshall, Nancy Rose Marshall. *City of Gold and Mud: Painting Victorian London*. New Haven, CT: Yale University Press, 2012.

Massey, Doreen. "Flexible Sexism." *Environment and Planning D: Space and Society* 9 (1991): 31–57.

Masterson, Margery. "Dueling, Conflicting Masculinities, and the Victorian Gentleman." *Journal of British Studies* 56 (2017): 605–628.

Mayhew, Henry. *London Labour and the London Poor*. London: Griffin, Bohn, 1862.

Mayhew, Henry, and John Binny. *The Criminal Prisons of London and Scenes of London Life*. London: Griffin, Bohn, 1862.

McClintock, Anne. *Imperial Leather: Race, Gender, and Sexuality in the Colonial Contest*. Hoboken, NJ: Taylor & Francis, 2013.

Meacham, Stanish. *Toynbee Hall and Social Reform 1880–1914*. New Haven, CT: Yale University Press, 1987.

Meah, Angela. "Materiality, Masculinity and the Home: Men and Interior Design." In *Masculinities and Place*, ed. Andrew Gorman-Murray and Peter Hopkins, 209–226. Farnham: Ashgate, 2014.

Meller, Helen. *Leisure and the Changing City*. London: Routledge, 1976.

Melman, Billie. *The Culture of History: English Uses of the Past, 1800–1953*. New York: Oxford University Press, 2006.

Melville, Herman. *The Melville Log: A Documentary Life of Herman Melville, 1819–1891*. New York: Gordian Press, 1969.

"The Paradise of Bachelors and the Tartarus of Maids." In *The Piazza Tales and Other Prose Pieces*, ed. Harrison Hayford, Alma A. MacDougall, G. Thomas Tanselle, and Merton Sealts, 316–335. Evanston, IL: Northwestern University Press, 1987.

Middleton, Richard. "The Royal Horticultural Society's 1864 Botanical Competition." *Archives of Natural History* (2014): 25–44.

Milne-Smith, Amy. *London Clubland: A Cultural History of Gender and Class in Late Victorian Britain*. New York: Palgrave Macmillan, 2011.

Mitchell, Rosemary. *Picturing the Past: English History in Text and Image, 1830–1870*. New York: Oxford University Press, 2000.

Mogg, Edward. *Mogg's New Picture of London and Visitor's Guide to Its Sights*. London: E. Mogg, 1843.

Morgan, W. John. *Law and Opinion in Twentieth-Century Britain and Ireland*. New York: Palgrave, 2003.

Mort, Frank. *Dangerous Sexualities: Medico-Moral Politics in England since 1830*. London: Routledge, 2000.

Mossman, Mary Jane. *The First Women Lawyers: A Comparative Study of Gender, Law and the Legal Professions*. Portland, OR: Hart, 2006.

Munby, Arthur. *Munby, Man of Two Worlds*, ed. Derek Hudson. Boston: Gambit, 1972.

Murdoch, Lydia. *Imagined Orphans: Poor Families, Child Welfare, and Contested Citizenship in London*. New Brunswick: Rutgers University Press, 2006.

Nead, Lynda. *Victorian Babylon: People, Streets, and Images in Nineteenth-Century London*. New Haven, CT: Yale University Press, 2000.

Newnham-Davis, Lieut.-Col. *Dinners and Diners: Where and How to Dine in London*. London: Office of the Pall Mall Publications, 1899.

Ngai, Sianne. *Our Aesthetic Categories: Zany, Cute, Interesting*. Cambridge, MA: Harvard University Press, 2012.

Noel, Gerard. *A Portrait of the Inner Temple*. Norwich: Michael Russell, 2002.

Nord, Deborah. *Walking the Victorian Streets: Women, Representation, and the City*. Ithaca, NY: Cornell University Press, 1995.

Normanton, Helena. *Everyday Law for Women*. London: Ivor Nicholson and Watson, 1932.

Olsen, Donald J. *The Growth of Victorian London*. New York: Holmes & Meier, 1976.

Oram, Alison. *Women Teachers and Feminist Politics, 1900–39*. Manchester: Manchester University Press, 1996.

Otter, Chris. *The Victorian Eye: A Political History of Light and Vision in Britain, 1800–1910*. Chicago: University of Chicago Press, 2008.

Owen, David. *The Government of Victorian London 1855–1889: The Metropolitan Board of Works, the Vestries, and the City Corporation.* Cambridge: Belknap Press, 1982.

Owen, Nicholas. *The British Left and India: Metropolitan Anti-Imperialism, 1885–1947.* Oxford: Oxford University Press, 2007.

Paige, Harriette Story. *Daniel Webster in England: Journal of Harriette Story Paige, 1839,* ed. Edward Gray. Boston: Houghton, Mifflin, 1917.

Parry, Jonathan. *The Rise and Fall of Liberal Government in Victorian Britain.* London: Yale University Press, 1993.

Perkin, Harold. *The Origins of Modern English Society, 1780–1880.* London: Routledge, 2002.

The Rise of Professional Society: England since 1880. London: Routledge, 1989.

Petrow, Stefan. *The Metropolitan Police and the Home Office in London, 1870–1914.* Oxford: Oxford University Press, 1994.

Picker, John M. *Victorian Soundscapes.* New York: Oxford University Press, 2003.

Polden, Patrick. "Portia's Progress: Women at the Bar in England, 1919–1939." *International Journal of the Legal Profession* 12: 3 (2005): 293–338.

Poole, Adrian. *Shakespeare and the Victorians.* London: Arden Shakespeare, 2004.

Popplewell, Richard. *Intelligence and Imperial Defence: British Intelligence and the Defence of the Indian Empire 1904–1924.* London: Frank Cass, 1995.

Porter, Bernard. *The Lion's Share: A Short History of British Imperialism, 1850–1970.* New York: Longman, 1996.

Potvin, John. *Material and Visual Cultures beyond Male Bonding, 1870–1914: Bodies, Boundaries and Intimacy.* Burlington, NJ: Ashgate, 2008.

Prest, Wilfrid. *The Rise of the Barristers: A Social History of the English Bar, 1590–1640.* Oxford: Clarendon, 1986.

Price, Leah. "Stenographic Masculinity." In *Literary Secretaries/Secretarial Culture,* ed. Leah Price and Pamela Thurschwell, 32–47. London: Routledge, 2005.

Prochaska, Frank. *Women and Philanthropy in Nineteenth-Century England.* Oxford: Oxford University Press, 1980.

Pue, W. Wesley. "Moral Panic at the English Bar: Paternal vs. Commercial Ideologies of Legal Practice in the 1860s." *Law & Social Inquiry* 15: 1 (Winter 1990): 49–118.

Ransome, Arthur. *Bohemia in London.* New York: Dodd, Mead, 1907.

Rappaport, Erika. *Shopping for Pleasure: Women in the Making of London's West End.* Princeton: Princeton University Press, 2000.

Reader, William Joseph. *Professional Men: The Rise of the Professional Classes in Nineteenth-Century England.* New York: Basic, 1966.

Readman, Paul. "The Place of the Past in English Culture c. 1890–1914." *Past and Present* (2005): 147–199.

Reay, Barry. *Watching Hannah: Sexuality, Horror and Bodily De-formation in Victorian England.* London: Reaktion, 2002.

Reclus, Élisée. *Londres Illustré Guide Spécial Pour L'Exposition de 1862.* Paris: Libraire de L. Hachette, 1862.

Report of the Commissioners Appointed to Inquire into the Arrangements in the Inns of Court. London: George Edward Eyre and William Spottiswoode, 1855.

Ringrose, Hyacinthe. *The Inns of Court. An Historical Description of the Inns of Court and Chancery of England*. Oxford: R. L. Williams, 1909.

Roberts, M. J. D. "The Politics of Professionalization: MPs, Medical Men, and the 1858 Medical Act." *Medical History* 53 (2009): 37–65.

Rodrick, Anne Baltz Rodrick. "'Only a Newspaper Metaphor': Crime Reports, Class Conflict, and Social Criticism in Two Victorian Newspapers." *Victorian Periodicals Review* (Spring 1996): 1–18.

Rose, Gillian. "Review of Edward Soja, *Postmodern Geographies* and David Harvey, *The Condition of Postmodernity*." *Journal of Historical Geography* 17: 1 (January 1991): 118–121.

Rutherford, Emily. "Arthur Sidgwick's *Greek Prose Composition*: Gender, Affect, and Sociability in the Late-Victorian University." *Journal of British Studies* 56 (January 2017): 91–116.

Schlesinger, Max. *Saunterings in and about London*. London: Nathaniel Cook, 1853.

Schneer, Jonathan. *London 1900: The Imperial Metropolis*. New Haven, CT: Yale University Press, 1999.

Searle, G. R. *A New England? Peace and War, 1886–1918*. New York: Clarendon Press, 2004.

Sedgwick, Eve Kosofsky. *Between Men: English Literature and Male Homosocial Desire*. New York: Columbia University Press, 1985.

Epistemology of the Closet. Berkeley: University of California Press, 1990.

Shannon, Brent. *The Cut of His Coat: Men, Dress, and Consumer Culture in Britain, 1860–1914*. Athens: Ohio University Press, 2006.

Shapely, Peter. "Charity, Status and Leadership: Charitable Image and the Manchester Man." *Journal of Social History* 32 (1998): 157–177.

Shaw, Charles. *The Inns of Court Calendar*. London: Butterworths, 1878.

Shoemaker, Robert Brink. *The London Mob: Violence and Disorder in Eighteenth Century England*. New York: Hambledon Continuum, 2007.

Showalter, Elaine. *Sexual Anarchy: Gender and Culture at the Fin de Siècle*. New York: Viking, 1990.

Siegrist, Hannes. "Professionalization with the Brakes On: The Legal Profession in Switzerland, France and Germany in the Nineteenth and Early Twentieth Centuries." *Comparative Social Research* 9 (1986): 267–298.

Sinha, Mrinalini. *Colonial Masculinity: The "Manly Englishman" and the "Effeminate Bengali" in the Late Nineteenth Century*. New York: St. Martin's Press, 1995.

Sinnema, Peter W. "Reading Nation and Class in the First Decade of the *Illustrated London News*." *Victorian Periodicals Review* (Summer 1995): 136–152.

Smith, Harold L. *The British Women's Suffrage Campaign 1866–1928*. Harlow: Pearson Education, 2007.

Smith, Phillip Thurmond. *Policing Victorian London: Political Policing, Public Order, and the London Metropolitan Police*. Westport, CT: Greenwood Press, 1985.

Snyder, Katherine V. *Bachelors, Manhood and the Novel, 1850–1925*. New York: Cambridge University Press, 1999.

Soja, Edward. *Postmodern Geographies: The Reassertion of Space in Critical Social Theory*. New York: Verso, 1989.

Sorabji, Cornelia. *India Calling*. London: Nisbet, 1934.

Sorabji, Richard. *Opening Doors: The Untold Story of Cornelia Sorabji: Reformer, Lawyer and Champion of Women's Rights in India*. London: IB Taurus, 2010.

Spilsbury, William Holden. *Lincoln's Inn: Its Ancient and Modern Buildings. With an Account of the Library*. London: Reeves and Turner, 1873.

Standford, Terry. *The Metropolitan Police, 1850–1940: Targeting, Harassment and the Creation of Criminal Class*. PhD thesis, University of Huddersfield, 2007.

Sutcliffe, Anthony. *London: An Architectural History*. New Haven, CT: Yale University Press, 2006.

(ed.). *Metropolis 1890–1940*. Chicago: University of Chicago Press, 1984.

Tabili, Laura. "A Homogenous Society? Britain's Internal 'Others,' 1800–Present." In *At Home with the Empire*, ed. Catherine Hall and Sonya O. Rose, 53–76. Cambridge: Cambridge University Press, 2006.

Thackeray, William Makepeace. *The History of Pendennis*. New York: Start, 2013.

Thane, Pat, and Esther Breitenbach. *Women and Citizenship in Britain and Ireland in the Twentieth Century: What Difference Did the Vote Make?* London: Continuum, 2010.

Thurley, Simon. *Hampton Court: A Social and Architectural History*. New Haven, CT: Yale University Press, 2003.

Tosh, John. *A Man's Place: Masculinity and the Middle-Class Home in Victorian England*. New Haven, CT: Yale University Press, 2007.

"Masculinities in an Industrializing Society: Britain, 1800–1914." *Journal of British Studies* 44 (2005): 330–342.

Tyack, Geoffrey. "The Rebuilding of the Inns of Court, 1660–1700." In *The Intellectual and Cultural World of the Early Modern Inns of Court*, ed. Jayne Elisabeth Archer, Elizabeth Goldring, and Sara Knight, 199–203. Manchester: Manchester University Press, 2011.

Tyler, Melissa, and Laurie Cohen. "Spaces That Matter: Gender Performativity and Organizational Space." *Organization Studies* 31 (2010): 175–198.

Van Teslaar, James. *Sex and the Senses*. Boston: Gorham Press, 1922.

Vicinus, Martha. *Independent Women: Work and Community for Single Women, 1850–1920*. Chicago: University of Chicago Press, 1985.

Vincent, John. *The Formation of the British Liberal Party*. New York: Scribner, 1967.

Visram, Rozina Visram. *Asians in Britain: 400 Years of History*. London: Pluto Press, 2002.

Walkowitz, Judith R. *City of Dreadful Delight: Narratives of Sexual Danger in Late-Victorian London*. Chicago: University of Chicago Press, 1992.

"Going Public: Shopping, Street Harassment, and Streetwalking in Late Victorian London." *Representations* 62 (Spring 1998): 1–30.

Nights Out: Life in Cosmopolitan London. New Haven, CT: Yale University Press, 2012.

Prostitution and Victorian Society: Women, Class, and the State. New York: Cambridge University Press, 1980.

Ward, H. Snowden, and Catherine Weed Barnes Ward. *The Real Dickens Land*. London: Chapman & Hall, 1904.

Weinstein, Benjamin. *Liberalism and Local Government in Early Victorian London.* Suffolk: Boydell & Brewer, 2011.

"Metropolitan Whiggery, 1832–1855." In *London Politics, 1760–1914,* ed. Matthew Cragoe and Anthony Taylor, 57–74. New York: Palgrave, 2005.

White, Jerry. *London in the Nineteenth Century.* London: Jonathan Cape, 2007.

Whyte, William. *Unlocking the Church: The Lost Secrets of Victorian Sacred Space.* Oxford: Oxford University Press, 2017.

Wiener, Martin. *English Culture and the Decline of the Industrial Spirit: 1850–1980.* New York: Cambridge University Press, 1981.

Winter, James H. *London's Teeming Streets: 1830–1914.* London: Routledge, 1993.

Wohl, Anthony. *Endangered Lives: Public Health in Victorian Britain.* Cambridge: Harvard University Press, 1983.

The Eternal Slum: Housing and Social Policy in Victorian London. Montreal: McGill-Queen's University Press, 1977.

Woolley, David. "The Inn as a Disciplinary Body." In *A History of the Middle Temple,* ed. Richard O. Havery, 357–372. Portland, OR: Hart, 2011.

Index

214   Index